The Decline and Fall of America

By Walter Lamp

OTHER BOOKS BY WALTER LAMP

Offshore Plundering by American Companies   © 2013
   The US Tax Incentive to Move Operations Offshore
   How America Lost Trillions in Tax Revenues
   How Our Economy Was Ruined ISBN #9780983495444

99 Prescriptions for a More Ethical Society   © 2008
   Combating the Major Ethical Abuses of the Day:
     Governance,   Excessive Compensation,
     Subsidies,   Information Suppression
     Lies and Spins, & More   ISBN #9780981668116

Biblical Verses, A Frank Study of the Old Testament and
              Hebrew Bible   © 2012
   How the Scripture and the Religion Changed Over Time
   What the Old Testament / Hebrew Bible Actually Says
   Explaining Conflicts & Inconsistencies in the Scripture
   Better Understanding All the Abrahamic Religions;
     Judaism, Christianity and Islam ISBN#9780983495420

Koranic Verses, A Frank Study of the Koran   ©2009
   How the Koran is Honored & Dishonored in Practice
   Understanding Islam's History   ISBN #9780981668123

The Decline and Fall of America

By Walter Lamp, JD (Yale), CPA

RunningLight Publishing Company
Reno, Nevada

© Copyright 2014, Walter Lamp

All rights reserved. No part of this work may be reproduced in any way without prior written permission from the author or publisher, except for brief quotations in articles or reviews.

The Decline and Fall of America   by Walter Lamp
   1st Edition.

United States-
1. Political Science   2. Economic Policy   3. Democracy
4. Personal Freedoms   5. Economic Inequality   6. Politics
6. Political Parties 7. Voting 8. Law 9. Ethics 10. History
12. Tax Policy   13. Industrial Policy   9. Trade Policy

ISBN-13: 978-0-9834954-5-1 (paperback)

Library of Congress Control Number: 2014908801

321 LAM 2014   10 9 8 7 6 5 4 3 2

Table of Contents

Introduction   1

1. Dysfunctional Democracy   7
2. Anemic Economy   139
3. Economic Inequality   261
4. Government Programs & Laws   313
5. Personal Freedoms   369

References   419

Index   421

("List of Topics" follows)

List of Topics

	Page

Dysfunctional Democracy — 7
- Dysfunction Prevails — 8
- The Danger to Our Democracy — 11
- Protecting the Minority — 12

Buying Elections — 13
- Limitations on Campaign Contributions — 14
- Using Super PACs to Buy Elections — 17
- Tax Deductions for Buying Elections — 19
- "Name" Celebrities Buying Elections — 20
- Use of Advocacy Groups — 21

Buying Influence / Corruption in Government — 23
- Corruption in Government — 24
- Restoring Public Trust — 26
- Use of Term Limits — 29
- Political Extortion — 29
- Corruption in Administrative Bodies — 31
- Corruption in Congressional Rule-Making — 33
- Corrupting Influence of Money in Politics — 34

	Page
Lobbyists Dominate Our Democracy	35
Setting the Legislative Agenda	35
Incentive to <u>Not</u> Solve Problems	37
Silencing Trade-Organization Members and Lobbyist's Clients	38
Issue Framing By Lobbyists	41
Lobbying Your Former Congressional Boss	43
Lobbyists' Money Funds Lawmakers Gracious Living	46
Politicians Nullifying Election Results	47
Nullifying an Election by Impeachment	49
State Recall Procedures	50
Advice and Consent of the Senate	52
The Senate's Internal Rules	55
The Senate's "Blue Slip" Blackball	59
The Senate's "Hold"	62
Amending the Constitution	63
Nullifying Enacted Laws	65
Putting Aside Federal Supremacy	65
Tactics Used	67
The New Dysfunctional Standard	70
Nullifying "One Person, One Vote"	71
One Nation, Out Of the Many (E Pluribus Unum)	74
Obliteration of the "Melting Pot" Concept	75
Diversity Can Be Dysfunctional	76
Keeping the "Other" From Voting	78
Gerrymandering	82

	Page
Leadership in a Democratic Society	85
Disenfranchising the Elected Legislator	86
Presidential Leadership	88
Leadership and Minority Treatment	89
Resolving Issues	91
The Needed Change of Attitudes	92
Making Our Democracy Work	93
1. End gerrymandering.	95
2. Adopt strict term-limits for Senators and Representatives.	97
3. Adopt California's "top-two" voting system.	102
4. Adopt term-limits for Supreme Court judges or limit filibusters.	106
5. End Senate confirmation of presidential appointments.	109
6. Adopt national identification cards.	111
7. Don't use public funds to match small-donor campaign contributions	113
8. Limit contributions to political advocacy groups.	115
9. Retain the primary systems of the major political parties (if no "top-two" voting).	119
10. Don't fine eligible voters for not voting.	122
11. Move elections from Tuesdays to weekends.	123
12. Inaugurate the President-elect two weeks after the election.	125
13. Treat legislators as being opposed to functional government.	126
14. Shun encouraging distrust and disobedience of duly passed laws.	128

	Page
15. Bypass our dysfunctional federal government when useful.	131
16. Improve the public debate about the role & size of government.	132
17. Rethink our views on the apt role of government in our lives.	135
Who Governs?	136

Anemic Economy — 139

Debt Levels, Tax Revenues & Spending	142
The Non-Existent Debt Ceiling	142
Austerity versus Stimulus	146
Dealing Out the Hand Unevenly	150
Unfairly Burdening the Next Generation	151
Redistribution & Class Warfare	154
Fairness Is In the Eyes of the Beholder	156
Subsidies	159
Giving Away Rights Owned By the Public	161
Governments Granting Exclusive Licenses	164
Matters of Public Policy	165
Unintended Consequences	167
User Fees & Carbon Taxes	170
Using the Tax Laws to Provide Subsidies	173
Government Charging for Services.	179
Extorting Subsidies from State & Cities	181
The Need for Good Accounting	188
Failure to Record All Current Expenses	191
Not Reserving For Risk	193

	Page
Accounting for Executive Compensation	196
Accounting for the Stock Option Rip-Off	197
Hating the Internal Revenue Service	199
Competition & Industrial Policy	203
Creating an American Industrial Policy	211
Protecting American Companies	214
Trade Treaties and Trade Policy	215
Board of Directors Responsibility	218
Government Regulation	220
Does America Overregulate Business?	220
Is More Regulation Needed?	222
Protecting the Public against Harm	226
Different Approaches to Regulation	228
Taxation as Regulation	231
Safety Oriented Regulations	232
Debunking Regulation	235
Innovation, R&D, Intellectual Property Rights	237
The Two Facets of Innovation	239
R&D Budgetary Cuts	240
Anti-American Commercial Espionage	241
Buying High-Tech American Companies	242
Innovation Is Not a Job Killer	244
Fostering Innovation	245
Educating American Engineers	248
Outsourcing American Innovation	250
Can the Ominous Trends Reverse?	253
Ignored Expropriation Risk	256
Protecting Intellectual Property Rights	258

	Page
# Economic Inequality	261
## What Can Be Done On the Low-Income End?	265
Enhancing Family Life	267
Long and Short-Term Programs	267
Increasing the Minimum Wage	268
Job Creation	271
Increasing Worker Mobility	273
Social Programs	274
Lower Product Prices for the Poor	277
## What Can Be Done on the High-Income End?	277
Redistribution Argumentation	278
Class Warfare Argumentation	279
Excessive Executive Compensation	280
Limiting Various Executive Packages	282
Limiting Executive Salaries	287
Executives of Non-Profit Organizations	290
Forbidding Use of Stock Options	292
Tax the Higher Income Group	297
Funding the Internal Revenue Service	302
Closing the Tax Havens	303
Keeping and Extending the Estate Tax	306
Steeply Progressive Estate Taxes	309
Cutting Through the Noise	310

	Page
Gov't Programs & Laws	313
Going Too Far With:	
Extending the Corporate Veil	314
Perpetuating Government Programs	320
Counter-Productive Incentives	324
Perpetuating Fraud-Prone Programs	326
Gaming Contract Law	329
The Uneven Litigation Playing Field	337
Equity versus the Letter of the Law	341
Pursuing Favorites & Lacking Balance	346
Affirmative Action in Education	347
Exporting Democracy	354
Reciprocity with Tax-Haven Countries?	356
Teachers' and Professors' Tenure	358
Efforts to Rehabilitate Prison Inmates	361
Protecting Intellectual Property Rights	364
Abuses by Owners of Patents	366

	Page
# Personal Freedoms	369
Going Too Far With the Right to Privacy	370
Limitations on the Right to Privacy	372
Data-Mining and the Right to Privacy	372
Undercutting the Right to Privacy	374
Going Too Far With the Right to Bear Arms	376
Going Too Far With the Freedom of Religion	381
Establishment of Religion	381
Religious Freedom Overriding Civil Law	384
Taking Advantage of Religious Freedom	388
Going Too Far With Free Speech, Free Press & Free Assembly	391
Right to Free Speech	393
Freedom of the Press	394
Right of Assembly	397
Equality, Protecting Minorities & Freedom of Choice	398
Equality	400
Protecting the Minority	403
The "Right" to Choose	405
Corporate "Rights" Taken Too Far	406
Barring Corporate Veils for Subsidiaries	408
Limiting Lawsuits Against Corporations	409
Forced Arbitration Clauses	411
The Corporate Cloak of Secrecy	412
Is There A Constitutionally Granted Corporate Freedom of Speech?	417

Introduction

I write *The Decline and Fall of America* as an observer; as a child of America seeing, feeling, and appreciating what is going on around me and having access to the appalling facts the advanced information age puts at my disposal.

In contrast, Edward Gibbon wrote his book "The History of the Decline and Fall of the Roman Empire" as a historian, as he had to do so since he wrote in the 18th century about the 1st through 16th centuries. He used the sources available to him as a historian would use, not being there to view any part of the process through his own glasses and having to rely on others and what they chose to write.

The analogy between Rome and America cannot be avoided. Rome was the mightiest of the then existing nations and it declined through internal rot, not external factors. America is now the mightiest of nations and the internal rot is showing.

The fall of America would be in the future, not an accomplished fact as was the case with Rome when Gibbon wrote. Being in prospect, America can still avoid the fall, reverse or mitigate it.

This, rather than delving into the details of the decline of America, is the focus of this book. The rot is identified and the focus is on what might be done about it.

Alexis de Tocqueville, a French historian and politician, published his book *"Democracy in America"* in 1835 after a few years of travel in the United States in order to see things first hand.[1] Things were much simpler then, and America's democracy was his primary interest.

In the current era and with this book having a much broader scope, limited personal observation and reflection is not enough. A much fuller portrayal of what is going on in America is presented by thousands of newspapers reporters writing in a host of newspapers, on which this book primarily relies. These reporters record history every day.

The middle of the 20th century was the turning point for America. In the 1950's, when I was in my twenties, America was at or near its zenith. America had recently become a superpower and such innovation began to flow in America as the world hadn't yet encountered.

Aviation had come of age and America started to dominate it upon the invention of the jet. Nuclear fission had

---

[1] His observations and reflections focused primarily on the political and on America's democracy. At the time France was ruled by a monarchy. After the French Revolution (1848), he was elected to the ruling assembly and had a hand in writing the French Constitution.

been invented here, and nuclear power came on the scene in a more reliable form then our foremost competitor, Russia, could achieve.[1] Communications exploded from the foreign-invented radio to American TV, to American satellite coverage, to American cell phones, and soon to a real Dick Tracy communications watch.

The computer was developed in America and was reduced in size from gigantic[2] machines to desktops, to laptops, to pads and ultimately to glasses that Dick Tracy would also love. The internet was invented in America. America began to excel in medicine and the American pharmaceutical industry became the world leader, ultimately leading to the American discovery of the genome and its potential for human healing and plant production.

In addition to the sciences, the cultural aspects of American life started to be envied and copied abroad. America took the motion picture to new heights and new forms of entertainment evolved. New York City, Hollywood and Las Vegas were American inventions, as was Disneyland. American fashions and foods started to go abroad, not dominating high fashion or the culinary scene but adding and dominating the new casual and fast-food aspects.

America promised and delivered new personal freedoms to immigrants and citizens. The American military became

---

[1] A cousin of mine was with the Argonne National Laboratory during the years when nuclear fission was first converted to peaceful electric power production.

[2] Gigantic, unwieldy and stupid machines according to an aunt of mine, a mathematician who had the "displeasure" of working at the University of California at Berkeley with an early computer.

foremost in the world with America taking on to itself the role of policeman to the world.

America was clearly riding high through the 1950s through the 1970s but then something started to happen. America still rode high but it did not dominate as before and flaws and fissures started to appear.

This book address the flaws or fissures, the ones that have clearly appeared and the potential ones in the embryo stage. The fine aspects of our society continue, in some instances frayed, but the underlying trends point to significant and continuing erosion.

We may have considered ourselves No. 1 in the world, but a Social Progress Index shows us in 16th place.[1] Our standard of living has become stagnant if not deteriorating for large segments of our population. Our educational system has fallen behind for our young children, although our universities still manage to excel and educate the world. We can no longer provide jobs for our workers although our corporations prosper.

We can no longer balance our budgets, forcing gridlock as there is no longer enough tax money to go around. We don't collect the taxes owed to our government, and tax cheating on Main Street is rampant. Americans work more and more for personal benefit in opposition to America's interests. Tax havens and offshore American business operations deplete America's tax revenues and promise to

---

[1] Kristof, Nicholas, "We're Not No. 1! We're Not No. 1!" The New York Times, April 2, 2014.

bleed America more in the future. America is forced to cutback on its military, on education, on research and other important keys to the future.

More than ever before, as individuals we attempt to impose our views on others or restrict what others might do. Our society has become belligerent. We litigate and litigate. We no longer speak civilly to one another. Lobbyists now drive decisions in Washington. We are no longer a nation of, by, and for the people, rapidly becoming a nation of, by, and for the wealthy.

Most of what America basically stands for is good, is to be admired and not to be deprecated. However, as a nation, we have a tendency to take things too far. This book focuses on where America has gone too far with good things. It also addresses the economic bind America finds itself in and the ever increasing economic inequality in America. And the book points out how our democracy is disappearing and our government becoming structurally dysfunctional.

This book propose solutions to America's problems but only as a means of helping readers focus and clarify their thoughts. Having a concrete suggestion in hand, one that you might or might not agree with, forces consideration of the merits. The proposals advanced are just starting points for consideration that will hopefully lead to better paths.

Neither the Democrat nor the Republican path is clung to in either thought or approach. Each matter is dealt with on the merits, which haphazardly winds up supporting either the

Republican or Democrat camp. Keep score and you'll find both camps presented.

A basic purpose of this book is to create awareness of what we are actually doing to ourselves as a nation. America is in decline and it is up to us to stop this decline before it becomes a free fall. If you don't contribute, who will?

Chapter 1

Dysfunctional Democracy

Our democracy is in clear decline. We go through the formalities of voting amid political battles that outwardly speaks of democracy, but we no longer have a government of, by, and for the people. Money and pressure groups command the legislative agenda.

Voters recognize that our government is dysfunctional. Legislators are held in the lowest regard. Political disillusionment is rampart.

The melting pot has failed. We are not one people and the concept of citizenship is being lost. We gerrymander so as to make the other guys' vote worth less than our vote. We prevent the other guy from physically getting to the ballot box, if not deliberately miscount the vote.

Even if every voter should get to vote on an equal basis, the elections themselves have become farces. It is no longer the case of the better candidate winning. Elections are won by money spent, won by slogans and disinformation, won by charisma, won by anything but merit. Only the open microphone or the taped private conversation brings reality to an election.

DYSFUNCTION PREVAILS

Even should electorate clearly state it preference at the ballot box, the opposition can and does keep the newly elected from governing. Senate confirmation of executive and judicial appointments still face obstruction even though the filibuster has been jettisoned, except for Supreme Court appointments and normal day-to-day legislation. The legislation that actually gets through can no longer address the major issues facing the country. Gridlock dominates Washington. Federal laws that have been duly enacted years ago are undermined on the state level.[1]

When it comes to actual legislation, the real power is not with the elected legislators. Commercial enterprises, or even a single large corporation, effectively wield the legislative power today. That is, they have the power to both block unwanted legislation and also to promulgate self-serving legislation (and even to reverse their positions when their

---

[1] Re nullifying all federal gun laws in the state: Schwartz, John, "Gun Bill in Missouri Would Test Limits in Nullifying U.S. Law," The New York Times, August 28, 2013.

Re state undercutting federal benefits for same-sex couples: Editorial, "The National Guard's Defiance on Civil Rights," The New York Times, October 20, 2013.

Re states opting out of new health care law: Stolberg, Sheryl Gay, "States Are Focus of Effort to Foil Health Care Law," The New York Times, October 18, 2013.

business model changes).[1] They actually set the legislative agenda.

A legislators' primary interest is on re-election, which only too frequently depended on money and what that money wants. The voter is usually secondary. Special interests direct a legislators' vote, sometimes in direct opposition to the legislator's constituency.

When the legislator votes in accordance with the wishes of her constituency but against the wishes a special interest group, the legislator nowadays faces the possibility of being unseated by the special interest group in the next election. Obedience to the powerful, and not fidelity to the electorate, has become the primary prerequisite for re-election.

Unyielding sectarian loyalty has replaced the consensus so necessary for democracy. Uncompromising mindsets control. Knowingly pursuing deliberate harm to America has become an acceptable alternative to yielding on anything. Sequesters, closing the government, and devaluing our debt has become acceptable alternatives as has endlessly piling up government debt.

The traditional categorizations such as conservative, liberal, reform, libertarian, or populist no longer define the issues that separate us. There are different views within these groups, as well as between these groups, as to foreign aid, gay marriage, military, marijuana, drugs, immigration, taxation, stimulus, spending, health care, social services and most everything else. We are polarized on everything.

Perhaps the basic issue that separates us to the greatest extent falls under the rubric of "redistribution," where, like

---

[1] Editorial, "Fairness on Sales Taxes," The New York Times, May 1, 2013.

Robin Hood, the government takes money from the rich and gives it to the poor. Robin Hood is no longer a hero. He has been transformed into a villain. Religious and ethical concepts of caring for the poor so as to create a better society for everybody, and traditional concepts like the ability to pay, have fallen by the wayside. So has the traditional role of the poor changed from asking for help to the belief in an entitlement to help.

In the past, only higher tax rates were viewed as being "redistributive," but now "redistribution" also includes spending on a variety of programs, on health-care, on job stimulation, on education and even on infrastructure. It seems that only spending on the military receives collective support.

Slogans have replaced consideration on the merits. Spins, misinformation and even direct lies are so widespread that voters rarely have a true picture of the issues. A question has even been raised as to whether our political system has been so degraded by misinformation and disinformation that it can no longer function?[1]

While there is some decree of functionality on the state and local levels, the electorate has become disillusioned with Washington and with our Senators and Representatives. Washington is no longer functional. Power is being grabbed by political factions, taking advantage of the rank and file reluctance to put themselves out by voting in party primaries. It seems that only the highly committed extremists vote in primaries, which gives us extremist "no-compromise" legislators.

---

[1] Krugman, Paul, "Moment of Truthiness," The New York Times, August 15, 2013.

THE DANGER TO OUR DEMOCRACY

Political disillusionment is now widespread in America, the same disillusionment that can and is leading to anarchy abroad.[1] It can happen here.

The dysfunctionality in America's governance may have accelerated when Rush Limbaugh's stated goal became the failure of the President-elect, later echoed by the Senate minority leader.[2] Whether that indicated the failure of America was an acceptable consequence was not explicitly stated.

On the other side, an unbridled rush to enact expensive stimulus packages to replace the jobs lost in the ongoing recession was right in the face of the unbelieving opposition.

A dysfunctional government can lead to public protests and strife by advocates for another system of government, abandoning democracy as we know it. Protests in Thailand, a democratic nation, called for substituting a "people's council" consisting of selecting professionals of different kinds and dumping democratic voting.[3]

Dysfunctionality in our government has already contributed to the decline of America, and if not reversed, can lead to the failure of our democracy and America.

---

[1] Editorial, "Europe's Populist Backlash," The New York Times, October 15, 2013.
[2] Egan, Timothy, "Rooting for Failure," The New York Times, November 28, 2013.
[3] Fuller, Thomas, "In Thailand, Standing Up for Less Democracy," The New York Times, December 16, 2013.

PROTECTING THE MINORITY

Democracy does not mean that the majority has a right to oppress or tyrannize the minority. While it's not a legal right, the minority has an ethical or intangible right to be heard and respected in a democracy dominated by those with different beliefs and outlooks.

On the other hand, protection of the minority can be taken too far with the majority denied its due. Obstruction by an empowered minority can become the order of the day. The resultant dysfunction can become more rampart to the point where nothing gets done. If and when that happens, a dedicated minority might even seek to dump democracy in favor of another form of government. Thus, it is in the majority's self-interest to give the minority a fair shake.

Protecting the minority should not allow disruption of the majority's right and duty to rule. A fair election had given the majority the right to govern until the next election, and the majority has a duty to do so. Thus, in protecting the minority, where should the line be drawn?

Certainly, the minority has a right to be heard and the majority has the obligation to let them be heard. The minority has a right to see pertinent available information, the same right as the majority. The minority has a right to present its views, to educate and attempt to convince, and democracy contemplates that the majority should welcome that.

The minority should have no right to block nominations or legislation. It should have no right to insist on supermajority votes, to filibuster, to "hold" matters from getting to the floor for a vote, or to obstruct proceedings with all sorts of delaying tactics. All these things keep the majority from getting its due, as the voters had decreed in the last election.

Buying Elections

We all make, or should make, campaign contributions to help finance the election of our favorite candidates on the federal, state and local levels. It is really our civic duty to do so. As our contributions are to candidates of like-mind, there is normally an expectation that the candidate will vote the way we want when she or he gets elected. However, with so many contributors, the elected cannot be said to have a personal commitment to so many people with different priorities.

Yet the process can and is abused by a donor who contributes so much money to a candidate's election that a personal commitment does arise. Frequently, the contribution is large enough that an "investment" is being made in the candidate with the payback being voting in the legislature as the donor directs.

The more money behind the candidate, the more likely the candidate will win the election. Big donations smack of buying elections.[1] Where big donors contributed to both candidates in an election, it would seem as though elections have merely become a way to settle disagreements between the wealthy.

---

[1] *See* Editorial, "Politicians for Sale," The New York Times, October 7, 2013.

Through buying the election, the big donor buys influence in, if not control of, how the candidate votes in the legislature after being elected. However, influencing how a legislator votes on a specific matter need not depend on having made campaign contributions to that legislator. Money can also flow to a legislator after he or she had been elected, usually aimed at influencing votes on specific matters and helping in his or her re-election. This is covered in the next section, *"Buying Influence / Corruption in Government."*

LIMITATIONS ON CAMPAIGN CONTRIBUTIONS

From what would appear to be clear limits enacted by Congress on contributing money to federal elections (to candidates, political campaigns, political parties and committees), the ingenuity of our courts and our politicians/lobbyists/pressure groups have so emasculated the original legislative intent so as to make all the limits meaningless.

An individual was limited to contributing a total of about $120,000 every two years, with no more than about $2,500 to each candidate. Within those limitations, there were sub-limits as to contributions to various political committees and the like. Corporations and unions were not allowed to make any political contributions. Now the fun begins.

Notice that these limitation only apply to federal elections. States and localities have their own rules with respect to state and local elections. In other election areas, federal powers have been used to overcome state and local rules, but not yet with respect to state and local political contributions. Of course, the candidates are different on the state and local levels, but the political parties aren't, which allows for a degree of hanky-panky. But this is merely speculative as it would be most difficult to determine if it did exist. The point of mentioning the state and local side is to show that much more money goes into politics than is addressed by the federal rules.

Getting back to the federal side, Political Action Committees or PACs (sometimes labelled committees or funds) were invented to bring more money into elections. Corporations and unions that could not make election contributions could pick up the cost of forming and administering the corporate/union PAC and soliciting contributions from its managers and owner/shareholders (in the case of corporations) and union members (in the case of unions). The individuals so contributing are still subject to the federal limits and the PACs are essentially viewed as a bundling or pass-through vehicle.

Since the corporations and unions are allowed pick-up all the PAC expenses, the amount of money going into federal elections is expanded. It is expanded by the amount of money the corporations and unions spend on the PAC activities that can be considered administrative or soliciting expenses. The scope of such expenditures are what the corporations and unions could make of it, perhaps including the think-tank type staffs that identify, lay out and explain the issues involved in the political campaigns, tilted as their biases direct.

Then there are the "leadership" PACs that allow political leaders to receive more campaign contributions than they need. For example, a big name leader with a safe seat doesn't need much money to campaign but collects plenty from those who want something. The leadership PAC confers added power to the leader by allowing her or him to recycle those contributions to the candidates she or he favors.

At first blush, it would appear that leadership PACs don't add to the total amount of money in politics, but merely makes for the efficient use of campaign contributions. However, it is said that legislative leaders and committee chairmen run a "tollbooth" (the tollbooth being the leadership PAC) that interested parties contribute to in order to move a deliberately delayed bill through a committee or the floor, or deliberately introduce "milker bills" so as to obtain donations from those threated by the bills, or to pit industries against one another ("double milkers").[1]

It has also been suggested that leadership PACs are used as slush funds to finance personal spending that wouldn't be allowed using funds obtained from direct campaign contributions or contributions to dedicated campaign committees.[2] Also, forbidding politicians from receiving campaign contributions during legislative sessions, while enacted by many states and presumably effective on the state level, would not appear effective on the federal level.

---

[1] Schweizer, Peter, "Politician's' Extortion Racket," The New York Times, October 21, 2013.
[2] Peters, Jeremy W., "Special PACs Spent Money at Resorts, Book Says," The New York Times, October 21, 2013.

USING SUPER PACs TO BUY ELECTIONS

It wasn't until 2010 when the Supreme Court's decision in the Citizens United case[1] allowed corporations and unions to fund all the activities of what came to be called Super PACs.

Before that decision, the corporations and unions could just shoulder administration and soliciting expenses, which could include issue development like that of think-tanks. With that decision, as much corporate and union funds could be contributed to the Supper PACS as their consciences would allow, and the Super PACs could also solicit unlimited contributions from anyone. These Super PACs (also known as Independent Expenditure Committees) significantly added to the amount of money going into elections.

The Super PACs are considered nonprofit, social welfare organizations described in 501(c) (4) formed for the specific purpose of communicating (broadcasting, printing materials, using films, and presumably whatever else advertisers would use to communicate, including blimps) and advocating the election or defeat of specific political candidates. Somehow social welfare got to include political electioneering.

Super PACs cannot coordinate their activities with, or seek the approval of, the candidates or their political committees in what the Super PAC proposes to do. That is, the Super PAC must act independently of the candidates and the political party machine even though the Super PAC founders, contributors and everyone else knows who and what the Super PAC will support or oppose. Essentially, the Super PAC was allowed to do what the favored political

---

[1] Liptak, Adam, "Justices, 5-4, Reject Corporate Spending Limit," The New York Times, January 21, 2010.

machines like the ancient Tammany Hall would do, but only do it independently of the political machines.

The qualifying Super PACs can receive and spend unlimited amounts of money received without limitation from anyone, including corporations and unions. This is justified by viewing the Super PAC as merely representing the freedom of speech all individuals and organizations had back when advocates took to the soap-box in public parks to rant for or against any political candidate or on any issue.

However, a corporation is not a living person. It is an entity created by law. The issue as to whether corporations have a "right" to freedom of speech is covered in the chapter *"Personal Freedoms."*

The resultant situation could be equated to a newspaper editorial coming out in favor of a particular candidate and the costs related to that (salaries, paper, ink) being considered a business expense and not a political contribution. Because of this, newspapers had and still have extraordinary political clout.

The newspaper, usually a corporation, could not make political contributions, but could run their own campaigns in favor of political candidates and now can also make unlimited contributions to their favored Super PACs.

The Super PACs are just getting into their stride and there is no telling how they'll grow or how they'll be used.

All indications are that their growth will be phenomenal and they will be used for all kinds of purposes and in all sorts of elections. Trying to get the government to tax your business competitor or a competing industry looks like a newly developed political tacit, and a Super PAC has been used for that very purpose.[1] A Super PACs has also been used to invade the normally stodgy and lackluster nonpartisan judicial races that heretofore didn't attract much money.[2]

TAX DEDUCTIONS FOR BUYING ELECTIONS

Business expenses are normally tax deductible and it would appear that that the expenses of a newspaper in running their political campaigns and the contributions of all corporations to a Super PAC would appear to be tax deductible. The corporation would presumably have or claim a business interest in the issues at stake in the election as the newspaper has in covering politics for its readership.

In the Citizens United case, the Supreme Court's 2010 decision treated the corporate contributions as the cost of independently communicating under the court's broad view that freedom of speech extends to corporations.

The court's holding that corporate contributions to Super PACs are not political contributions that corporations are barred from making, coupled with the decision that corporations can legally make the contributions to Super PACs and bear the expense, would seem to make these expenditures tax deductible.

That is unfair. Individual should also be able to tax deduct their contributions to Super PAC as being aimed at preserving their jobs or the like. Preferably, none of these

---

[1] Editorial, "The Koch Attack on Solar Energy," The New York Times, April 26, 2014.
[2] Eckholm, Erik, "Outside Spending Enters Arena of Judicial Races," The New York Times, May 5, 2014.

expenditures should be deductible by either corporations or individuals.

Thus, while many if not most Americans would view contributions to a Super PAC as political contributions, they now also have to deal with the probability that corporations will get tax deductions for their contributions to Super PACs. Corporations, like individuals, are not supposed to get tax deductions for political contributions.

Thus, Super PACs not only allow corporations to buy elections, it appears that they can do it on a tax deductible basis. Unions can also buy elections, but tax deductibility is not an issue since they are non-profit, non-taxable organizations.

"NAME" CELEBRITIES BUYING ELECTIONS

Anyone can form and run a Super PAC. A well-known comedian has formed a Super PAC, presumable because he could attract sizable contributions to his Super PAC.[1] Any celebrity (athlete or otherwise famous person) who is so inclined could presumably form a Super PAC and use her or his name to attract sizable contributions from individuals as well as corporations.

So now we could have elections that are effectively between celebrities who disagree with each other instead of merely between billionaires who disagree with each other. Nevertheless, this would broaden our democracy somewhat, and might be very positive if it serves to bring out those who want to serve society as contrasted to serving special interests.

---

[1] Cordes, Nancy, "Colbert Gets a Super PAC," CBS News, June 30, 2011.

USE OF ADVOCACY GROUPS

Outright vote-buying with booze and cash at wild parties had been eliminated from the democratic process decades ago. It is much more sophisticated today. Non-profit advocacy groups effectively allow unlimited cash contributions to be used for the benefit of specific political candidates and also allow the donors to hide their identities.

These organized advocacy groups have become a vehicle for the very wealthy, frequently billionaires, to push their own philosophies and keep their contributions secret. The donors were legally able to keep their identities secret by using a chain of organizations in making their contributions even though the last organization in the chain might possibly (usually, infrequently) incur fines and penalties for not disclosing where the money came from.[1]

These advocacy groups were initially used to combat the candidates of the opposing political party. The scope has been extended exponentially to also oppose upstanding candidates in one's own political party, the target candidate having to be brought into line on a party issue or on the contributor's issue.[2]

Adding still more levels of sophistication, the well-funded advocacy groups are able to employ bussed-in, compensated crews from other districts or states to wage street and door-to-door campaigns aimed at helping the candidates of their political party or aimed at destroying the other political party's candidates. These guerilla tactics can

---

[1] Editorial, "A Victory Against Dark Money," The New York Times, November 2, 2013.

[2] E.g., *see* Stolberg, Sheryl Gay, "States Are Focus of Effort to Foil Health Care Law," The New York Times, October 18, 2013.

be aimed at intimidating, impeaching, or politically destroying already elected local legislators who have contrary views on specific issues.

Another version of this would be a national one-issue organization funding efforts to find and run candidates in federal, state or local primaries so as to defeat the re-election of office holders opposed to that one-issue organization. These organization might even create a viable candidate in the district (where none had existed before) committed to their views.

In one fashion or another, legions of bussed-in "volunteers" could be employed by advocacy groups to create opposition that would not otherwise appear in a state or district. It is as if our democracy wasn't already riddled with too much conflict between by diverse groups not willing to come together, we condone the fabrication of still more controversy that serves particular political interests.

Thus, in addition to these advocacy groups being used as a means to avoid or evade election laws, they also find use in allowing out-of-state or out-of-district money to impact and local elections.

A local electorate driving local elections has always been a basic feature of our democracy, but advocacy groups representing out-of-state/district interests are now destroying that. These advocacy groups diminish our democracy, diminishing America, and yet we condone it by not taking the steps necessary to restore our democracy (discussed later).

Buying Influence / Corruption in Government

"Buying Influence" and "Corruption in Government" are two sides of the same coin. For each person who buys influence, there is a corrupt politician who does the selling. They go hand in hand, one party giving and the other taking.

And the first step isn't necessarily taken by those who are on the buying side. The sell-side politician could be the initiator seeking a buyer. Both are corrupt. What might appear to be a bribe could turn out to be an extorted payment. This is corruption at the most sophisticated level.

Corruption in government is also found in the operation of government agencies, boards, committees, and commissions dominated by partisan politics, and in the internal rulemaking of the legislators themselves. To various extents, these situations are akin to the wolves guarding the hen houses.

The administrative bodies are administered in the public interest only in the rare occasion when the partisan or bipartisan political interests don't dominate.

Legislative rule-making serves to enhance the power of both political parties (there is bipartisan cooperation in this) rather than be primarily aimed at making government work smoothly and efficiently.

Countless examples show that self-interest (partisan and bipartisan) comes first, which is also corrupt.

CORRUPTION IN GOVERNMENT

Corruption in government always existed to some extent, but seldom were there exposés as to what is really going on behind closed doors. The eye-opener came when an independent commission was appointed by a state governor to study the matter after a number of scandals had rocked the state.[1]

The commission took its job seriously, perhaps too seriously as there were unconfirmed reports that the governor's office later tried to limit its scope. Yet, the final report accomplished the purposes the governor had in mind by revealing (without naming names) a multitude of wrong or potentially illegal activities and making specific recommendation to reduce corruption.

The commission showed that donors made campaign contributions with the expectation of an adequate payback, effectively buying the legislation they wanted with their targeted campaign donations.[2] Some legislators sought to bill travel expenses twice, once to their campaigns and again to the state. Sham non-profit organizations were funded by the state, apparently at the behest of legislators.

The commission was quietly disbanded, with one of the co-chairmen publically acknowledging the inability of the commission to force the legislators to disclose what they did

---

[1] Kaplan, Thomas, "Panel Appointed by Cuomo Says Corruption Is Commonplace in Albany," The New York Times, December 2, 2013.

[2] Kaplan, Thomas, and McKinley, Jessee, "Corruption Panel's Report Offers Look at the Payback Culture in Albany," The New York Times, December 3, 2013.

to earn so much outside income,[1] a most important indicia of corruption.

Money did influence legislation and some laws were custom-tailored for the donors. A real estate developer could get a tax abatement and a large retailer could get an exemption from a wage-law. The commission used sophisticated intelligence gathering firms to uncover hard-to-trace relationships, like large hidden contributions to both political parties after specific legislation was enacted.

It would appear to be against a politician's self-interest to curtail the flow of campaign contributions which allows them to perpetuate their employment by getting re-elected and continue to earn a living from politics.

The state's bipartisan Boards of Elections is made up of politicians who would seem to have a similar self-interest in the flow of campaign contributions; so it is no surprise that the independent commission's report showed that the Board of Elections did not enforce the election laws.

The report showed that the Board of Elections enabled a culture of corruption in the state. The commission called for tighter limits on campaign contributions and stopping politician's from using those contributions for personal use.

The commission also recommended a new way (independent of the Board of Elections) to enforce the election laws, recommended making it criminal for public officials not to report bribery, and recommended baring public officials and legislators from influencing state

---

[1] Kaplan, Thomas, "With Panel Gone, a Move to Monitor New York Lawmakers' Income Is Thwarted," The New York Times, April 16, 2014.

contracts where they have a financial interest.[1] There was also a report that almost 10% of state legislators leaving the legislature since 1999 exited under known allegations of criminal or ethical violations.

RESTORING PUBLIC TRUST

With about 10% of the legislators exiting the state legislature having been known to face accusations of criminal corruption, the incidence of corruption in government must be much higher when the unseen is considered. As with the analogy to an iceberg, the known is just the tip with much more unseen under the surface. It could indicate that 20% or 30% or more of our legislators are criminally corrupt or unethical.

Whatever the percentage, which of course cannot be known, drastic steps are required to restore public trust in government. Not only should corrupt and unethical conduct be stamped out, it is equally important to keep the greedy from viewing and entering politics as being an easy road to riches.

Success in deterring the greedy from undertaking careers in politics would hopefully leave more room for those who really want to serve society. We have to remove politics as a path to riches and do more to attract those who really want to serve the public. Strict term-limits, discussed later, would deter the greedy from entering politics and make room and induce others to actually serve society for a while.

---

[1] Editorial, "New York's 'Legalized Bribery,'" The New York Times, December 4, 2013.

With more than half of those presently in Congress being millionaires,[1] it becomes difficult to determine whether the rich are entering politics because they want to serve or whether they got rich after they became politicians. Reviewing net worth disclosures over time might be a way to explore this.

But requiring a politician to make annual disclosures of net worth and income is frequently of little avail (but should nevertheless be mandatory) as tainted funds are frequently ferreted away with family members or hidden in other ways. As we know, most legislative salaries are not that great and would not support an expensive lifestyle.

Investigating politicians lifestyles might place some in jail but, more important, such a widely disclosed investigatory process would act as a deterrent to the greedy considering politics as a career.

To some people, such a mandatory and dedicated investigatory process might smack of a police-state, yet there seems to be no other way to deal with the matter. It is to be noted that the law already treats those who enter politics as having waved the normal rights citizens have, like the right to privacy. So, for politicians, additional and even harsh inquiry and disclosure rules would not be inappropriate.

Financial disclosures necessarily leave big loopholes for squirreling away money with others. Only lifestyle gives away the existence of hidden wealth. The greedy considering politics as a career to get rich would lose the incentive if it became known that the lifestyles of politicians are constantly

---

[1] Kristof, Nicholas, "A Nation of Takers?" The New York Times, March 26, 2014.

being scrutinized. The public spirited would welcome such scrutiny.

Voters should rightfully wonder why politicians are particularly successful in their personal investments.[1] If statistics were compiled showing that to be the case, the implication would arise that investment suggestions ("tips" in the vernacular) are substituted for or augment political contributions made in the form of cash.

More and better disclosure laws have to be enacted on the financial end in order to catch the corrupt and, more important, to deter the greedy from seeking to make a fortune by entering politics. Not only should the total invested and the earnings thereon be disclosed, but there should be an item-by-item listing of each investment with names and description so that associations can be made and questions asked.

For example, how did the mayor come to invest in the named cement company that happened to start getting city contracts, or how did the legislator come to invest in the land adjacent to a real estate development seeking approval?

We should also make it a criminal offense for public officials and legislators not to report bribery and bribery attempts. Bribery attempts might be difficult to define but, still, having such a law even if it is somewhat vague would be a great deterrent. The publicity involved in an allegation of failure to disclose would likely destroy re-election prospects, so politicians are likely to modify their behavior somewhat even though the prospect of going to jail is not great.

---

[1] Peters, Jeremy W., "Special PACs Spent Money at Resorts, Book Says," The New York Times, October 21, 2013.

An expansion of the whistleblower laws to include bribery and attempted bribery would increase the risk in unduly trying to influence government action.

It would also be very useful to require and publicize that all government employees must log (on a confidential government website) all telephone calls, messages, notes and letters received from seated legislators and public officials (logging only name, date and time). This should not invade privacy rules and it would be of great use to investigators, to say nothing about being a deterrent to the undue use of influence by public officials and legislators.

These are admittedly hard measures, but experience has by now shown that we need to take off the gloves to deal effectively with corruption, and by so doing deter the corrupt from entering politics.

USE OF TERM LIMITS

Another effective way to deter the greedy and the potentially corrupt from entering politics is to have term-limits, very tight term limits. A limit to one-term only would be particularly effective in keeping those who aim to get rich from politics out of politics.

Pro's and con's of tight term-limits are explored in detail in the section *"Making Democracy Work."*

POLITICAL EXTORTION

Political extortion can exist in all levels of government, perhaps more so on the state and local levels than on the federal level.

Corruption on the state level wasn't much of a surprise to those who follow the political scene. "Paying-to-play," meaning requiring campaign contributions or other payments to legislators in order to do business (play) in the state, is commonplace in many states and essential amounts to extortion by legislators. But there are some potential surprises for politically savvy observers on the federal level.

Congressional leaders and committee chairpersons have created what is known as a "tollbooth" to extort contributions by obstructing or delaying the passage of legislation anxiously awaited by those who would benefit from the legislation.[1]

They also extort by their use of "milker bills."[2] A "milker bill" allows the extortion of contributions from parties who would be disadvantaged by the bill the legislator introduces. More profitable would be a "double milker" that attracts donations from two parties (two industries) on both sides of a bill designed to help one and penalize the other.

A legislator aiming to get appointed to a particular committee could be motivated by the large cash contributions members of that committee attract. Joining such a committee wouldn't appear to be extortion because the contributions flow readily from the industry dealing with that committee. Perhaps wanting to join such a committee merely indicates a desire to sell one's influence, but when the committee has deliberately been made super-sized, it does smack of

---

[1] Schweizer, Peter, "Politicians' Extortion Racket," The New York Times, October 21, 2013.
[2] *Ibid.*

extortion. It seems that the Financial Services Committee of the House of Representatives is such a "cash committee."[1]

CORRUPTION IN ADMINISTRATIVE BODIES

We believe government bodies will be fairly administered if we have rough political party balance in running government agencies, boards, committees, and commissions, with the party in control of the executive branch either making all the appointments or appointing a majority with the losing political party effectively appointing the minority as in a 3 to 2 board.

But in some bodies, like the Federal Election Commission (FEC), consist of six commissioners who are split strictly according to political party affiliation. They can be relied to vote the party line. So with an equally balanced board, nothing gets done on controversial matters.

But should the political parties agree in their self-interest on something that benefits both of them, that would surely get done whether it benefits the public or not. What we get is bipartisan cooperation in evading the assigned responsibilities or in feathering their own nests, which is another form of corruption.

The designated responsibility of the FEC is to police the money used in political campaigns and determine whether campaign activities comply with the campaign laws. As both political parties are the beneficiaries of ill-gotten political contributions and other dubious activities, there is a natural

---

[1] Editorial, "The Cash Committee," The New York Times, August 17, 2013.

conflict of interest. Calling for a nonpartisan, independent board[1] makes sense.

The administrative agencies and commission that actually govern the activities of an industry can serve to benefit the industry interest rather than the public interest. But where the industry interest is split between two groups having different party affiliations, a politically balanced board would be unable to take action. As industries do have a history of contributing to both political parties, they have the power of influence administrative action as long there is agreement within the industry, making the public interest irrelevant and usually not present.

Every appointee by politicians to these governmental administrative boards is partisan. We should give up the fiction that politicians can be trusted to appoint truly non-partisans, independent people to these boards.

So the matter has to resolve down to using some judicial or quasi-judicial body to select administrators from amongst their membership. Or use academic or quasi-academic bodies, or the like. Perhaps a combination. Perhaps only the retired who formally worked in the industry (and thus knowledgeable) should be eligible to serve.

The point is that America is now in the clutches of the political parties and so far no way has been developed or even suggested as to how truly independent administrative bodies can be established. We must find a way to get the heretofore politically-balanced agencies, boards, committees, and commissions out of the clutches of the political parties and under truly independent control.

---

[1] Editorial, "Dangerous Inaction by the Election Commission," The New York Times, January 19, 2014.

CORRUPTION IN CONGRESSIONAL RULE-MAKING

The purposes of the legislature is to fulfill its constitutional responsibilities in governing America. The purpose of Congress is to legislate and its rule-making should facilitate the process of legislating.

Instead the internal rule-making in both legislative houses is aimed as arrogating more power to the particular house and to its members. Rules that promote simplicity, efficiency and speed should prevail but they don't. Instead the legislators have given themselves "blue slips" and "holds" that outwardly call for more careful deliberation but in reality are mechanisms to enhance power. So are the filibuster rules and the need for supermajorities that the constitution does not call for. And various rules can be used to obstruct and delay.

But why is all this considered corruption? It is because the legislators are not fulfilling their duty but are instead serving themselves. They are enhancing themselves over serving the public. Taking power not granted is analogous to taking cash not earned. It is corruption.

A simple solution would be to have efficiency and other experts determine the internal rules of the legislative bodies instead of having the legislators themselves do it. There are nonpartisan people outside of government who understand government and how it should work. Again the rub is finding them and establishing a mechanism to have them write the internal rules that the legislators previously had responsibility for. It should be part of any reform package.

CORRUPTING INFLUENCE OF MONEY IN POLITICS

It has been shown that money influences government action and that there is too much money in politics. Limiting the amounts that can be contributed to political campaigns is the preferable way to go, and we already have such laws. And those laws don't work. In practice, there are no limits to the amount of money that can go into politics.

Matching small public campaign donations with state funds would merely be a raid on the public treasury with still more money going into elections. And the amounts collected are not likely to make a dent in balancing the flow of funds from the rich and super-rich.

The problem we have had with money in politics is that there are too many ways to avoid the limitations[1] and hide the donors.[2] The limitations becomes unenforceable if the donors cannot be identified. So the first order of business is to strengthen the disclosure laws.

As we would be averse to having each individual who makes a political contribution report that contribution in some way, the recipient of each contribution must record and report each contribution received with a trail going back to the specific individual who was the source of the funds. Thus, contributions could not be taken from an organization unless the organization supplied a listing of all individual contributors to that organization, going back tier by tier until

---

[1] Lipton, Eric, "A Loophole Allows Lawmakers to Reel In Trips and Donations," The New York Times, January 19, 2014.
Peters, Jeremy W., "Special PACs Spent Money at Resorts, Book Says," October 21, 2013.
[2] Editorial, "The Koch Party," The New York Times, January 25, 2014.

all the funds can be traced to specific individuals. Those listings need not be made public but would be available to any election or other body that should have access. If such a requirement is considered too unwieldy, donors always have the option of making direct contributions.

The source of funds that go into political issue advertising or into allied use should also be subject to strict disclosure requirements. All violations should have appropriate penalties involved, sufficiently severe so as to deter evasion.

Lobbyists Dominate Our Democracy

Lobbyists garner political influence for themselves and for their clients, it being difficult to ascertain which comes first for the lobbyist. Nevertheless, it is clear that lobbyist have extraordinary muscle in our legislative process. In reality, it might be government by, for and of the lobbyists rather that by, for and of the people.

SETTING THE LEGISLATIVE AGENDA

Government of, by, and for the people would exist if the President and Congress elected by the people actually set the legislative agenda and voted their conscious or voted in accordance with the wishes of their constituents. After all, the administration and Congress has the constitutional mandate to propose and depose and they are supposed to represent the public.

Yet, it isn't clear whether the legislative agenda is set by the administration and Congress, or set by lobbyists, or set by corporations, or set by any of the three as the occasion arises. It is frequently difficult to tell who the moving party is. It may be apparent that the administration and Congress are setting the legislative agenda on public policy issues that they initiated, but not where business interests are involved.

Corporations might be seen setting the legislative agenda when they openly initiate a proposal, and even draft the legislation, garner support themselves and work with lobbyists to smooth the way with the administration and legislators. Or it could be the lobbyists employed by the corporations that really set the legislative agenda, proposing the legislation that benefits their corporate clients. The role of lobbyists in setting the legislative agenda is not always apparent as they work behind the scene in mysterious ways.

The muscle of lobbyist becomes apparent when they can get legislators to reverse themselves on an issue. For example, Congress had enacted a cut in a program the administration had proposed with the support of more than 100 legislators who later reversed their position after industry lobbyists started a repeal effort.[1] On occasion, the lobbying muscle becomes apparent when it can be attributed to the lobbyists having been former aids to powerful committee chairman.[2]

Sometimes the lobbyist muscle becomes apparent as they so kindly volunteer to help legislative committees draft the

---

[1] Lipton, Eric, "In Congress, a Bid to Undo Dialysis Cuts," The New York Times, August 28, 2013.

[2] Lipton, Eric, "Tax Lobby Builds Ties to Chairman of Finance Panel," The New York Times, April 6, 2013.

bills of interest to their clients.¹ The muscle of lobbyists can also be seen as they overcome decades of intra-industry controversy and legislative stalemate when industry positions change and manage to get bipartisan legislative support.²

It is clear that the lobbyist's represent their corporate clients, and the lobbyists have the muscle to get things done. However, it would outwardly appear that the corporations they represent are the ones setting the legislative agenda when the matter is not a public policy issue dominated by the administration or legislators. After all, the corporations pay the lobbyists' bill and ultimately call the shots.

But the lobbyists know the Washington scene and have a good understanding of what their clients would want, so it is no more than feathering their own nests when they offer lobbying proposals to their clients. The lobbyists might represent a single corporation, a group of corporations or even the entire industry as the occasion might arise. The lobbyist muscle flexing must be at its utmost when only a single corporation is behind the lobbyist's effort and is setting the legislative agenda.

INCENTIVE TO <u>NOT</u> SOLVE PROBLEMS

In my naïve youth, I was warned by a friendly person who ran a corporate political office in Washington D.C. to be

---

[1] Lipton, Eric, and Protess, Ben, "Banks' Lobbyists Help in Drafting Financial Bills," The New York Times, May 23, 2013.

[2] Streitfeld, David, "Internet Sales Tax Coming Too Late for Some Stores," April 26, 2013.

Editorial, "Fairness on Sales Taxes," The New York Times, May 1, 2013.

beware of the staffs of industry trade organizations and of lobbyists because their primary concern is to remain employed and earn ever-continuing fees. Look at it at the extreme I was told. The lobbyists and the trade organization executives would be out work if they could magically solve all of their client or member problems all at once. Obviously, they can't solve all the problems all at once so they remain employed, being careful not to do too much real problem solving lest their billings deteriorate and have to reduce staff levels.

I cannot vouch for the truth of what I was told, but I have seen a couple of indications over time that smacks of it. Normally, there is a natural conflict of interest situation where one party pays and the other receives so normal diligence is required. It seems to me that clients and members should be especially wary when dealing with their lobbyists and trade organization management.

SILENCING TRADE-ORGANIZATION MEMBERS AND LOBBYIST'S CLIENTS

Trade organizations can be used and are used to silence the less powerful members (usually the smaller corporations) under the rubric that the organization must provide a united front. It would seem that merely joining such an organization could be against a smaller corporation's interest as it could destroy its ability to speak out on an issue where its economic interest is contrary to the bigger members. But it needn't be big verses small, for the divergence of interests can arise in different ways.

Take the issue of the US tax incentive for American corporations to operate abroad through foreign subsidiaries, which insulates the parent company from US tax on foreign earnings while the parent company continue to include the earnings of those foreign subsidiaries in its Annual Reports to shareholders and its filings with the SEC. This loophole in America's worldwide taxation system is mostly used by large American companies and has reduced US tax collections by trillions of dollars and ruined the American economy, reducing domestic purchasing power of workers who still find domestic jobs.

This works to the distinct disadvantage of US corporations that cannot or do not choose to go offshore (e.g. local retailers, domestic service companies, utilities). A person might imagine that they would be eager to close the foreign subsidiary loophole for they are being called to pay the tax that the offshore operators have avoided or evaded.

The domestic operators also lose part of their market base as American jobs are shifted abroad and their remaining customers have less purchasing power as American wages stagnate and so many American workers are unemployed.

These domestic corporations should be fighting for the elimination of the foreign subsidiary loophole in our worldwide tax system, but that cannot be seen in the positions of their trade organizations. They are being muzzled because they joined trade organizations that don't really represent them.

Yet, this is not seen or heard of as there is no reporting on it. Numerous domestic industries should be fighting this battle but nothing is being said publically by them.

Perhaps the business leaders in these domestic industries are not aware of the matter. These corporate leaders are business men who know their shops and are probably happy to delegate the political chore to the so-called professionals, not even questioning the motivations the others might have.

Perhaps these amenable domestic business leaders were even selected as compliant figureheads by their trade organizations so as to silence other members in similar domestic industries.

Perhaps some of these business leaders are aware of the situation but are being restrained by the rubric of a united front. Arguments extolling a united front, stopping the camel from getting its nose under the tent, and the like are predicated on the proposition that people, voters, legislators and the business leaders themselves are not capable of making distinctions and drawing lines. This is nonsense, and yet the united front argument is successful in muzzling dissent.

It would appear that lobbyists face the same issue as the trade organizations face when their clients are not allied on an issue. Lobbyists can ill afford to represent clients both sides of an issue although they would gladly do so if they could. So lobbyists might attempt to keep the conflict from being known, or attempt to muzzle a client, or even use misinformation.

The fact remains that splits in corporate America are not frequently seen. The hundreds of thousands of domestically operating corporations are not seen complaining about the offshore tax incentive and perhaps other issues that would appear to be equally divisive. It can only be attributable to their lobbyists and trade organizations muzzling or misinforming them, because we have seen how politically aggressive corporations can be when they want to.

ISSUE FRAMING BY LOBBYISTS

There are those who can frame issues so cleverly that even the politically savvy don't know what is really going on. On occasion, sufficient information leaks out to show that things might not be as they outwardly appear.

Take the medical device industry fighting a discriminatory tax on their products while no other group in the broad health care industry was subject to such a tax. Very appealing arguments can and were made to repeal that obviously discriminatory tax, yet those appeals un-understandably failed time after time. It is un-understandable only if you do not know what had gone on behind the scene.

The industries that would benefit greatly from the expanded coverage of the new healthcare law (put aside whether you agree or disagree with the new law) were expected to contribute to the cost of the new law with price discounts or policy changes. Deals were worked out with these industries, but the medical device industry wanted a free ride.

Congress worked out the math in a manner that was accepted by both political parties and that included placing a tax on the medical care industry to put it in the same position as the other health industries that voluntarily agreed to such deals. Thus, the tax was not discriminatory but merely to even the playing field so as to keep one segment of the health industry (the medical device industry) from getting an advantage the others did not get.

Whether things just happened to turn out that way, or whether it was planned that way by some clever executive or lobbyist, or whether the macho just took advantage of the situation cannot be known. The medical device industry wound up getting an outwardly appealing issue that it could fight (a discriminatory tax) so as to achieve an advantage no other healthcare industry got and their lobbyists wound up getting still another source of fees.

How the system works was recently revealed by showing how the medical device industry was able to influence or pressure local politicians.[1] The medical device industry was actually able to recruit Senators who had voted for the medical device tax, but now citing spurious dire consequences for the industry and local jobs.

The industry is very profitable and faces little price competition[2] and it would seem the industry could raise prices to pass on the tax without seeing much if any reduction in sales -- if so, it would make one wonder why the industry is still fighting the tax, paying millions in lobbying fees and probably spending many times that in support of selected politicians.

The repeal of the tax comes up time and time again, with seeming success until actual repeal is merely put aside by the legislators. The industry gets to the goal line and then losses. Perhaps repeal is put aside because of the realization that the tax not paid by the medical device industry will ultimately be

---

[1] Lipton, Eric, and Meier, Barry, "Tax on Medical Devices Becomes Recurring Theme in Budget Debate," The New York Times, October 22, 2012.

[2] Spiro, Topher, "The Myth of the Medical-Device Tax," The New York Times, October 16, 2013.

shifted to others, including those who made concessions. Perhaps it is all politics, making it appear the industry has support in the legislature while it is actually looked at differently.

The actual roles of the various parties (the lobbyists, corporations, and the politicians) in all of this would be very interesting, but probably never to be known. Why couldn't or wouldn't the medical device industry work out a deal as the other industries did? Who were the moving parties and the decision makers? In the end, so far, it seems like the lobbyists and the legislators were the only beneficiaries. Does this say something?

A much more prevalent situation where the public does not realize what is going on is where a seeming public purpose "institute" is formed, one the public could trust to tell the truth. These "institutes" abound, and their names are beguiling, but they are merely the lobbying vehicles of an industry or labor union group.

In one situation, the "institute" had no staff, all the work being done by a lobbying firm that billed its services to the "institute" an hid the names of the corporations participating in the lobbying effort.[1] Something must be done to get such organizations to insert the words "a lobbying organization" wherever their title appears, which is not likely to happen.

LOBBYING YOUR FORMER CONGRESSIONAL BOSS

After a lobbying scandal that made the front page for weeks, in 2007 Congress tightened its ethical rules to assure

---

[1] Lipton, Eric, "Fight Over Minimum Wage Illustrates Web of Industry Ties," The New York Times, February 9, 2014.

that at least a year passes before departing legislative aids could lobby and take advantage of their old connections and friendships. As one might expect of the lobbyists, they made sure that the new restrictions would be meaningless and Congress went along with it. Or it could have worked the other way with the legislators wanting to help their loyal servants and stay in touch with them when they become lobbyists, which never hurts.

Either way, it becomes apparent that Congress cannot be trusted to limit rather than expand its own rules. Why should we expect it? Power is the name of the game in Washington and nothing really effective in limiting the power and wellbeing of legislators should to be expected.

Within a year after leaving government, 1,650 congressional aides registered to lobby,[1] showing that the restrictions Congress made to its ethical rules in 2007 didn't work. We should not be surprised at this because legislators are not about to diminish their power or weaken valued contacts. When forced to legislate, the law is unlikely to work but merely aimed at relieving the pressure encountered.

Lobbying has been a growth industry, with lobbyists having prior government experience nearly quadrupling in the last 14 years.[2]

Severe term-limits for legislators, as has been suggested, would also serve to go far in limiting the power of lobbyists, particularly former staff members. While severe term-limits would not stack the legislative bodies with only public-

---

[1] Lipton, Eric and Protess, Ben, "Law Doesn't End Revolving Door on Capitol Hill," The New York Times, February 1, 2013.

[2] Editorial, "The Capitol's Spinning Door Accelerates," The New York Time, February 2, 2014.

spirited citizens eager to serve rather than achieve personal gain, it would go far in that direction and thus make it harder for lobbyists to influence Congress. These one-term legislators would hire staffs (there would be no term-limits for staff) of like mind, in time making for an experienced staff to help successor legislators. That staff would also tend to be of the more public-spirited types rather the get-ahead types eager to get rich in subsequent lobbying.

Pragmatically, there is no substantive reason why those leaving government in any capacity should be allowed to ever lobby that government. The public-spirited would not be any less likely to serve in government if they knew in advance that could not later lobby that government in any way. The get-ahead types seeking riches in politics would look elsewhere for employment if they knew that lobbying wouldn't be available to them. The question is why America leans over backwards to create, foster and enrich lobbyists.

The answer is that individual Americans would probably agree on baring lobbying by ex-government employees if it would be put up to a vote. It is the politicians who stand to benefit from the present situation allowing such lobbying, and the politicians are not likely to give the public a choice unless forced to.

Yet the rhetoric continues without being backed-up by any showing that the present system induces the best and brightest to join government as legislators and staff. A better argument can be made that the present system deters the best and the brightest from going into government.

Rather, it would appear that the most aggressive, power-seeking and greedy are attracted to government, although there would naturally be exceptions. Strict term-limits (that is, one term only) would go far in turning the tables, attracting the best and the brightest while deterring the greedy power-seekers.

Other than backing strict term-limits, there doesn't seem to be anything the public can do to change the current system. As we've seen with reform in simply delaying lobbying for a year, it just doesn't work.

We cannot ask Congress for true reform because we've rarely gotten it. And when it seems that Congress is willing to entertain reform, the reform turns out to be a nullity and things remain as they were before. The only effective thing votes can do, if they are of that mind and organize for it, is to push for one-term limit in Congress, which would surely change Washington.

LOBBYISTS' MONEY FUNDS LAWMAKERS GRACIOUS LIVING

It might well be said that the primary interest of all politicians is getting re-elected (self-preservation) while the secondary interest for some (probably most) is leading the good life or a gracious life. Sometimes the two dovetail nicely.

Whether a lobbyist is pursuing a client's pet project or just building a personal relationship with a legislator, lobbyists are able to flow money to legislators despite the 2007 law that prohibited lobbyist from making personal-use gifts to legislators. One ploy is for a legislator's campaign committee or a leadership PAC run a fund-raiser, which is perfectly fine way to raise funds that can only be used for campaigning and not used for the personal living expenses of the legislator.

It becomes a ploy when the fundraiser is held at a destination resort, usually an expensive one, in vacation havens of various types (like ski resorts, famous golf courses, five star hotels, hunting preserves, and other hot spots) that could even be outside the United States.[1]

Lobbyists and business interests attend these affairs and make contributions to the hosting campaign committee, which of course can legally pay the legislator's expenses in attending the fundraiser and participating in its activities. The legislators expenses are a cost of conducting the fund-raiser, and those who contribute to the fundraiser are making campaign contributions, not personal gifts to a legislator.

The legislator might pick-up the expense of the ski lift ticket or the gun ammunition, while all the transportation, food, hotel, and entertainment expenses are paid by the campaign committee.

Politicians Nullifying Election Results

American voters conferred on the President-elect the constitutional right and obligation to run the executive branch and administer the government. Upon winning the election, the President-elect's political party takes on the position of power.

---

[1] Lipton, Eric, "A Loophole Allows Lawmakers to Reel In Trips and Donations," The New York Times, January 19, 2014.

Yet many practices have evolved over the years that allows the minority (the political party that lost the election) to keep the majority (represented by the President who won the election) from pursuing its due. When this happens, the politicians in the minority effectively nullify the election results.

Impeachment is the most direct way of nullifying election results as it can oust the new President. State and local governments might also allow for impeachment of a governor or mayor, but are more likely to allow recall elections that also results in unseating the elected. But impeachments and recall elections are rare and it is the everyday tactics used by the minority party that allows it to block what the newly elected should be able to do.

Through the adoption and use of a variety of rules practices by the U.S. Senate, the Senate has snatched for itself the power to keep the President's appointed team, necessary to run the government, out of office. The foremost tactic is the use of the right of the Senate to reject presidential administrative (and judicial) appointments pursuant to the constitutional requirement that the President obtain the "advice and consent" of the Senate by a majority vote. The Senate had managed to convert that into a supermajority vote, which confers this extraordinary blocking power on the minority.

Then there are the Senator's "blue slips" and "holds" submitted under the internal Senate rules that can allow a few Senators to actually blackball the President's appointments, or to endlessly delay their confirmation. In addition, internally adopted rules govern the operation of Senate committees, which are famous for their ability to procedurally bottle up the consideration of presidential appointments and keep them from getting to the floor of the Senate for a vote.

Where the majority in the Senate is of the opposing political party, the Senate would have the power, based on the constitution and not merely internal rulemaking, to keep the President's nominees from being seated by just voting against the appointments. Of course, the Senate (or for that matter, the House of Representatives) can also vote against the bills offered by the President. But the power the Senate has to keep the President's team from taking office can keep the newly elected President from exercising the administrative powers that goes along with the office, which is a way of nullifying the election.

All this has contributed to the dysfunctional government we now have. It cries for change. It calls for eliminating the internal Senate rules and procedures that arrogate power to the Senate and Senators. It also suggests a constitutional amendment to eliminate or modify the "advice and consent" provision -- the passage of time and our changing society has served to pervert what our founding fathers had sought with this provision.

NULLIFYING AN ELECTION BY IMPEACHMENT

The constitution provides for the impeachment of any officer of the federal government, including the President, Vice President, lesser officers and judges for high crimes, misdemeanors, treason or bribery.[1] A majority vote in the House of Representatives is necessary to bring the

---

[1] Article II, section 4.

impeachment case, and a two-thirds majority is required in the Senate to convict after holding a trial.

On the state level, there are a variety of impeachment procedures as determined by the state constitutions. A number of governors have been removed from office through impeachment proceeding but never a President of the United States.

Impeachments of federal officials, including the President, causes the convicted person to lose their job. With the Vice President being the successor to a convicted President, the executive branch of government remains in the hands of the same political party. And with a two-thirds majority being required in the Senate to convict, removal of a President isn't very probable. Thus impeachment would be of little avail politically, except for the embarrassment it causes which can result in the loss of the next election.

Thus, the impeachment process is more likely to be a vendetta pursued to embarrass the President and hurt the President's political party in the next election, rather than being a way to combat treason or other high crimes as our founding fathers visualized. The impeachment process on the federal level has become a political gamesmanship tool perverting the original intent of our founding fathers, as does so many other constitutional provisions perverted by our dysfunctional Congress.

STATE RECALL PROCEDURES

Many states have procedures that allows the recall of an elected official based on a vote of the electorate. This seems to be democratic since the electorate gets to vote on the recall, however it is grossly unfair in that recall does not depend on wrongdoing but can be politically based on the way the legislator voted. Recall, like impeachment, should be based on wrongdoing and not merely on how the elected representative chooses to vote.

In the general election, the electorate considers all aspects of a candidate's qualifications and the candidate's viewpoints on numerous issues. The electorate balances all that in voting for a candidate. Recall can be based on a single-issue vote by the elected candidate, an issue that didn't loom large in the election but can be blown up in devastating ways.

Two state senators were recalled because they voted for a gun control law that was passed in the state and became state law.[1] The opposition saw an opportunity in their small districts to have these senators recalled even though that would not repeal the gun control law disliked in that district. The districts became a battle ground for out-of-state interests interested in that one issue. One of recalled senators was the Senate President and when he lost, he was replaced by his ballot challenger who had lost the election.

It is most difficult to justify recall procedures that are not based on wrongdoing. Elected candidates should be allowed to vote as they would for their entire term and not be subject to political gamesmanship if the electorate changes in the interim, or if the electorate in the district is made to focus on just a single issue. It is procedures like this, that sound good because the electorate gets to vote, that become instruments of abuse.

---

[1] Healy, Jack, "Colorado Lawmakers Ousted in Recall Vote Over Gun Law," The New York Times, September 11, 2013.

This contributes to dysfunctional government and impinges on other voters who rely on one person, one vote. These recall laws should be rewritten to require a finding of wrongdoing by some legislative or quasi-judicial body.

ADVICE AND CONSENT OF THE SENATE

The United States Constitution requires[1] the Senate to "approve" (that is, give its "advice and consent" to) treaties entered into by the President by <u>a two thirds vote</u> of the Senators present; and approve by <u>a majority vote</u> the President's appointment of Ambassadors, Judges of the Supreme Court and lesser judges, officers and officials.

The Senate was given the constitutional discretion to forego its vetting of the lesser nominations, and it has exercised that discretion to some extent. The President was given the power to make recess appointments, which is being challenged.[2]

While the constitution governs the required "advice and consent" votes on the floor of the Senate, it is the Senate's own internal rules that govern the procedures used in bringing appointments to the Senate floor. The treaties and appointments go to the relevant Senate committees that discuss approval and send the matter to the floor of the Senate for the up-and-down (yes or no) vote.

Because Senate debates can be endless, the Senate also has internal procedural "cloture" rules providing for the closing of debate. Thus, a cloture vote of the Senate is

---

[1] Article II, Section 2, paragraph 2.
[2] Editorial, "Protect the President's Appointments," The New York Times, January 11, 2014.

necessary to stop endless committee debate and delay by a determined minority wanting to block appointments. While the constitution required only a majority vote on the floor if the Senate for confirmation, stopping the minority from blocking appointments in committee required a supermajority vote that greatly empowered the minority at the expense of the elected majority.

Initially, there was no Senate rule to end debate. In 1917, President Woodrow Wilson got the Senate to adopt a cloture rule requiring a two-thirds majority, destroying the power, he said, of a small number of "willful men" in the Senate to render the government helpless.

The Senate further reduced the required vote for cloture to three fifths in 1975. Three fifths required that a supermajority vote of 60 out of the 100 Senators were needed to vote for cloture, while only a majority vote was required to change the Senate procedural rules.

On November 21, 2013, a majority of the Senate voted to change its procedural rule to allow cloture with a simple majority.

Thus from 1975 to 2013, the appointment of federal judges and executive branch nominees to the Cabinet, to executive departments and to federal agencies required a supermajority vote of three-fifths (60 votes) for the cloture of debate and getting the appointment to the Senate floor for a yes or no vote. Where the elected majority could count on the votes of 51 Senators (a simple majority) but not 60 Senators (the required supermajority), the minority could block nominations from ever getting to the floor of the Senate.

This allowed the minority to pick and choose who would govern and thus nullify the previous election. By 2013, strong opposition to the status quo became apparent.[1]

President Barack Obama, echoed the century old view of President Wilson, saying the supermajority vote and the pattern of obstruction it engendered was "not what our founders envisioned. A deliberate and determined effort to obstruct everything, no matter what the merits, just to refight the results of an election is not normal, and for the sake of future generations we can't let it become normal."[2]

So now the constitutional mandate of a simple majority vote (51 votes) for approval on the floor of the Senate is mirrored by the Senate's new procedural rule providing the same simple majority for cloture (51 votes) in committee. The political party that won the Senate would normally have the simple majority necessary to approve the slate of appointments by a President of the same political party. If they are not of the same party, the old style Senate blockage can still arise inasmuch as the opposition has the majority to vote against approval in committee and on the floor of the Senate.

---

[1] Peters, Jeremy W., "G.O.P. Delays on Nominees Raise Tension," The New York Times, May 11, 2013.

Peters, Jeremy W., "Between Democrats and a Push for Filibuster Change, One Nominee," The New York Times, October 29, 2013.

Peters, Jeremy W., "Abortion Cases in Court Helped Tilt Democrats Against the Filibuster," The New York Times, November 29, 2013.

Editorial, "The Politics of Petulance," The New York Times, October 31, 2013.

[2] Peters, Jeremy W., "In Landmark Vote, Senate Limits Use of the Filibuster," The New York Times, November 21, 2013.

Thus, it is only when the same political party wins both the presidency and the Senate can the elected President be confident of being able to govern. When the President-elect's political party losses the Senate, the new President would face a tremendous handicap in governing.

The "advice and consent" provision of the constitution allows a Senate dominated by the other political party to keep a newly elected President from governing, which calls for repeal of the advice and consent provision by a constitutional amendment.

THE SENATE'S INTERNAL RULES

The Senate's own internal rules contribute mightily to the dysfunction in the Senate, at times shutting down the entire government. Committee bottlenecks, filibusters, obstructions, and delays are the minority's stock in trade.

Curiously, both political parties had agreed upon and approved the dysfunctional rules by a majority vote, and yet it came to be viewed as a "nuclear event" when the majority voted to curb a dysfunctional rule, as was the case with changing the cloture rules in 2013.

The new Senate rule of a simple majority for cloture on appointments was not extended to Supreme Court appointments even though only a simple majority is constitutionally required in voting yes or no on a Supreme Court appointment on the floor of the Senate. Thus, the Senate deliberately left that as a fertile field for filibuster and blockage. Nor does the new cloture rule extend to the ordinary, day-to-day legislation that flows through the Senate and does not involve appointments.

Thus, the filibuster remain alive and functioning, courtesy of the Senate's internal procedural rules. Also alive and functioning are the numerous procedural rules that govern the operation of Senate committees.

All the internal rules that allow for obstruction and delay represent tools used by the Senators to arrogate power to themselves. They effectively enable other Senators to obstruct and delay so that they too can also do so in the future when it benefits them, enhancing the personal power of each Senator. As to this, Senators cooperate nicely.

Some people were of the opinion that partisan fever was likely to increase due to the 2013 "nuclear event" of changing the cloture rules.[1] Increased use of other obstruction and delay tactics might be a possibility if a person actually believes that those tactics were not already being used to fullest. Hopefully, the new cloture rule will favor the moderates and tame partisan fever in the Senate, but don't count on it.[2]

While the 2013 change might possibly lead to other filibuster changes,[3] the Senate did deliberately allow the continued use of filibusters to obstruct day-to-day legislation

---

[1] Weisman, Jonathan, "Partisan Fever in Senate Likely to Rise," The New York Times, November 21, 2013.

Editorial, "Government in Slow Motion," The New York Times, November 28, 2013.

Peters, Jeremy W., "With Filibuster Threat Gone, Senate Confirms Two Presidential Nominees," The New York Times, December 10, 2013.

[2] Peters, Jeremy W., "White House Steps Up Effort to Confirm Federal Judges," The New York Times, April 28, 2014.

[3] Editorial, "Democracy Returns to the Senate," The New York Times, November 21, 2013.

from proceeding to a floor vote and to obstruct the appointment of Supreme Court judges.

A voter might well ask why their elected majority in the Senate had been willing to abandon the mandate their political party was given in the last election by not eliminating all the supermajority rules that could be constitutionally eliminated. The answer could have uncovered what is really going on with the Senate's internal rules.

The Senators might say that they have a longer range view and are thus willing to limit their power today so that they would have greater power in the future should they find themselves in the minority. That is the usual stated rationale for allowing filibusters and other obstructions -- they themselves want the power to be the future obstructers should the occasion require it.

What appears on the surface is that the Senate rules empower Senators at the expense of the executive branch. That enhances an incumbent's position, fundraising and re-election prospects.

Voters should determine for themselves what the underlying rationale of the legislators might be, because the voters put those legislators in office. Surely something is going on behind the scene to account for elected legislators to work with the opposition in establishing rules so as to arrogate power to themselves and by doing so undermine those who put them in office.

With the horrendous situation of so many appointments being recently blocked by the minority, why did it take so long for the majority to call a halt to it? Could it be that retaining personal power was more important than having a functional government? Perhaps the majority was forced to act for the dysfunction went beyond the level of tolerance.

Yet, when the majority did act, they did so only partially, keeping the supermajority rule intact in other areas (Supreme Court judges, day-to-day legislation) apparently so as to hold on to personal power, aid in future fundraising and re-election.

Each political party yielding to extortion by the other party through filibusters has to be a zero sum game over time, so why should both parties be so interested in preserving their filibuster prerogative over time? Obviously, Senators are reluctant to give up their prerogatives, reluctant to yield the power they snatched for themselves at the expense of a truly functional democracy of, by and for the people.

Our founders obviously felt we should have a greater consensus (two thirds) when we enter into treaties with other nations, but a simple majority was found sufficient for domestic matters. Obviously, our Senators want something else, which accounts for their procedural rules that benefits only themselves and leads to dysfunctionality.

In addition to keeping the elected President from fulfilling the voters mandate to govern, the Senate procedural rules operate in a disturbing fashion that doesn't meet the eye. Difficulty in getting appointments approved results in the administration being reluctant to rid itself of poor or embarrassing performers because it recognizes that it would be difficult to get a replacement appointment approved.

The question arises as to how the people can regain control of their own Senate, a matter more fully discussed later under the heading of *"Making Democracy Work."* Right now it seems that haranguing the political party responsible for defeating a popular measure is the only available remedy.

To illustrate, the vote in favor of increasing the minimum wage was 54 to 42 but the bill lost since it didn't have a supermajority. Republicans voted solidly along party lines so as to keep the Democrats from having the needed 60 vote supermajority to move the bill to a vote on the Senate floor where the simple majority of 54 would have passed the bill.

Yet the bill was popular amongst American voters, a poll showing that Americans (both Republicans and Democrats) overwhelmingly favored an increase in the minimum wage (62% to 38%). After the defeat of the bill due to the lack of a supermajority the President asked voters to punish the Republicans and put them out of office if they continue putting politics ahead of voters' wishes.[1]

A more effective and permanent solution would be found in instituting a term limit for Senators (only one term) so that Senators would not be so interested in arrogating power to themselves through unnecessary and unfair supermajority rules. The objection to a term limit is that the Senators would focus on their next job outside the legislature, which would probably serve America better than their present focus on re-election to the legislature and a lifetime of power grabbing.

THE SENATE'S "BLUE SLIP" BLACKBALL

The "blue slip" procedure provides another way the electorate's vote can be nullified. Under the rules of the

---

[1] Peters, Jeremy W., "Democrats Assail G.O.P. After Filibuster of Proposal to Raise Minimum Wage," The New York Times, April 30, 2014.

Senate, the chairman of the judiciary committee can refuse to schedule the necessary hearing on an administration appointment if either of the Senators of the state where the judicial vacancy exists objects to the appointment by filling out a blue slip.[1]

That is, Senators of either party of a particular state can personally stop the appointment of any judge in that state, a right not conferred by the constitution but conferred by other Senators who also want to wield the same power in their states.

The chairman of the judiciary committee is naturally of the political party that won a majority in the Senate. That majority is now sufficient to confirm Presidential judicial appointments (except for Supreme Court judges where a supermajority is still needed). If the President is of the other political party, obstruction wouldn't be anything special.

But where the President is of the same political party as the judicial committee chairman, a voter might logically expect that presidential appointments would sail through confirmation. The blue slip practice denies that by allowing Senators in the same political party to face off against a President in the same political party.

Giving three Senators (the two Senators from a given state and the Senator chairing the judiciary committee) the ability to veto Presidential appointments contributes to our dysfunctional government. Although the constitution gives the Senate the right to confirm or deny judicial appointments,

---

[1] Savage, Charlie, "Despite Filibuster Limits, a Door Remains Open to Block Judge Nominees," The New York Times, November 28, 2013.
Editorial, "The Senate's Discourtesy to Judges," The New York Times, March 30, 2014.

that right is given to the entire Senate and not just to two or three Senators.

Thus, it becomes clear that where the Senate and the President are of the same political party, the blue slip procedure operates as a power grab by the Senate -- that is one body of our government is grabbing power at the expense of the other. Where two different political parties control Senate and presidency, the blue strip procedure is basically irrelevant.

The party that won the Presidential election should have the right to govern and nominate federal judges throughout the land. Senators from the state where the federal judge would sit should have no say in this just because the court sits there. That court just deals with federal matters, not state matters.

The state courts are the bailiwick of state and local interests and voters. The federal court system belongs to the nation. Arguments that the blue strip procedure would be useful where wackos are appointed are merely spin. All appointments by both parties are vetted because nobody needs to or wants to appoint wackos.

America would be well served by a rule that all appointments go to the floor of the Senate for a yes or no vote within 60 days of the submission of the appointment, with the Senate holding as many committee hearings it wants within those 60 days. That would serve the constitutional purpose better and destroy the potential for obstruction and dysfunctionality

But would the Senate ever yield any power it could arrogate to itself? Probably, not. But it would be worthwhile to push for it, to see which Senators would publically standup to support their dysfunctional practices and whether there would be support for a constitutional amendment.

The constitution separation of powers was a brilliant move by our founders and should be honored and, like everything else, not be carried too far. The founders' mandate was to have the Senate accept or reject the appointments the President makes. This certainly contemplates a vote on the floor of the Senate within a reasonable time frame. Anything less should not satisfy the constitution.

Any restrictions, limitations, scheduling, blue or other slips goes too far, which we have a tendency to do as a nation. It goes too far because it is not necessary to satisfy the constitutional mandate, because it leads to obstruction and dysfunctionality in the operation of our system of government, and because Washington has clearly shown it is dysfunctional and that it is about time the voters did something about it.

THE SENATE'S "HOLD"

Under another internal procedural rule, a single Senator has the power to place a "hold" on voting on a nomination. This inexplicable rule states that "no motion to proceed to the consideration of any bill, resolution, report of a committee, or other subject upon the Calendar shall be entertained by the Presiding Officer, unless by unanimous consent…" Imagine requiring unanimous consent in the Senate.

Thus, any Senator who objects to the bringing of a bill or nomination to a vote on the floor of the Senate might make his or objection known (the act being considered a "hold' on the motion) and stop consideration of the bill or nomination. With a rule like this it is a wonder how anything gets done. Again, the trade-offs involved in placing a hold and the machinations to free the hold confers much power on each Senator and the party leaders in the Senate.

The stated justification for a "hold" is frequently that the objecting Senator needs more time to study the bill, as if he or she were the only slow kid in the class and only his or her constituents have a special interest in the bill. What the real reasons are and what goes on behind the scene are not known.

Yet, one Senator recently appeared honest about it. He announced he will place a "hold" on an important nomination and block every appointment until he gets the hearings he wants on an entirely unrelated matter.[1] The "hold' is another contributor to our dysfunctional government that has to be eliminated.

AMENDING THE CONSTITUTION

The confirmation process our founders had in mind no longer functions in this age of political parties and reluctance to compromise, which appears to be the norm from now on. As our society has changed, we should amend the constitution to accord with the present situation.

Many persons would insist, reputedly including George Washington, that it is up to the President alone to select the nominees he or she wants. The President might take or seek the advice of Senators in making the selection, but there is no requirement that the advice be sought or accepted.

---

[1] Collins, Gail, "The Art of Senate Stoppage," The New York Times, November 13, 2013.

As the constitution is worded, the word "advice" adds nothing because the constitutional provision address the consent of the Senate after the nomination has already been made, whereas advice to be pertinent should be offered before the nomination is made.

Thus, the constitution as written contemplates a voluntary co-operative effort for consensus amongst the Senators, while today we face deliberate adversarial efforts by Senators to obstruct.

Today, the President's nominee can be rejected by the Senate and the replacement nominee also rejected, going on endlessly and destroying the will of the electorate. The majority who elected the President would expect, and so would logical people everywhere, that the President would nominate people of like mind.

The Senators also know and expect that. However, willful for the politicians amongst them this is set-up for the use of extortion in order to get a candidate of their liking or exact a deal for something else.

Perpetuating the constitutional provision for "advice and consent" as originally drafted no longer makes sense and should be eliminated or amended, perhaps along the lines suggested below in the section "*Making Democracy Work*."

That section also offers suggestions on how to stop the politicians from arrogating power to themselves through their rulemaking.

Nullifying Enacted Laws

Some States believe that they have the right to disregard federal laws that have national application. When this occurs, and it has occurred from time to time, the State is effectively nullifying an already enacted law as far as the State's citizens are concerned.

The Constitution of the United State provides in Article VI that the laws of the Federal government "shall be the supreme Law of the Land; and the Judges in every State shall be bound thereby, any Thing in the Constitution or Laws of any state to the Contrary notwithstanding."

Notwithstanding this constitutional "supremacy" mandate, a State governor or a state legislative branch or judiciary occasionally strives to nullify the application or execution of a federal law within the State.

PUTTING ASIDE FEDERAL SUPREMACY

Supreme Court has the ability to declare a law unconstitutional. It also has the ability rewrite the law by the way it "interprets" the law that it declares constitutional. By putting aside the federal supremacy clause so as to allow the states to opt out of a law, it blatantly changes the way the law applies.

By doing so, the Supreme Court can effectively grant the states the power to nullify the application of federal laws in their states even though the enacted law did not provide for that. That would be the clearest illustration of the Supreme Court legislating.

The Supreme Court had put aside the supremacy clause so as to allow states to opt out of a federal law expanding Medicare (and Medicaid, technically, the "Affordable Care Act" which opponents label "Obamacare").[1]

The expansion of Medicare became a federal law applicable across the entire United States. The expansion was highly controversial and America was largely divided on it. Some state governors were against the expansion and lawsuits were filed seeking to declare the expansion unconstitutional.

It would appear that the Supreme Court found a ground for compromise, preserving the constitutionality of the new law and yet allowing the opposing states to nullify it as far as their citizens were concerned.

Many people would applaud the Supreme Court for doing this, as it would tend to bolster our democracy in matters as divisive as this one was. A person can only speculate about what would have happened to our democracy if the Supreme Court had declared the Medicare expansion unconstitutional, or had declared it constitutional without giving the hostile states a way out. It appears that the court adopted a middle ground.

The approach disregards the principle of one person, one vote. State citizens denied the benefit of expanded Medicare in states that opted out did not achieve equal protection promised throughout the land by duly passed federal legislation. Yet, expanded Medicare was pulling the nation apart as no other issue had ever done.

The divisiveness even got to the point where the US government was actually closed down for a while because of

---

[1] Stolberg, Sheryl Gay, "States Are Focus of Effort to Foil Health Care Law," The New York Times, October 18, 2013

it. Opponents of the Medicare expansion at first threatened and then voted to shut the federal government down by prohibiting the federal government from paying its debt if the Medicare expansion was not repealed.[1]

To avoid hitting the federal debt ceiling, which is usually extended by Congress before it is breached, the government closed down to save the cash needed to pay outstanding US debt as required[2] by the constitution. As the administration refused to consider repeal of the Medicare expansion because it was blackmail, the tactic failed badly and created so much electorate resentment that the tactic is not likely to ever be used again.

But, in the meantime, the Supreme Court did legislate by allowing putting aside federal supremacy. And it appears to have been a good thing that it did.

Who said the courts shouldn't legislate? All the courts on all levels do so whenever they address a new issue.

TACTICS USED

Filing lawsuits is the primary tactic aimed at nullifying or modifying federal law. Legal challenges to the expanded

---

[1] Krugman, Paul, "One Reform, Indivisible," The New York Times, August 18, 2013.

[2] Section 4 of the 14th Amendment provides that the "validity of the public debt of the United States, authorized by law, including debts incurred for payment of pensions and bounties for services in suppressing insurrection or rebellion, shall not be questioned." Thus, all debts arising from payments authorized by Congress, pensions being only one such payment, are authorized by law and must be treated as valid public debt; meaning the debt must be paid whatever the debt-level. This view also seems to deny the existence of the so-called "debt ceiling."

Medicare still abound.[1] Just as the Supreme Court was able to handle the basic constitutional challenge, the lesser courts are perfectly capable of dealing fairly with the lesser challenges.[2]

Another tactic is to make enforcement of the federal law within the state a crime, which can potentially land federal enforcement officials in jail. The state of Missouri is poised to enact such a law with respect to enforcement of a federal gun law within the state.[3] Such a law would pit the states' rights provision[4] against the federal supremacy provision of the constitution.

Still another tactic is for the local law enforcement officials to refuse to enforce the law, whether it is a federal or state law.[5] The gun control laws are a frequent target because of the constitutional right to bear arms. When law enforcement officials refuse to enforce a gun law, they are effectively maintaining that right to bear arms had been abridged by that law.

---

[1] Stolberg, Sheryl Gay, "A New Wave of Challenges to Health Law," The New York Times, December 2, 2013.
[2] Editorial, "Health Care Reform Survives a Lawsuit," The New York Times, January 16, 2014.
[3] Schwartz, John, "Gun Bill in Missouri Would Test Limits in Nullifying U.S. Law," The New York Times, August 28, 2013.
[4] The 10th Amendment provides that "the powers not delegated to the United States by the Constitution, nor prohibited by it to the States, are reserved to the States respectively, or to the people." The federal government has the power to enact laws and enforce them. While a state might raise a question as to whether the federal government can force the state to enforce a particular federal law or regulation, in this instance the federal government is enforcing its own law.
[5] Goode, Erica, "Sheriffs Refuse to Enforce Laws on Gun Control," The New York Times, December 15, 2013.

Sometimes the claim is that the gun control law is constitutionally vague so they need not enforce it.

Many law enforcement officials feel that they have wide discretion in enforcing laws and they exercise that discretion by not intervening to enforce a federal or state law, which is akin to refusing to enforce the law.

The abortion rights issue gave rise to another type of tactic, one involving the states right to regulate where a valid purpose is served.

Texas required that abortion doctors have local hospital admitting privileges pursuant to its duty to protect the health and safety of Texans, even though opponents claimed that regulation would close the abortion clinics.[1]

Placing obstacles in the way of a law is another tactic to keep the law from being implemented. The obstacle can be the refusal to process a required application, to make it difficult to obtain and file what need be filed, or just to delay processing. Such tactics were used to deny same-sex military couples the federal benefits they were entitled to claim.[2]

Requiring a state license to conduct an activity mandated by federal law is still another sabotage tactic. The federal law required the employment of counselors who had to meet federal standards with the state adding a requirement of a state license, which the courts struck down as an

---

[1] Eckholm, Erik, "In Reversal, Court Allows Texas Law on Abortion," The New York Times, October 31, 2013.

[2] Editorial, "The National Guard's Defiance on Civil Rights," The New York Times," October 20, 2013.

impermissible obstacle to the implementing of the federal law.[1]

It seems that what had heretofore been viewed as "state's rights" aimed at keeping the big, bad federal government from taking advantage of the states has now been subverted into a tool for the states to sabotage the federal government. Fortunately, the founders (in anticipating this?) allowed federal law to pre-empt state law.

America needs to stop the endless battles concerning already enacted federal laws where the states through their representatives were able to weigh in against the federal law before it was adopted. Once duly adopted, the federal law should be obeyed.

Both the public and federal officials should be vigilant in identifying and publicizing state sabotage and look forward to law enforcement and the court system handling it. Any state law or practice that operates as an obstacle (whether or not deliberately designed to do so) to the administration of federal law should be stricken.

THE NEW DYSFUNCTIONAL STANDARD

The new standard, especially with regard to the very controversial issues (e.g., guns, Medicare expansion, abortion, gay marriage), is to never accept defeat and continue fighting to curtail, limit, or nullify at all costs. This is a phenomenon of the current decade. In previous decades the controversy ended when the law was enacted.

---

[1] Editorial, "Roadblocks on Health Reform," The New York Times, January 28, 2014.

This is another aspect of our dysfunctional government. Continued fighting and taking advantage of everything the democratic process possibly allows is claimed to be the right of a minority in a democratic society.

However, reason would suggest that the fight is over once the law is passed. The continued fighting shows that nothing is ever settled. The 1973 decision in Roe v. Wade has been fought for 40 years.

This constant opposition is time consuming and diverts attention from other matters that should be addressed. It creates ever more animosity in its path. It is destroying America.

Nullifying "One Person, One Vote"

The US constitution adopted the concept of "one person, one vote." It is not just that each voter gets to vote only once in each election. Our founders used that concept so that each voter in a state would have equal weight in electing representatives.

A periodic census is used to redraw voting districts so that each district would have approximately equal populations. This is what enables the one person, one vote concept to operate. But even with this, voting equality issues lurk.

The number of voters in a district might be measured by head-count or measured by the number of persons eligible to vote, with the weight of court decisions being on head-count even where much of the population is ineligible to vote (e.g., children, immigrants). The Supreme Court hasn't yet addressed this.[1]

In the 1960's, the US Supreme Court had addressed whether the one person, one vote concept extended to state and municipality elections and found it did, including both houses of a bicameral state legislature.

Yet our founders were forced into compromising one person, one vote and put principle aside so as to induce the smaller states to join the union without fearing domination by the larger states (the "Connecticut Compromise"). They split the legislature into two houses, with only the voters for representatives to the House of Representatives being subject to one person, one vote and state redistricting every 10 years.

Voters in each state get to vote for two Senators, providing unequal representation in the Senate as the states vary greatly in population. Voters in low population states are over-represented while voters in high population states are under-represented. Thus, the equality amongst states in the Senate effectively disenfranchises voters in the large population states to some extent.

The staggered six year term in the Senate, as compared to the two year term in the House, also serves to disenfranchise voters but in a very different way. It serves to keep voters from making large, fast swings in their governance.

While the large/small state compromise and the staggered votes serves the purposes of balance, it should be recognized that balance itself disenfranchises because it keeps the majority from doing its will. There is some justification for

---

[1] Liptak, Adam, "One Person One Vote (or Was That One Voter One Vote?)" The New York Times, March 18, 2013.

this in terms of protecting the minority, but our democracy cannot be said to fully subscribe to voting equality.

Worse, although the founders did not anticipate it, the bicameral legislature did not give America a better government balanced between the interests of large and small states.

Today, the un-proportionate voting in the Senate allows the political party in control of the Senate to confound the will of the majority of the American population as represented in the House on issues that have absolutely nothing to do with big state vs small state.

Thus, a minority of Americans having control of the Senate not only gets their minority rights respected on big states versus small state issues, but allows that minority to overrule the majority of Americans on any issue.

So much for the legislative intent of the founders writing the constitution. No constitution is perfect to begin with. Not only are there un-anticipated consequences, things also change in time. The constitution has undergone many amendments, showing it wasn't perfect or showing it needed to change in order to keep up with changes in our society.

More amendments can be expected as our society changes. And more amendments should be sought as our democratic government gets more and more dysfunctional in ways never envisaged.

There are ways people in power can keep the "other" from voting or can dilute the other's vote by tactics like gerrymandering. Even if there were no structural flaws in our constitution, various impediments have been developed by the nefarious or evolved naturally that does not strictly accord with one person, one vote and call for amendments to the constitution.

Splits in America have become wider and deeper since America has stopped striving to become one nation out of the many ("E Pluribus Unum"). That has led to even more disenfranchisement and more dysfunction.

ONE NATION, OUT OF THE MANY (E PLURIBUS UNUM)

Equal voting by state in the Senate cannot be changed by amending the constitution,[1] which is the only limitation on amending the constitution other than two provisions that couldn't be changed before a specific date, 1808.

Not being able to change equal state "suffrage" in the Senate emphasizes the separate identity and status of the various states.

That also serves to preserve and accentuate state and regional differences in opposition to being one nation. If we were indeed "one nation," there would be less pressure and fewer attempts to disenfranchise the "other" voter.

As initially adopted in 1782, the Great Seal of the United States had the motto "E PLURIBUS UNUM" which, when literary translated from the Latin, stands for "out of many, one" or one nation out of the many.

It means that out of the many nations or peoples coming together, the new nation makes them one. This portrayed the prevailing democratic philosophy when our country was founded. But in 1956, Congress saw fit to change this motto on the Great Seal to "In God We Trust" although E

---

[1] Article V: "... no state, without its consent, shall be deprived of its equal suffrage in the Senate."

PLURIBUS UNUM remains on the official seals of the President, Vice President, the Senate and House and the Supreme Court.

The 1956 change in motto had no legal significance but does show how American society changed since its founding era, effectively laying to rest the one nation out of the many, melting-pot concept.

OBLITERATION OF THE "MELTING POT" CONCEPT

Assimilation or melting together (the "melting pot") as one people had been the prevalent belief from the time of America's founding through the waves of immigration lasting to the mid-1900s.

The push for diversity or multiculturism in America might be ascribed to the years after the World War II. It may have been attributable in part to the holocaust and in part to America's failure to assimilate the black community which had to coalesce and strike off on its own and eventually create its own voting caucus and voting bloc.

Striving for diversity was full blown by the 1970s, about the time the decline of America started as a matter of coincidence or as a partial result.

America started off with a major contradiction that later contributed to the ultimate domination of diversity in the cultural scene. The treatment of each state being equal in the Senate preserved colonial divergences' instead of making one nation out of the many. Regional attitudes and voting blocs ensued, and disenfranchising the "other" voters became widespread.

Our founders, off on a new venture, built-in many checks and balances but that too has been carried by us too far as we have a tendency to do with a good thing.

We now have an established nation, the uncertainties surrounding the foundation of the nation having been overcome. We no longer need to include balances in what we now do because unneeded balances stifle and lead to more dysfunction in government.

We need measures that bring us together, not more opportunities to shackle the other guy.

DIVERSITY CAN BE DYSFUNCTIONAL

There is support for the proposition that radically diverse communities are dysfunctional. The various groups in these diverse communities, not viewing themselves as one with their communities, frequently do not trust the other groups or their governments and institutions.

In addition to less trust, there might be less invested in infrastructure, less charity, less helping others, and less consensus in government, all leading to dysfunctional government.

In these diverse communities, there is more group internalizing, more economic inequality, more demands for special rights, more demands for separation and self-determination, and more actual inter-group hatred.

Diversity and multiculturalism allows for more individual self-expression. It provides a richer community mosaic of ethnic, religious and cultural differences, and the comfort arising from being in sync with one's ancestors. Unfortunately, it requires the adoption of special measures to assure minority group participation, to assure minority group access to societal resources and to assure national unity, which measures are lacking too frequently.

As contrasted, assimilation would have naturally led to more societal cohesion and universally shared values and norms. History exhibits the prevalence of exclusion, conflict, and even genocide in diverse societies, but not where assimilation has taken place.

A new element recently entered the scene and seems to be expanding. Corporations had set up campuses for its employees, some even supplying housing and food services. They allowed the upmost of personal freedom, in hours worked, in the manner of dressing and in almost everything else. It appeared to work in terms of fostering creativity but it also represents the making of still another type of community separated even more from the other diversified societies in our midst.

Fostering creativity through self-expression, one of the benefits of diversity, doesn't go very far in justifying diversity as the standard for society in general, aside from its being very limited in scope. Today, corporate campuses are being taken further with the campuses including shops, like cleaners, that can be used only by employees.[1] It seems that we are no longer dealing with diversity at all, but rather with a new form of monasteries, single-purpose institutions.

The concern in this book is the decline of America, and solely that. From that viewpoint alone, the present emphasis on diversity and multiculturalism has failed America since it

---

[1] Arieff, Allison, "What Tech Hasn't Learned From Urban Planning," The New York Times, December 13, 2013.

contributed to dysfunctionality in government and to internal strife that stultifies.

Perhaps it is once again America's tendency to go too far with a good thing. Diversity, honoring one's background, should not keep a person from fitting into the mainstream, whether in language, dress or in other ways, but some carry it too far. We should no longer identify ourselves as Italian, Iranian or Indonesian. It's okay to have an ethnic, racial, religious, or other soul, but we should all consider ourselves Americans first and foremost.

When it comes to voting, we speak of equality of treatment but instead get the opposite of group thought, of voting blocks and of disenfranchising the other.

We should be putting the brakes on diversity and multiculturalism, maintaining a neutral attitude toward it while aiming for assimilation. We should not let the melting pot grow cold.

KEEPING THE "OTHER" FROM VOTING

Voter registration laws, regulations and rules were aimed at enabling voters to exercise their right to vote at the appointed time and place. The laws were designed to prove their entitlement to vote, but to vote only once in the relevant elections and referendums.

However, these laws, regulations and rules can also be used by the persons controlling the voter registration process to exclude the "other" from voting.[1]

---

[1] Yaccino, Steven, and Alvarez, Lizette, "New G.O.P. Bid to Limit Voting in Swing States," The New York Times, March 29, 2014.

The "other" could be those of particular racial, ethnic or religious groups. Since discrimination of this nature is unconstitutional, indirect methods are used that are not discriminatory in themselves but have the effect of discrimination because they fall more heavily on a particular group.

In its simplest and most obvious forms, keeping the "other" from voting would include situating a voting location in a difficult place to get to, in having cramped voting space, in being short of balloting equipment, in having insufficient or inconvenient voting hours, and anything else that forces unconscionably long lines to vote or keeps the targeted "other" voter from getting to the voting booth.

It could merely be the removal of names from a voting role, perhaps a last minute purge, without enough time to accurately evaluate data bases.[1]

More sophisticated approaches to lowering the "other" vote would include the absence of measures that make voting easier; like advance voting, absentee ballots, additional voting hours for the elderly, and assistance to the disabled.

There are also more subtle ways to disenfranchise potential voters by requiring identification documents that some groups are less likely to have,[2] like the dearth of drivers' licenses amongst the very poor and the scarcity of original birth certificates amongst the elderly.

---

[1] Alvarez, Lizette, "In Florida, Bid to Cut Voter Rolls Is Set Back," The New York Times, April 2, 2014.

[2] Alvarez, Lizette, "Ruling Revives Florida Review of Voting Rolls," The New York Times, August 7, 2013.

Davey, Monica, and Yaccino, Steven, "Federal Judge Strikes Down Wisconsin Law Requiring Photo ID at Polls," The New York Times, April 29, 2014.

There should be ways to prove the existence of unequal voting facilities, equipment and the like, and mechanisms exist to rectify that. The requirement of identification documentation is more difficult to deal with.

As a general proposition, it seems appropriate to require a voter to be able to identify herself or himself as a member of the voting community. And identification is needed in order to keep a person from voting more than once. The problem is to be able to do this without the requirement falling unevenly and thus discriminatorily.

Federal law continues to bar states from have election rules that discriminate racially. The Voting Rights Act had required advance Washington approval for certain states with a history of voting discrimination to change their voting laws. The Supreme Court struck down that part of the law because society had changed so much since it was enacted.[1] However, the Voting Rights Act still prohibits state and local racially discriminatory voting laws.

A case went to the Supreme Court involving Wisconsin, a state that did not have a discriminatory history requiring advance approval to change its voting law. Wisconsin required government issued photo identification (e.g., state driver's license, federal passport) for voting.[2] Although well meaning, statistics were cited that tended to show that the Wisconsin identification law discriminatorily fell heavier on black voters.

---

[1] Liptak, Adam, "Supreme Court Invalidates Key Part of Voting Rights Act," The New York Times, June 25, 2013.

[2] Editorial, "Voter ID Gets Another Day in Court," The New York Times, November 30, 2013.

And now, States previously requiring advance approval to change their voting laws are free to do so without approval and they are adopting more voter identification requirements.[1]

A brazen in-your-face claim is presently being made that discrimination based on political party affiliation is permissible. It is claimed that partisan discrimination is not legally barred since the Voting Rights Act bars only racial discrimination.[2] It is claimed that it doesn't matter whether that partisan discrimination happens to fall more on minority voters who tend to favor one political party over the other political party.

While the power over federal elections clearly rests in the government in Washington, the states are now asserting that they have the power to enact laws governing state and local elections, effectively demanding a two-tier voting system in America.[3]

A federal law (the National Voter Registration Act of 1993) allows a voter to sign a form asserting US citizenship without having to provide proof. That does not satisfy the states now wanting to set up their own proof requirements for state and local elections. This will surely go to the US Supreme Court.

The issuance and use of a national identification card (as suggested in the section "*Making Democracy Work*") is favored for a host of reasons not related to voting. It appears

---

[1] Alvarez, Lizette, "Ruling Revives Florida Review of Voting Rolls," The New York Times, August 7, 2013.

[2] Hasen, Richard L., "Voter Suppression's New Pretext," The New York Times, November 15, 2013.

[3] Santos, Fernanda, and Eligon, John, "2 States Plan 2-Tier System for Balloting," The New York Times, October 11, 2013.

that the time has come for such a national identification card, perhaps coordinated with state drivers' licenses so that only one card need be carried.

As voting rights can be abused with stringent state identification requirements, the federal government could go to special lengths to issue a national identification card to everyone in America with acceptance of the card being required for state and local voting purposes.

With reasonable exceptions for infants and others not having use for identification cards, the federal government can use its experience with the census to identify where people might be and actually locate them, noting their place of residence on the issued card. This could include going to the homes of the elderly and infirmed to issue the cards there, on the spot.

The obvious objections to a national identification based on the right to privacy would seem to be carried too far if those objections are allowed to interfere with present day security needs. Persons who favor security in law enforcement and in combating terrorists are probably the same persons who favor security in elections, and they might well support national identification cards.

GERRYMANDERING

Legislators elected to the House of Representatives must come from state electoral districts of approximately equal population size, based on the census done every ten years by the federal government. The aim is to give each voter an equal say in elections, fulfilling a requirement of "one person, one vote."

The requirement of equal population districts for federal elections was extended to the states and state elections, including both houses of a bicameral state legislature. The only exception is the election of federal Senators where each state has two Senators regardless of population size, which was the price paid to induce the less populous states to join the union.

The process by which each electoral district is re-sized in accordance with the ten year census is called redistricting. Redistricting is done by the states using a variety of rules and methodologies, with one fixed requirement; each district must be contiguous -- it cannot consist of geographically separate parts.

The term "gerrymandering" came from Massachusetts Governor Gerry redrawing voting district lines into a mosaic that looked like a salamander since each district must be contiguous. Bunching the opposition political party's votes into one gerrymandered district, which the opposition handily wins, leaves the opposition with fewer votes in the other districts which the opposition would have to lose. Thus, even though the opposition might actually have an overall majority of the voters in a state, the minority political party once having achieved control can gerrymander victory for itself in elections to come. In so doing, the political party in control automatically creates "safe seats" for its party members. It'll take a truly colossal event for the opposition to upset the apple cart and prevail in a meticulously gerrymandered state.

Even where the state is not under the clear control of either political party, the two political parties can get together in a so-called "true" bipartisan fashion to redistrict the state so that incumbent legislators of both parties would have "safe seats." For instance, after a California bipartisan redistricting in 2000, only one incumbent lost an election during the next ten years.[1]

This means that those on the bipartisan committee cooperated superbly to assure that all of them, all the incumbents, would get re-elected because of their bipartisan gerrymandering. Only one incumbent losing in the ensuing ten years exhibits how effective gerrymandering can be.

The California episode also shows that principle, party, and beliefs can be and are put aside by politicians as they gladly work with the "devils" on the other side of the aisle so as to assure their own re-election. Re-election comes first, nothing else matters.

In addition to serving the personal self-interest of legislators in getting re-elected, gerrymandering perpetuates political party control.

The next California redistricting in 2010 was done by a truly independent, non-partisan commission, which rid California of gerrymandering and allowed the state to honor the voter mandate and allow the State to function better.[2]

Gerrymandering is probably the most effective way of disfranchising the "other guy" although the public might not recognize it for what it is. The "other guy" still gets to vote, not recognizing that her or his vote had been diluted by redrawn voting districts.

Getting rid of gerrymandering is probably the most important single thing America can do to restore true

---

[1] Nagourney, Adam, "California Set to Send Many New Faces to Washington," The New York Times, February 13, 2012.

[2] Nagourney, Adam, "California Sees Gridlock Ease in Governing," The New York Times, October 18, 2013.

democracy on its shores. A later section devoted to *"Making Democracy Work"* contains suggestions that would destroy gerrymandering and give true meaning to one person, one vote.

Leadership in a Democratic Society

Leadership entails either following your own conscious or adhering to the views of your constituents. To have been elected, the executive and the legislators would have necessarily been chosen by a majority of the electorate. The elected would ordinarily be of the same or similar view as their constituents, but issues do arise where the elected feels differently about an issue.

Some people would say the elected officials must represent the majority that put them in office, which means that they must following the dictates of that constituency. Other people would say that the constituents voted for the person, implicitly trusting the elected make the right decision by following her or his judgment (or conscious).

Both views have merit, but the reality is that the elected legislators for the most part do neither.

Legislators normally vote on public policy issues as they are told to vote by their political party. This would accord with the view that most voters vote for the party, not the issues and not the person. On occasion a voter would vote a single issue if that issue was personally important enough and election campaigning brought that issue to the forefront. Normally, voters vote for any candidate their political party chooses to run, so in reality voters wouldn't be voting for the person.

Voters normally vote their political party. On rare occasions the political party might be under the control of an unpopular intramural faction, might not be in touch with their general membership, or might nominate a particularly unattractive candidate and find members crossing-over to vote for the other political party's candidate.[1] For the most part, Americans now elect political parties, not individuals. The individual candidates merely carry the party flags.

DISENFRANCHISING THE ELECTED LEGISLATOR

A legislator is usually constrained to vote on public policy issues in a certain way because his or her party leadership demands it. The individual legislator is disenfranchised in the sense that he or she can neither vote his or her judgment nor vote as the majority of his or her constituents would want.

Public policy issues are the important issues that frame the path of America. The vote on those issues is directed by the political party leadership, leaving individual legislators free to vote as he or she wills only on unimportant matters.

If the vote is going to be close, it becomes imperative that the legislator vote as the party dictates. It is only when the political party is assured of winning the vote (that is, the party has the vote "nailed") that the leadership might allow the legislator to vote his or her conscious or as his or her continuants want.

---

[1] Gabriel, Trip, "Virginia G.O.P. Assesses Loss to Rival It Saw as Weak," The New York Times, November 6, 2013.

Thus, the legislators effectively gets to vote on unimportant matters and on the important public policy issues when his or her vote doesn't matter; otherwise, he or she is effectively disenfranchised.

Individuals or factions within a political party who are powerful enough will choose the party leaders. The party leaders control the legislative agenda, control party funds and also determine how their legislators vote. The party leaders who dominate the party caucuses determine the party's position on the important issues. Discipline within a political party can be severe when the occasion warrants.

None of this was envisioned by our founders, although some of them fumed against the formation of political factions. They envisioned legislators debating issues on the merits and arriving at a consensus of what is good for America.

Instead, the founders got political parties that are focused on winning every issue, on winning re-election, and on blaming the other political party when things go wrong.

The founders wanted and envisioned a cooperative government working within a framework of balanced powers and instead got an adversarial government carried to such an extreme as to become dysfunctional.

Getting the legislators re-elected is important to the political party and the party leaders. It is their source of power, so they would help legislators raise campaign funds by sponsoring special legislation, legislation not particularly important to the future of America but important to the sponsors of the legislation and their lobbyists. And the legislator might be helped by the party in invading the public treasury so as to benefit local constituents and thus help re-election. It's called pork.

PRESIDENTIAL LEADERSHIP

Once elected, the President can lead as he or she wishes. Leadership does not mean domination because the President might lead but not control the outcome. In terms of legislation, the checks and balances built into the constitution limits the power of the President but not the capability of the President to lead. The President is free to lead in accordance with the dictates of his or her conscious or the dictates of his or her constituency.

The President always gets to propose, gets to be heard, gets to advocate, gets to approve or disapprove, and gets to execute the law. But it doesn't mean that the President will always be successful. The President cannot be silenced as a legislator might be silenced by his or her political party or caucus. The President cannot be disenfranchised, but the President can lose.

Yet, today, a committed opposition can obstruct, delay and deny the President the appointments needed to run the executive branch, and to that extent hamstring the presidency. The committed opposition is the opposing political party.

Individual legislators don't have the clout. It awaited the development of political parties to restructure the checks and balances built into the constitution. An individual can propose that the President must be made to fail, but only where the opposing political party adopts that position does the President's constitutional powers face erosion.

Some of our founders and initial leaders, including George Washington, feared the formation of political parties, and rightly so. The political parties divert the constitutional separation of powers from being an instrument that yields better legislation to an instrument used to obstruct and obtain political advantage.

The President is the figurehead leader of his or her political party, very influential but not necessarily dominant. Others in the party can and do disagree with the President. Sometimes the disagreement comes out in the open, showing interplay that is basically what our founding fathers would have wanted.[1]

LEADERSHIP AND MINORITY TREATMENT

Inherent in democracy is the belief that the majority should not tyrannize, oppress or disregard the minority. Since the minority has lost the election, laws can be and are passed that disadvantages the minority or conflicts with their ideology. Our constitution anticipated this and attempted to improve the position of the minority with its checks and balances.

Initially, before the advent of political parties when matters were decided on the merits and everyone participated in arriving at a consensus, it would have even been difficult to identify a minority group. Now, with the dominance of political parties, the minority stands out and is frequently the target of both legislation and denigration.

---

[1] Peters, Jeremy W., "Obama Faces Barrier in His Own Party on Syria," The New York Times, September 4, 2013.

It ultimately falls to the majority party leadership to give the minority appropriate recognition, certainly in granting them opportunity to convince and in granting them the right to ask questions and be heard. However, leadership with goodwill and a willingness to compromise is not always present in the majority, which can lead to endless delay if not outright obstruction on the part of the minority. It becomes a two-edged sword. Just as the majority can tyrannize the minority, the minority might attempt to tyrannize the majority, as, for instance, by filibuster.

Of course, this leads to dysfunction in government except when one party is in clear control of both the legislature and the executive office. But where there is a split, let's say with each party controlling one of the legislative houses, havoc and dysfunction can be expected. It appears to be at its worst when the minority party is split between factions and a second battle, an internal battle for dominance, is also being fought.[1] Dysfunction on the federal level does not necessarily carry over to the state level as the state political make up is frequently very different.[2]

---

[1] Lipton, Eric, "Tangled Role in G.O.P. War Over Tea Party," The New York Times, January 3, 2014.
Lipton, Eric, "In G.O.P., a Campaign Takes Aim at Tea Party," The New York Times, November 5, 2013.
[2] Nagourney, Adam & Martin, Jonathan, "As Washington Keeps Sinking, Governors Rise," The New York Times, November 9, 2013.

RESOLVING ISSUES

All is not lost because our democratic system sometimes works. Where one party controls the legislature and the other party controls the executive office (President or governor) it is possible for one branch to convince the other that they are going astray. It just doesn't happen very often.

The executive, even when his or her party is in a very weak minority position in the legislature, always has the opportunity to speak out and be heard, and sometimes the executive will prevail. In one situation, a very committed and aggressive governor facing an overwhelming majority in the legislature that could easily override his vetoes of controversial tax-cut and gun-control bills was able to take his case to the public and force opposing legislators to allow his vetoes to stand.[1] It just doesn't happen very often.

However, opposing politicians usually work together superbly when they don't have a real interest in addressing an issue. They can claim credit for reaching a compromise[2] that essentially did nothing but kick the can down the road. But the major issues are seldom resolved.

The major issues[3] facing America include economic and foreign policy, foreign aid, gay marriage, drug laws, marijuana, criminal-justice reform, sentencing reform, taxation, regulation, level of social services, public sector

---

[1] Eligon, John, "Missouri Republicans Fail to Block Vetoes on 2 Bills," The New York Times, September 11, 2013.
Editorial, "A Governor Battles Against Ruinous Tax Cuts," The New York Times, September 10, 2013.
[2] Calmes, Jackie, "A Dirty Secret Lurks in the Struggle Over a Fiscal 'Grand Bargain'," The New York Times, November 18, 2013.
[3] Douthat, Ross, "Libertarian Populism and Its Critics," The New York Times, August 16, 2013.

unions, bailouts, stimulus, sequester, military and other spending levels, immigration, health insurance, subsidies (to the poor, to the wealthy, to businesses) and more.

Another version of the major issues[1] facing America includes repairing crumbling infrastructure, investing in intercity rail transportation, renovating highways and bridges, creating safe water systems, refurbishing waterways and coastlines, increasing energy production, creating safe hydraulic fracturing and horizontal drilling practices, investing in low-carbon solar, wind and nuclear energy production, pursuing carbon capture and sequestration, supporting electric vehicles and other smart technologies, improving job skills and adopting apprenticeship practices. In the past, the US government invested, with success, in long-term projects like the internet, but now research and development funding faces curtailment.

The lists of issues needing to be addressed are long and differ depending on the glasses one wears. Yet, in the current dysfunctional environment cooperation only exists in kicking the issues down the road

THE NEEDED CHANGE OF ATTITUDES

Many if not most of the issues facing America are issues of principle (yes, issues of spending and taxation have become matters of principle), and legislators are not normally willing to compromise on their strongly held principles.

Yet, they have compromised in the past. That had been what democracy was all about. It was not a matter of "my

---

[1] Sachs, Jeffrey D., "On the Economy, Think Long-Term," The New York Times, March 31, 2013.

way or no way" or of "winning." America was founded on compromise and it grew mightily with it. Now, there is little interest in compromise. It has become a "winner take all" proposition which cannot work in a democracy and thus is doomed to failure, taking America down with it.

We, the voters, have to do something about this. It is our own principles that we must learn to compromise. Compromising on the unimportant is meaningless. Compromise must be on the meaningful, on the strongly held views, on principles. And it is clearly the time to step in, change our attitudes and do an about face.

We all see that we have a dysfunction government and one likely to remain so. We have to do something about lest the decline of America actually result in the fall of America.

We have to stop being in lock-step with our political parties. We have to think for ourselves. We have to search our own conscious and determine where we can live with compromise and then about-face and actually vote for candidates committed to compromise.

Making Our Democracy Work

With voters holding our legislators in the lowest regard ever and with our government becoming so dysfunctional that closing the government down had become an actual option, it is about time the citizenry acted to make our democracy work. What can be done runs from unobjectionable to the more consequential, from the needed to the inadvisable, as discussed in the following order:

1. End gerrymandering.
2. Adopt strict term-limits for Senators and Representatives.
3. Adopt California's "top-two" voting system.
4. Adopt term-limits for Supreme Court judges or limit filibusters.
5. End Senate confirmation of presidential appointments.
6. Adopt national identification cards.
7. Don't use public funds to match small-donor campaign contributions.
8. Limit contributions to political advocacy groups.
9. Retain the primary systems of the major political parties (if no "top-two" voting).
10. Don't fine eligible voters for not voting.
11. Move elections from Tuesdays to weekends.
12. Inaugurate the President-elect 2 weeks after the election.
13. Treat legislators as being opposed to functional government.
14. Shun encouraging distrust and disobedience of duly passed laws.
15. Bypass our dysfunctional federal government when useful.
16. Improve the public debate about the role & size of government.
17. Rethink our views on the apt role of government in our lives.

In order to get our democracy back on track, each one of us should choose or originate remedies that appeals to us personally and pursue them. Most of the suggestions presented here curtail the power of our legislators so you can expect them to resist. Our democracy is the backbone of America and we must stem the dysfunction which emanates from our legislators.

1. END GERRYMANDERING.

The elected politicians controlling a state legislature are the ones with the power to gerrymander, except where the state has established a truly independent, non-partisan commission to draw district lines. Once a state has been gerrymandered by its politicians, it becomes extremely difficult for the opposition to win elections, to unseat incumbents or beat down referendums.

Gerrymandering can assure political victory for long periods of time even where the party then in control has the loyalty of only a minority of the voters.

For decades the two political parties gerrymandered and re-gerrymandered the State of California. At a time when California wasn't firmly in the hands of either political party, in the year 2000 California redistricted under a new census using a bipartisan committee that insured "safe seats" for incumbents of both parties for the ensuing ten years. That is, the incumbents of both parties cooperated in assuring safe seats for themselves.

At that time, California probably had the most dysfunctional government in the United States, even more dysfunctional than the federal government in Washington.

With grassroots pressure to reform, the next California redistricting in 2010 was done by an independent commission (non-partisan) that protected neither party nor incumbents, resulting in healthy elections and a state legislature that is now applauded for its functionality.[1]

While the State of California was successful in having a non-partisan, independent commission redistrict the state without gerrymandering, that cannot be expected across the nation. State redistricting committees usually consist of politicians, and even where lip service is given to non-partisanship and independence, the states that are committed to gerrymandering will select compliant people for their redistricting committees. It happened to work in California. It was unexpected in California and it remains unexpected elsewhere.

Yet, there may be ways to defeat gerrymandering. One way is to federally mandate the use of a specific methodology for redistricting after each census.

Say the methodology would require redistricting into the same number of squares and rectangles (using straight lines) as the state has seats in the House of Representatives, with each square or rectangle having equal population. There would be no more salamanders, no more odd shapes.

For instance, if the state gets 20 seats in the House of Representatives, it would have 20 districts and the state would have to be redistricted into a total of 20 squares and rectangles of equal population size.

To be sure, some communities would be split and some people might have to go further than others to vote, but one person would truly have one vote. Minor community and

---

[1] Nagourney, Adam, "California Sees Gridlock Ease in Governing," The New York Times, October 18, 2013.

distance exceptions (strictly defined) could be allowed without offending the mandated requirement.

Of all the proposed changes to make our democracy work, ridding America of gerrymandering ranks as the most telling and most important. If only one change is to be made, this is the one to choose.

2. ADOPT STRICT TERM-LIMITS FOR SENATORS AND REPRESENTATIVES.

Severe term-limits would bring more functionality to our government. Congress is now controlled by vested legislators having safe seats that assure re-election no matter how the mood of voters change.

These long-term legislators have their constituents in their pockets, not necessarily because they are personally liked by their constituents, but rather because incumbents can have invincible positions under our electoral system. Illustrative of how safe legislative seats can be, during the ten year period before California changed its election laws only one seat changed hands between the political parties in 255 elections.[1]

Political pressure groups now have more influence with the long-term legislators than the legislators' own constituents. Lobbyists swamp our legislators, to say nothing of the activist trade organizations and activist public groups who have managed to develop teeth.

Legislators have learned to obey these pressure groups lest a group target the legislator's seat for replacement.

---

[1] Nagourney, Adam, "California Set to Send Many New Faces to Washington," The New York Times, February 12, 2012.

Legislators fear these groups more than they fear their constituents as their seats would remain safe but for payback attacks by pressure groups if the legislator should cross them.

    A severe term-limit, like the very short one-term only, allows the legislator to view matters on the merits and not be concerned about re-election. Lobbyists and activist groups should and will continue to exist as they do play an information role, but they will no longer be in a power position to intimidate the legislator. Pressure groups could not dominate government because the short term-limit allows legislators to disregard them.

    It is claimed that the adoption of a short term-limit would lead to legislators being more concerned with their next job than in doing a good job while in office. Yet, the person who deliberately takes a short-term job is likely to be less concerned with the next job, or he or she would not have even considered a temporary job.

    History has shown that long-term legislators have re-election constantly on their minds, eclipsing anything else they might think about. After all, the long-term legislators have chosen to make their living from politics from the moment they entered politics and that necessitates the constant focus on re-election.

    With stringent term-limits, a legislative candidate knows in advance that it will be a temporary job providing a temporary living. The temporary legislative job would appeal to a person who is truly interested in public service. The legislative job could be a stepping stone to other gainful employment, but there would be less pressure while in the legislature to temporarily feather one's own nest or build relationships with pressure groups that supply re-election campaign contributions.

Stringent term-limits would also be a great help in deterring the greedy from trying to make a living or a killing in politics. There is probably no better way to rid politics of the greedy than to have a one-term, term-limit for legislators.

"We'd get inexperienced legislators" would be the rallying cry of those who don't want term-limits, and there would be some truth in this. However, legislative staffs would not be term-limited and they would likely have the experience and background to help their legislator. In addition to relying on staff, the new incumbent can always access the specialized experience and historical perspective in the executive branch which proposes legislation.

On the other side of the coin, the so-called experience of long-term legislators can be overrated. Only too frequently it is the leaders and the experienced staff employed at the political party headquarters that call the shots for members of that party, the experience and even the viewpoint of individual legislators being irrelevant. With views and positions on pending issues being controlled by party headquarters, too much is being made of the experience of long-term legislators, as if they actually had any real experience. Legislators are given position papers to follow. They don't author the position papers, nor can they edit them.

Thus, the experience of long-term members of a legislature might well be overrated, as would be the need for experience. However, the new incumbent has access to the issue and procedural background and experience of her legislative staff, needs little of it because of domination by her political party, and always has the option of tapping the resources of the executive branch which proposes legislation and can supply background.

Failing that, there is always Google. Google is a great equalizer. The so-called experienced long-term members of Congress might or might not have actual experience or understanding since much of it could have been supplied by party headquarters with the legislator not really knowing the subject, or even caring about it. What happened in the past and the reasons for it can usually be found on Google and be of much more use to the new hot-shot as compared to the safe-seat occupant who is comfortable with the status quo.

We all get experience at something or other as we live through the years, but that says nothing about the quality or scope of the experience. Long-term legislators could merely be experienced in providing a voice for the talking points given them. And young, term-limited legislators lacking the years and much experience might be more inquisitive, have a fresher and more independent voice, and be likely to work harder.

The normal incentive for legislators to usurp as much power as possible should dissipate where there is no possibility of re-election. More is at stake for the legislator when a lifetime of added power is to be had. Much of the internal rules of the legislature is aimed at increasing the power of the legislators. With legislators serving only one term, arrogating power to themselves loses its importance.

The increase in power of legislators comes at the expense of the executive branch. By forcing the executive branch to make deals to get its appointments confirmed, the legislators arrogate power to themselves. When legislators can stop the approval of an executive branch appointment by "blue slipping" or placing a "hold" on the appointee (which is made possible by rules made up by the legislators themselves), the legislators are arrogating power to themselves. When their internal rules allow delays and obstruction of ordinary day-to-day legislation, the legislators are arrogating power to themselves. All this contributes to our dysfunctional government. All this dissipates with severe term-limits.

It has been suggested that we are better off as a nation when the presidency is strong than when, as is the case now, pressure groups are strong or Congress is strong.[1] A strong presidency is favored because it is possible for administration officials to reach policy conclusions while it seem impossible for Congress to do so.

Also, the special-interest pressure groups are less effective with administration officials than with Congress. And administrative officials have more specialized and historic knowledge than the legislators or their staffs, and have more flexibility to deal with things that go astray. But most important, the administration can be thrown out of office by the voters when the administration fails; while failing legislators are less likely to be thrown out by the voters since most legislative seats are safe.

Severe term-limits for legislators would significantly strengthen the presidency, and might be the most effective way to do that. To be sure, such a limitation was not contemplated in the constitution or by our founders, but it has been said[2] that the constitution was not a perfect document --

---

[1] Brooks, David, "Strengthen the Presidency," The New York Times, December 12, 2013.
[2] Greenhouse, Linda, "A Work Still in Progress," The New York Times, December 25, 2013.

it required a number of amendments, engendered a civil war, and needed a fundamental expansion of individual freedoms and humans rights. Now it needs to provide for strict term-limits.

Of all the proposed suggestions to make our democracy work better, stringent term-limits is the most extreme politically, particularly when insisting on only a single term. There is precedent in the two term-limit for the presidency.

The term-limit should be set at the point where it would deter the greedy from entering politics and induce public spirited citizens to take a sojourn in serving the public. Next to ridding ourselves of gerrymandering, adopting strict term-limits would be single best way to restore American democracy.

3. ADOPT CALIFORNIA'S "TOP-TWO" VOTING SYSTEM.

California's new top-two voting system applies to all elections except the election of the President of the United States and the election of political party governing committees. The new system has worked superbly so far, taking California from dysfunctionality to functionality.

While some people might argue for more experience with that system before adopting it on the federal level, its merits are so obvious that it deserves immediate attention. America is going downhill and we just can't afford to wait. We have to stem the decline now. It is not that the change can be made immediately for it would take a lot of time under the best circumstances. Thus the need to start now.

The 2013 state legislature was the first elected under California's top-two voting system, and also the first elected since California rid itself of gerrymandering. It might well be that the elimination of gerrymandering was the more important of the two, and only time will tell.

Ridding the many states of gerrymandering is very high on the list of proposals to restore our democracy, but that is on a different track since it requires only an act of Congress, while adoption of the top-two voting system requires amendment of the U.S. Constitution.

In 2013, California also approved extending its legislative term-limits to 12 years, but that had no effect on the superb legislative turn-around in 2013. Legislators elected when the more stringent term-limits were in effect were responsible for the success of the 2013 legislature. That would normally suggest that stringent terms-limits actually work but those legislators were largely of the old school, having entered politics years before and thus still of the mindset of having the job forever. The leopard doesn't change its spots and the old mindset legislators rushed to get the term limit extended. And you can be certain that they'll do it again and again.

It outwardly appears that the top-two voting system is based on open primaries, but California has really eliminated political party primaries. Under the top-two voting system, an election is held that is nominally called a "primary." It is not really that because all voters of any or no political party can vote in that election. But it is a primary election in that it is the first of two elections California holds.

Each political party no longer has its own primary, open or closed. In effect, there is no primary at all for the first vote is actually a pre-election to identify the top-two vote getters who face each other in a second, run-off, final election.

We can call the first vote a primary, an open primary, a pre-election, or simply a first election. The first vote merely selects the finalists for the second vote. The labels don't matter.

What matters is that the political parties are no longer the only ones to select candidates to run against the candidates of the other political party. Now, anyone who gets the required number of signatures can be a candidate.

What matters is that the first election has no winner, but is held only to identify the top-two vote getters who face each other in the final, run-off election.

The candidates could be and usually are affiliated with one political party or the other. One candidate in the first election would invariably have been selected by each of the political parties, but other party members could also run without their leadership approval. This, very cleverly, reduces the power of the political party bosses.

Thus, the first election (the so-called "primary") is a free-for-all open to everyone who can assemble the required number of signatures. The political party primary as we have known it has been eliminated in California, which now has an all-comers first election followed by a run-off election between the top-two vote getters.

Since the top-two vote getters can have the same political party affiliation (e.g. both can be Republicans, or both can be Democrats), the final or run-off election is not necessary between the two political parties. The final election might possibly be between candidates having no political party affiliation. Thus, the electorate is no longer voting for a political party but is now voting for the candidate. This has many ramifications and it made for a more functional California government. Our founders would have applauded a system that diminished political parties.

The elimination of gerrymandering in California also contributed to creating functionality. In every election in every district, the electorate was more balanced between the political parties because the district boundaries were set by an independent, non-political, non-partisan body. With the electorate in a district being more balanced, there were no more "safe seats" and the candidates had to appeal to a broader spectrum of voters. Although gerrymandering is not a factor in the federal Presidential election since all voters throughout a state vote as though they are in one district, Presidential candidates already have to appeal to a broader spectrum of voters.

With the top-two voting system, whether in state or federal elections, candidates could no longer stick exclusively to their party line and seek votes from only their own base in order to get elected. In California, that led to candidates adopting more moderate positions, diminishing the political party connection.

The top-two voting system also allowed the elected legislators to view matters on the merits since every vote was no longer a win or lose proposition in the battle between the political parties.

And the actual votes during the first year, 2013, has shown that California legislators affiliated with one political party became more amenable to positions usually associated with the other political party.

The same should be expected on the federal level elections upon adoption of the top-two voting system.

Possibly to be feared in California and elsewhere are elections dominated by celebrities. Even under the old voting system, a number of movie celebrities became governors of California.

In other states, other types of celebrities are foremost.

Under the top-two voting system, a celebrity that manages to come in as number 2 in the first election would be likely to win in the second election.

If so, is the lack of political experience a bad thing, or a good thing? Will the top-two voting system induce all sorts of celebrities to run in federal elections? Can these celebrities win nationally or is it just a state phenomenon? On the federal level, the top-two voting system would appear to be celebrity-neutral as witness Ronald Reagan winning the presidency under the existing voting system.

4. ADOPT TERM-LIMITS FOR SUPREME COURT JUDGES OR LIMIT FILIBUSTERS.

It has been suggested that a term-limit be set for Supreme Court judges; a term-limit of 18 years, staggered so that replacement nominations would come up every two years.[1] As a result, the entire bench of 9 judges would turn over every 18 years. The change would require a constitutional amendment.

It is said that this will result in the appointment of more older and thus more experienced judges. The present

---

[1] *See* Nocera, Joe, "Fixing the System," The New York Times, November 4, 2013.

lifetime-term prompts the appointment of younger judges so they can sit on the bench for decades on end, presumably perpetuating the harmonious views of the President nominating them. Senate confirmation of Supreme Court nominations are frequently acrimonious since the stakes are so long-term, the hope being that the shorter term-limit would reduce the partisanship.

It is not clear whether such a change is worth the candle. Voters might not accept the wisdom of the proposal. The proposal is likely to be controversial, hard fought and take decades to implement.

On the other hand, there is nothing detrimental in the proposal. A term of 18 years is long enough to provide lifetime or near life-time security for the judges, so their independence would essentially be assured. It is unlikely that nominees would be under 40 years old, so a term of 18 years would mostly take them into or near unusual retirement age.

The staggered term is a very desirable feature as it would lessen the gamesmanship involved as to when an incumbent judge should decide to retire. However, the acrimony encountered in the Senate approving Supreme Court nominations is likely to continue whether it's a lifetime appointment or an 18-year appointment.

An acceptable alternative to the proposed constitutional amendment might be the elimination of the Senate's internal requirement for supermajority vote to bring a Supreme Court judicial appointment out of committee and to a vote on the floor of the Senate. The constitution requires only a majority vote on the Senate floor, not a supermajority vote.

The supermajority vote necessary to get the nomination out of committee and to the Senate floor is a creation of the

Senate, using its ability to make its own procedural rules. It is not that the committee vote itself must be a supermajority vote, but rather a supermajority vote is necessary to vote cloture. That is, stopping the invariably endless filibuster in committee requires a supermajority vote. The supermajority cloture vote forces a vote on the nomination in the committee, which requires only a majority vote.

Thus, in an around-about fashion, the Senate had effectively imposed the need for a supermajority vote to confirm Supreme Court judges, which makes for more acrimony as a small group can thwart the majority. It is very difficult to get a supermajority in the Senate.

When the Senate in 2013 got rid of its supermajority vote for cloture of filibustering presidential appointments, reducing the vote for cloture to a majority vote, it did not apply the change to Supreme Court judicial appointments. Thus, a supermajority vote is still necessary to invoke cloture on the filibuster of Supreme Court judicial appointments. However, a mere majority vote of the Senate can change the Senate's internal rule, eliminate the supermajority requirement for cloture and substitute a majority requirement.

So an alternative to the proposed constitutional amendment to institute a term-limit for Supreme Court judicial would be for the Senate to reduce its cloture requirement and bring sanity to the approval of Supreme Court nominations. This should be easier to obtain than a constitutional amendment for an 18 year term limit, and it would be better for reducing acrimony. Whether Supreme Court judge appointments are for life-time service or for an 18 year term-limit, Senate acrimony would remain unless the requirement for a supermajority vote for cloture is eliminated.

5. END SENATE CONFIRMATION OF PRESIDENTIAL APPOINTMENTS.

The constitutional requirement for the Senate to consent to presidential appointments is another instance of a good idea that has gone bad. The consent requirement has been perverted in actual practice to such an extent that it destroys the very purpose of the constitutional requirement and makes it counter-productive.

Requiring the Senate to approve an appointee selected and vetted by the executive branch has become a mechanism to extort political concessions or to make headlines. The greatest harm is keeping vital governmental and judicial positions vacant. And for what?

So the opposition doesn't like a person the President appointed, but the President making the appointment liked that person, and the President did win the election. After having won the public mandate through an election, it should be expected and accepted that the President would appoint people of like mind to vital positions. And it can be expected that the person would be thoroughly vetted by the President and the President's staff, as they would naturally want to appoint qualified people of their political persuasion and reject turkey's and wackos.

In the initial days of the nation when there were no or minimal staffs, using the expertise of the Senators to vet nominees made sense. Nowadays, with the executive branch having large and expert staffs that would strive to avoid the embarrassment of a approving an unqualified person, and with the advent of political parties that destroyed the cooperative environment, the consent requirement had become an instrument of torture, extortion or obstruction.

If the Senate majority is of the same political party as the President, the President's appointment would, under normal circumstances, be confirmed. Extensive hearings allowing for deliberate delay and obstruction are just dysfunctional and waste time that can be devoted to meaningful matters. It is also extortion, demanding something (perhaps a nomination they like) in return for not delaying or obstructing the appointment.

If the other political party controls the Senate, there can and will be endless delays in confirming appointments until the President appoints candidates acceptable to the Senate majority. The party in control of the Senate could merely use its controlled committee to keep the appointments from reaching the floor for a vote.

Even if the matter should get to the floor, the party controlling the Senate can vote the appointment down and also vote down the next appointment. Creating an endless cycle of appointment rejections followed by new appointments could also prevent vital jobs from being filled and deny the President the fruits of her or his victory. This was not the intent of our founders. It is also extortion, the only potential restraint on the Senate majority being any concern it might have about necessary governmental or judicial positions remaining vacant.

Something more than a mere change in the Senate's internal procedural rules is required to bring reason back into the advice and consent process. The confirmation process our founders had in mind no longer functions in the age of political parties, which appears to be the norm from now on.

The best approach would be a constitutional amendment eliminating the advice and consent provision. Another approach could be mandating committee consideration and floor votes on appointments within a month of the appointment being made, and, if the first appointment is rejected, the replacement appointment would automatically be deemed approved.

Only something like this will allow the executive department to govern, as it was elected to do.

6. ADOPT NATIONAL IDENTIFICATION CARDS.

The time has come for a federal national identity (ID) card for everyone in the nation, with the concomitant adoption of measures and restrictions so as to keep America from becoming a police state.

Privacy and personal freedom concerns should not deter the establishment of a national ID card system. The concern for privacy and personal freedom should revolve around the rules to be adopted that determine when ID cards can be requested for examination. Authorities should be forbidden to merely stop somebody on the street to examine an ID card, just as it is forbidden to stop a car to determine whether the seat belt laws are being obeyed. Neither the seat belts nor the ID cards, in themselves, offend the right to privacy and personal freedom. Those rights are offended when there is no cause to stop the car or to ask for an ID card.

Everyone should be required to carry an ID card, citizens as well as aliens, residents and visitors from abroad, excepting only children and the infirmed. Each ID card should have a photograph, signature, fingerprint or digital eye scan, whatever modern technology allows. To avoid carrying too many cards, the national ID program should be coordinated with State drivers' licenses and state identification cards with one card serving all ID purposes. US passports could include a separable national ID card.

Our right to privacy is another good thing that America tends to take too far. What we now call our right to privacy has already been infringed in many ways. Technically, our right to privacy was invaded the moment our birth certificates were issued. Now we also have Social Security numbers, drivers' licenses, credit cards and internet search engine listings. The existence of national ID cards should offend no one's right to privacy any more than our right to privacy is already offended and found to be acceptable.

Going further than providing identification, like enabling ID cards to pinpoint location through global positioning as cell phones already do, is another matter.

Protecting our personal freedom should not perversely block us from protecting ourselves. We protect ourselves by helping law enforcement and homeland security, and a national ID card system would be of great help to them. It could also tell us that a person is not wanted by the police, that an alien is not overstaying a visa, that a person is an undocumented worker entitled to or barred from certain benefits, and so forth.

But we must exercise great care in delineating when the ID cards can be requested by law enforcement or other officials.

The benefits of a national ID card system are many and meaningful, including providing core voter registration information that combats voter fraud and also combats oppressive state voting requirements. Three large cities are providing them to anyone who can prove residence, but have not mandated that all residents obtain the IDs or have alternate identification.[1]

7. DON'T USE PUBLIC FUNDS TO MATCH SMALL-DONOR CAMPAIGN CONTRIBUTIONS.

In order to counter the undue influence of big-donor campaign contributions, it has been argued that we should use public funds to match small-donor campaign contributions so as to assist in leveling the playing field. Use of public funds in a 6 to 1 ratio ($6 public funds for each $1 of small-donor campaign contributions) has been found to be effective.[2]

However, the public funds even with the six-fold increase (presumably split among the candidates unless small donor preferences are publically disclosed) wouldn't go very far in leveling the playing-field when a big-donor enters the fray in favor of a particular candidate.

It is also said that public financing of elections would invite more competition for elective office and diminish the ability of incumbents to hold on to their seats.[3] To the extent that this reference to public financing means that only the public treasury is to be used for elections and all individuals would be barred from making any political contributions or advocacy expenditures, the statement holds water but there is absolutely no way our budgets could afford it. But if the

---

[1] Editorial, "Mr. de Blasio's Welcoming Gesture," The New York Times, February 12, 2014.
[2] Nocera, Joe, "Fixing the System," The New York Times, November 4, 2013.
[3] Editorial, "Gov. Cuomo's Cleanup Campaign," The New York Times, February 2, 2014.

reference is merely to have the public treasury match-fund small-donor political contributions, we are back to the proposition that it wouldn't make much of a difference.

But even if it would make a difference, use of public funds to match fund small-donor contributions at any multiple does not appear desirable.

Public match-funding not only has negative budget ramifications because it would be an added form of government spending, but, more important, public funding makes for even more money going into elections.

Rather, we should attempt to reduce the amount of money going into elections. Our focus should be on limiting the amounts that can be contributed to a candidate because a large contribution could still allow the big-donor to "own" the candidate no matter how much the small-donors contribute or the public treasury match-funds. Bringing still more money into elections through public matching of small campaign contributions is not the way to go.

Placing campaign contribution limitations on state ballots or seeking a constitutional amendment might be a way to stem large amounts of money going into political campaigns, but such approaches are unlikely to succeed.

The limitations and constraints that America had before the courts obliterated them weren't bad. But the trend to curtail those limitations continues with the ability of big-donors to influence elections being recently expanded by a Supreme Court decision.

It seems that fighting the judicial battle is the way to go. The judicial battle should be fought on every front, in every way, and at all times as courts and viewpoints do change. Obtaining new legislative limitations on contributions is unlikely as the legislators likely view themselves as being the beneficiary of unlimited contributions. Besides, legislative limitations had been enacted in the past, only to be diluted judicially. So the remedy has to be found in the courts.

8. LIMIT CONTRIBUTIONS TO POLITICAL ADVOCACY GROUPS.

While a person might reasonably view advocacy groups as properly being part of the democratic process, this view should not be extended to the manner in which many advocacy groups are funded and the tactics they utilize.

The wealthy buying elections through the use of advocacy groups is clearly offensive and should be stopped lest we wind up having a government of, by, and for the wealthy instead of, by and for the people.

The courts have bypassed political contribution limitations for advocacy group based on the courts' tendency, as is the case with Americans generally, to take good things too far. This time the courts equated the spending of money to some sort of speech protected by our freedom of speech, thus allowing issue advocacy to avoid political contributions limitations.

The use of money is not speech and should not be equated to speech. Even should spending money be viewed as speech, our freedom of speech has never been absolute. Speech has been limited when warranted (e.g., hate speech, yelling fire in a crowded theater, etc.) and preserving our democracy would warrant curtailing the flow of money in elections and strictly adhering to our election laws.

Recent Supreme Court and Second Circuit Court decisions effectively authorized unlimited political expenditures by advocacy groups,[1] increasing the flow of money into politics. This is said to help stem the influence of political party leaders[2] since the donors determine how the money is to be spent. The big donors will be in a position to squeeze the parties.[3] But these decisions also increased the flow of money to the political party leaders as courts put the political contribution limitations aside. Whether all this

---

[1] Kaplan, Thomas, "Court Lifts Limit on Contributing to Pro-Lhota PAC," The New York Times, October 24, 2013. This article covers the Second Circuit decision in a case brought by Alabama businessman Shaun McCutcheon who wanted to contribute more to a candidate for mayor of New York City (Joseph J Lhota) than New York election law allowed.

Liptak, Adam, "Supreme Court Strikes Down Overall Political Donation Cap," The New York Times, April 2, 2014 and Liptak, Adam, "Ruling's Breadth Hints That More Campaign Finance Dominoes May Fall," April 3, 2014. These articles cover Mr. McCutcheon's suit to allow him to contribute more to a number of candidates than federal election law allowed.

Liptak, Adam, "Justices, 5-4, Reject Corporate Spending Limit," The New York Times, January 21, 2010. This article covers the Supreme Court case brought by Citizens United, a non-profit corporation, which provided the basis for the foregoing cases.

Collins, Gail, "Surprise! The Rich Won One," The New York Times, April 2, 2014.

Editorial, "The Court Follows the Money," The New York Times, April 2, 2014.

Bittman, Mark, "Why Care About McCutcheon?" The New York Times, April 22, 2014.

[2] Brooks, David, "Party All the Time," The New York Times, April 3, 2014.

Also, Persily, Nathaniel, "Bringing Big Money Out of the Shadows," The New York Times, April 2, 2014.

[3] Editorial, "How to Squeeze the Political Parties, The Campaign Finance Ruling Helps Big Donors," The New York Times, April 3, 2014.

serves to help new candidates who face incumbents having a 4 to 1 spending advantage is unclear. But one thing is clear, more money will flow from the wealthy into politics, and big money signifies influence.

Huge amounts of money flow can into issue advertising protected by the courts freedom of speech approach. Although there are some rules that try to keep the political party or candidate from approving or consulting on such issue advertising, the sponsors of such advertising know the issues, have the funds to hire savvy campaign consultants and can go it alone without the help of the political party machinery or the political candidate.

Moreover, this restriction on issue advocacy is largely meaningless. The issue advertising is easily associated by the targeted voter audience with the candidate it aims to support, and the political message is as clear as that given in candidate endorsed commercials. But perhaps still more important, issue advertising has the dubious advantage of getting away with more cons and misrepresentations.

We should pursue campaign contribution limitations even though the Supreme Court decisions still stand, and also pursue overturning or limiting all the Supreme Court decisions that emaciated our election laws.

The amount an individual could contribute to advocacy groups should be limited, just as there are limits on direct political contributions. Even with these limits, permissible annual contributions may well exceed what most Americans make in a year, which would seem to be enough for a single individual to publicize a favorite issue but not for the truly wealthy who want no limitation.

Curtailing the flow of money into politics wouldn't curtail the ability of any individual, wealthy or not, from personally taking to the soap-box (or social media) and speaking out on an issue or on a candidate. But speaking through a TV, film, radio, or newspaper production or advertisement and paying for it would be the expenditure of funds, prohibited if the limitations were exceeded.

Of course, all this would be a nullity if the donor's identity is not disclosed and made available to public and media scrutiny. There would be no way to establish whether the limitations were violated if names weren't made available.

So each organization receiving advocacy contributions would have to keep and disclose the names of contributors and the amounts they contributed, even though its political advocacy may be only a small part of its activities. To do otherwise would invite gamesmanship. To stop the passing along of contributions though chains of organization so as to hide the name of the donor, each link in such a chain should be required to reveal donor names and amounts to the next link.

The limitations and disclosure rules should also apply to labor unions and other organizations if they used member dues for political advocacy. If this is found to be objectionable, separate advocacy entities could be formed to take the political contributions directly from those willing to reveal their names.

Inducing unions, corporations and other organizations to separate political advocacy from their normal activities seems desirable and equitable because all members, shareholders, participants, employees or volunteers are not usually of one political mind.

In addition, the tax laws should be changed to remove the possibility of advocacy expenses being treated as tax deductible business expenses or union dues.

Of course, none of this is likely to be in the interest of politicians of any political persuasion since they would all favor more money going into political campaigns, particularly their campaigns.

Thus the electorate should become aware that their public interest is not necessarily allied with the interests of the politicians or the political parties they favor. There is, in the true sense of the words, an inherent conflict of interest. However, voters should not let this derogate into a battle with an enemy. Rather, voters should seek and vote for enlightened politicians who realize that they would ultimately be better off with less money going into political campaigns.

9. RETAIN THE PRIMARY SYSTEMS OF THE MAJOR POLITICAL PARTIES (if no "top-two" voting).

Many people say that the primary system of the major political parties is flawed in that it produces extremist candidates for both parties. As the more highly motivated, extremist party members tend to vote more frequently in political party primaries than do the more moderate party members, it is said that the primary system tends to nominate more extremist candidates.

Although extremists could contribute to more dysfunctional government, we do tend to prejudge matters when we label a person an "extremist." The more highly motivated and the more activist are not always extremists. Even if they could be considered extremists, we can't say that extremists are always wrong. And we can't say extremists are always dysfunctional. Female suffrage marchers were extremists, but not wrong or dysfunctional.

As long as political parties are a permanent part of the scene, the parties must have some sort of process to cull down the number of candidates put before their membership for the next election. Instead of primaries, recourse could be had to town hall meetings, caucuses or other means of selecting nominees, but nothing would deter the more highly motivated from also dominating those venues. It is inherent in every organization; those who are most interested and commit the most time and effort are going to run the organization. If this is not to the liking of enough members, it is up to them to do something about it.

Of course, the political party could establish a nominating committee who would independently select a slate of acceptable candidates that the membership could vote on in a primary, or the committee could receive all applications so that they could vet the slate of nominees. However you cut-it, the most highly motivated would still be in control so, basically, no purpose is served by ranting against a presumed faction or against polarization.

It is up to the political party to police itself, change if indicated, or wait to change after its candidate goes down to defeat in the general election. Nothing changes if it is a one-party state where the same political party always wins; the only difference is that the battle is being fought within the political party rather than in the election.

An overriding majority of states, 44 of them,[1] have laws that prevent a person who lost in a primary from running in the general election under any party or independent designation. Although these laws could limit voter choice in the general election, it does prevent the loser from becoming a spoiler by diluting the vote the winner of that primary. Two candidates in a general election having the same party affiliation would necessarily dilute the party vote and help the opposition win.

Opening a political party primary to voters of all political parties is said to lead to the nomination of less extremist candidates, presumably candidates more willing to compromise and supposedly reduce dysfunctionality in government. Maybe. Nevertheless, opening the primary would also open the gates to gamesmanship, where one political party sees an advantage by ganging up to vote in the other political party's open primary, deliberately diverting the nomination to a weaker candidate.

Primaries should yield candidates that reflect the views of the political party and it is up to the political party itself to assure an adequate primary turnout of its own members to keep one faction from dominating. The party itself is responsible for harmony within the party and, if it is impossible to achieve, perhaps the party should be split.[2]

---

[1] Edwards, Mickey, "Perverse Primaries," The New York Times, January 23, 2014.

[2] *See* Peters, Jeremy W. and Martin, Jonathan, "G.O.P. Weighs Limiting Clout of Right Wing," The New York Times, November 6, 2013.
Robertson, Campbell, and Lipton, Eric, "In Alabama Race, a Test of Business Efforts to Derail Tea Party," The New York Times, October 31, 2013.

Our democracy should encompass diverse views and the primary system should not allow for gamesmanship. Opening primaries isn't necessary a good idea. Keeping them closed under our prevailing voting system would be preferable. Effectively eliminating primaries entirely through the adoption of the top-two voting system would be a better approach, but where the old voting system endures, maintaining closed primaries which produce more diverse choices for the electorate would seem to be what democracy is all about.

10. DON'T FINE ELIGIBLE VOTERS FOR NOT VOTING.

Levying fines on non-voters so as to force them to vote does seem to be invasive of personal freedoms. However, we use fines to force people to obey traffic and other laws, so fines for not voting cannot automatically be considered as unduly invasive. Australia uses them.[1]

Perhaps, it is the connection to voting which makes the use of force seem invasive. However, we are forced to serve on juries which is a civic duty similar to the duty to vote. And some states force voters to obtain certain types of documentation in order to be allowed to vote. So forcing people to vote might not be all that outlandish.

Yet, it seems that civic education is a better way to get people to vote. Perhaps American voting participation is low because legislators are held in such abysmal regard and our government is so dysfunctional. We should try to fix that

---

[1] Nocera, Joe, "Fixing the System," The New York Times, November 4, 2013.

first to see whether that would take care of the voter participation problems. If that fails, then we should consider fines. Since unpaid fines ordinarily involve jail, it is a drastic step.

11. MOVE ELECTIONS FROM TUESDAYS TO WEEKENDS.

Moving elections from Tuesdays to the weekends is a good idea.[1]

People don't usually work on weekends and mothers have more time then, making it easier to fit voting into their busy lives. While most of the employed seem to be able to take-off time during the work day, some workers can't. And they surely don't have the time to wait on long lines should those lines develop, which have become commonplace.

Voting on Tuesdays has become a deterrent to voting, although some people maintain that both Tuesday elections and long lines in some locations tools are deliberately aimed at reducing the voter turnout of the "other." Democracy calls for voter turn-out and moving the Election Day to the weekend will improve voter turn-out.

Religious reasons contributed to holding elections on a weekday. In the horse and wagon days, transportation difficulties contributed to the selection of Tuesdays which would allow farmers time to get to the city where voting takes place, vote and get back while leaving the weekend free for worship. Today, transportation is no longer a problem. Generally, Protestants, Catholics, Muslims and some Jewish

---

[1] Nocera, Joe, "Fixing the System," The New York Times, November 4, 2013.

denominations allow work on their day of worship and would condone voting.

Should voting on a weekend present a religious problem to some voters, today we also have recourse to advance voting and absentee ballots. Also, voting a day earlier could be allowed religious objectors. Weekend voting would answer objections of those who would look at the original religious reasons for weekday voting as a form of establishment of religion.

Weekend elections would also make it easier to find appropriate voting locations, attract more election volunteers, allow voters to stay up later to watch election results, and have longer late-night victory parties.

Weekend elections would benefit business interests as the mid-week election disrupt business operations and result in lost work hours that have to be paid for. In some states, Election Day is a legal holiday that increases the cost to business even more. As there is no free lunch, these costs get passed forward to customer or passed back to workers in the form of lower wages. And America losses some production.

Aside from indirectly earning less because of lost work time, a good number of workers and busy mothers would probably prefer avoiding a hectic election day by having elections on weekends and also avoid the guilt and next day disruption from staying up late for election results or missing election parties.

It does seem that the time has come holding elections on weekends. The Election Day can be changed by a vote of Congress.

12. INAUGURATE THE PRESIDENT-ELECT TWO WEEKS AFTER THE ELECTION.

As things stand today, we effectively have two Presidents during the two and a half month period[1] between the November election and the January 20 inaugural. This delay made sense 200 years ago in the days of horses, buggies, and crude roads, but today transportation takes a few hours. Communications are almost instantaneous. Most all things can be done faster and more efficiently.

There is no reason to perpetuate such a long lame-duck period. The lame-duck period was shortened once before as proposed in the early 1930s, when we didn't have interstates, jets, TVs and cell phones making for a faster life tempo.

The long delay may help by giving the victor more time to vet appointments. Some people would say part of this can be done during the long campaign periods we have gravitated to, but others would say that 100% of that time should be devoted to getting elected. A number of countries have much shorter interim periods between elections and inaugurations, and some even have full shadow governments ready to take office immediately. America should be able to do better than a 2½ month lag period.

Shorting the lag period could be dealt with, but it isn't clear that legislators would care to do so. It is again a matter of power and the lame-ducks retain their power. Perhaps they have greater power or flexibility during the lag period after

---

[1] Elections are held on the first Tuesday after the first Monday in November, done that way to avoid having the election on the first day of November should it fall on Tuesday. With elections taking place between November 2nd and 8th, there would be between 74 and 80 days to inaugural day, or say 2½ months.

they discover they didn't win re-election -- they can then do what they wouldn't have dared to do before. But, instead of 2½ months, they would still have 2 weeks for hanky-panky.

In the sense that no legislator gives up power voluntarily, the longer lame-duck period would likely be favored by legislators. Yet legislators did once vote for a constitutional amendment to move up the inaugural day from March 4th (the day the constitution came into effect) to January 20th.

Our present system is even more confused as the members of Congress are inaugurated on January 3rd while only the President and Vice-President have to wait for January 20th. Moving the inaugural of the President and Vice-President to November would force moving up the inauguration of the members of Congress.

Shorting the lame-duck period is necessary to avoid the chaos of having two Presidents at one time, which effectively means no direction in government, no meaningful action, and a long period for hanky-panky. The longer lame-duck period delays addressing the matters of concern the majority of the electorate based their votes on. There is no longer any compelling reason to wait 2½ months for the new administration to take over.

13. TREAT LEGISLATORS AS BEING OPPOSED TO FUNCTIONAL GOVERNMENT.

A good part of the dysfunctionality in government can be attributed to legislators causing dysfunction as they arrogate power to themselves.

In addition to outright abuse of the constitutional power given to them in advising and consenting to appointments, the legislators themselves have established internal legislative procedures that allow them to obstruct and even endlessly delay appointments. They created burying by delay.

The legislators have established "blue slip"[1] and "hold"[2] procedures that allows only one of them, a single legislator, to prevent nominations from being addressed in committee. The blue slip procedure inexplicably allows a committee chairman of the same political party as the President to block the appointment of a worthy nominee, forcing the judicial seat to remain vacant.[3]

This clearly shows that legislators are behind the dysfunctional government we have; they want it that way, they themselves made it work that way, and they are not to be trusted in any reform effort the citizenry undertakes.

Legislators might assert they favor a functional government, but these and a host of other examples show that they would not change any dysfunctional process that they or their predecessors of like mind established.

While there was a recent modification in the internal legislative filibuster procedures that allowed a minority to keep presidential appointments from getting out of committee and going to the floor for an up-and-down vote, the filibuster was kept available for legislators to use on other matters, perpetuating their use of that dysfunctional tool.

---

[1] Savagem Charlie, "Despite Filibuster Limits, a Door Remains Open to Block Judge Nominees," The New York Times, November 28, 2013.

[2] Collins, Gail, "The Art of Senate Stoppage," The New York Times, November 13, 2013.

[3] Editorial, "The Senate's Discourtesy to Judges," The New York Times, March 30, 2014.

Voters do get angry about dysfunction in government from time to time, not realizing that the legislators want to retain the tools of dysfunction. As there is no dysfunction when legislators in both political parties cooperate in self-serving matters, maintaining and using the dysfunctional tools is a matter of choice, their choice.

Adoption of a strict term-limit (one-term only) as proposed here would take care of the problem, but what else might be done? The only thing is for voters to be willing to vote their own favorites out of office if they don't pledge to change the procedural rules so as to make for a more functional government. But is hard to image that legislators would adhere to such a pledge, voluntarily giving up power and serving their constituents, as the avoidance of fulfilling pledges has become an art for them.

So this might just have to be done by the influential political donors who traditionally buy elections (the wealthy, the billionaires, the corporations and the unions) who are willing to look at the long-term benefits to America, and thus to themselves, in getting rid of dysfunctional government and putting America back on track. If this group has the mind to do so, they should be able to force legislators to change their internal rules.

14. SHUN ENCOURAGING DISTRUST AND DISOBEDIENCE OF DULY PASSED LAWS.

Advocating the distrust of government leads to questioning the "legitimacy" of the seated government, its competence to manage, and its authority to coerce its citizens.[1] When this is carried to an excess, it is corrosive to our society and sometimes leads to people to maintain they have a "right" to disobey laws enacted by such a government.

Upon analysis, distrust of government essentially depends on what is the eye of the beholder. Some people just don't like government and distrust everything the government does. Others trust government. They trust government to protect them with a superb military, to assure the safety of our medicines, food and water supply, to plan and oversee our transportation and energy needs and a host of other programs too numerous to count. Obviously, the programs include many massive ones that have been handled competently by the government.

Our most highly regarded and profitable business enterprises occasionally come up with a new project that fails, but rarely is the competence of that management berated because of that. Successful movie studios have flops. Some new car designs by top auto companies don't sell. And the computers of a leading retailer are hacked into.

It is assumed that these organizations will rectify their errors. Things don't always go as expected, in life, in business and in government, but only in the world of politics does failures lead to questions of legitimacy.

Let one thing go wrong in government and some people question the "legitimacy" of our government, whatever that means. A person might question the dysfunctionality in government that we now face, but to suggest that our government is illegitimate goes too far.

---

[1] Brooks, David, "The Legitimacy Problem," The New York Times, December 23, 2013.

Questioning the authority of the government to force its citizens to do things also goes too far. Our government can and has forced its citizens to join the military, to pay taxes, to get drivers licenses, to drive and the right side of the road, and to use coercion in a host of other things too numerous to count.

But let our duly elected and legitimate government enact a law that requires any action by those opposed to the law, and they'll claim they have a right ignore what that "illegitimate" government had done. They are effectively arguing for a "right" to disobey the law.

A group of ranchers faced off against the Bureau of Land Management (BLM) and refused to pay the BLM fee for the use of BLM property.[1] The ranchers brandished guns, the BLM backed off, and some in the media applauded the ranchers and demonized the government. The message to the public was destabilizing, suggesting that the ranchers had a right to disobey the law.

And the BLM agents backing away from a gun fight made the government look inept in the eyes of some people, while other people would consider it to be the prudent thing to do.

It is just plain politics to dredge up a "rights" argument when you don't like the law, as if you have the right to disobey the law. It reflects the dysfunctional animosity found in politics today, where the minority that lost the legislative

---

[1] Krugman, Paul, "High Plains Moochers," The New York Times, April 27, 2014.

Dowd, Maureen, "Slaves to Prejudice," The New York Times, April 26, 2014.

battle goes underground to continue to fight by attempting to nullify the law, nullify the election or undermine it.

Disregarding such nay-sayers is not enough. We must stand up and contradict them whenever and wherever they are encountered lest they, through repetition alone, undermine our democracy and our government. Perhaps we can no longer afford to be gentlemen and gentlewomen in this era of belligerence and resort to shoot-outs with the bullies if they resist arrest. Law and order is the corner stone of civilization, and America will surely fall if law and order vanishes.

15. BYPASS OUR DYSFUNCTIONAL FEDERAL GOVERNMENT WHEN USEFUL.

On occasion, it might be possible to achieve needed action through bypassing dysfunctional Washington. This is not a cure to dysfunctionality, but only a means to cope with it while other ideas are pursued to overcome that dysfunctionality.

Regional alliances between the states, sometimes including provinces of Canada, are starting to emerge so as to compensate for central government failures to act.[1] There is now a northeastern state alliance focusing on reducing power-plant emissions. A western state and province alliance is addressing climate and energy concerns.

The existence of such alliances confirms the dysfunctionality in our federal government and the need to address that with serious legal and constitutional changes so as to stem further decline.

---

[1] Editorial, "A New Alliance on Climate Change," The New York Times, November 13, 2013.

16. IMPROVE THE PUBLIC DEBATE ABOUT THE ROLE & SIZE OF GOVERNMENT.

Before we argue for a cut in government spending or an increase in spending we should be aware of the cost of a proposal. Only then can the spending be evaluated in terms of the value that expenditure will deliver for our society. It is only the unreasonable or outlandish in terms of cost and benefit that should automatically justify opposition.

Neither side should draw a line, like "not a penny more of spending" or "we need it no matter what." We've seen positions like those with respect to a number of issues facing us.

And what we're being told, even by those we trust, is not always so. It should be noted that government spending has dropped in recent years, that our debt level hasn't hurt US creditworthiness, and that spending cutbacks do harm in periods of economic weakness by perpetuating high unemployment.[1]

Voters are subject to so much deliberate misinformation and disinformation from the politicians they trust (and personally devote so little time to independently exploring, evaluating, and thinking) that a majority of voters have wrong understandings of the situations America actually face. This has raised a question as to whether our political system can still function.[2]

We should be honest with ourselves and try to spend where it makes sense and reduce spending where it makes

---

[1] Krugman, Paul, "The Biggest Losers," The New York Times, December 12, 2013.

[2] Krugman, Paul, "Moment of Truthiness," The New York Times, August 15, 2013.

sense, and not just parrot routine positions. We should eliminate government programs, pejoratively labelled "invasions," that are actually found to be unnecessary, found not to be worthwhile, found to be unmanageable, or found to serve no significant purpose policy purpose.

A good recent example of this would be the Internal Revenue Service taking heat for not being able to delineate the un-delineable line between social welfare and political advocacy in the tax classification of non-profit organizations, where the rational thing to do is draw no line and bar all tainted activity (which is actually what the law says). Or perhaps go further and suggest totally new law defining charitable contributions tailored to our era.

This would simplify government and reduce voter discord that leads to a dysfunctional democracy incapable of governing itself. This would also address the valid complaints about an outsized government by reducing the size of government.

On the other side of the coin, programs that make sense, appear popular to large segments of the population, and have some favorable attributes (like producing tax revenues and balancing budget) should be seriously considered even though there is vocal opposition.

For instance, why are we still fighting the legalization of marijuana which so many states of both political persuasions are pursuing. Legalization would do much to produce needed tax revenues without increasing taxes, provide the basis for reducing the population of our overburdened and expensive jails, and simplify law enforcement.

It is almost a repeat of the situation facing alcohol decades ago. The constitution was amended in 1920 to prohibit the use, manufacture and distribution of alcohol and amended again in 1933 to repeal those prohibitions, with the states taking over the chore of regulating alcohol if they wished to do so. They did, and found that they not only eliminated the financial burden of enforcement but found another source of tax revenue.

Much of what the government does is not worth the candle or serves no significant policy purpose. Those activities should be identified and eliminated no matter where or how the chips might fall. And new proposals should be considered on the merits and only the truly significant and meaningful ones pursued.

Unfortunately, our legislators tend to deal with the minor nits as they have to be seen as doing something and the minor nits are the pay-dirt for lobbyists and vested interests. Either that, or our legislators kick the important matters down the road so as to enhance their re-election prospects rather than make hard decisions and face their constituents who are on both sides of the pending issues.

We need more public debate on what the government should and shouldn't do, looking toward broad solutions and allowing the chips fall where they may. The rubric that we need complex laws that cover all situations so that we can void injustices is just as likely to create more loopholes and complexity for complexity's sake. One way for a special interest legislator to destroy legislation is to deliberately harp on minor aspects and confuse issues.

17. RETHINK OUR VIEWS ON THE APT ROLE OF GOVERNMENT IN OUR LIVES.

Some of us want to cut back our "outsized" government while others want the government to do more. We can help our democracy to function better by both limiting government involvement in some matters that should be avoided, and also by expanding government involvement is other areas where it is needed. This would be possible if we forgo our slogans and preconceived notions and focus solely on the merits of the suggested changes.

Complaints about the "outsized" role the government plays in our daily lives focuses on the negatives (the so-called "invasions" of government), like the levels of taxation and spending, the size of government debt, the "over-regulation" of business, the excessive hand-outs and so forth.

However, it must also be acknowledged that the government also engages in "outsized" beneficial roles (the so-called "benefits" of government), like making us more secure, improving our living conditions (air & water quality, safety of our food supply), funding health research and much more.

Whether the invasions outweigh the benefits or visa-versa is largely in the eye of the beholder. We should become more open on these issues and not just take positions that applaud or condemn. We should start to think about the merits of each position, listen to what the other guy says, and put aside our preconceived notions.

We should eliminate or reduce the negative invasions when it makes sense. Any negative invasion that truly causes meaningful harm should be up for elimination. The negative invasions that can and should be eliminated should not be perpetuated merely because of a vague belief that they are more than balanced by the benefits the government confers. Similarly, if there is truly a meaningful benefit to our society, we should not seek to bar its adoption merely because of an unsubstantiated belief that the government is already doing too much.

Whether the government is too big or too small is a matter of opinion with validity on both sides. We have got to stop marching in lock-step, kowtowing to those who claim to lead us, and start thinking on our own. The approach adopted in this book supports neither extreme; it supports whatever makes sense under the circumstances. This is the mindset that can make America functional again.

WHO GOVERNS?

The American government is no longer of, by and for the people. To be sure, we all get to vote. But, America is basically governed by the millionaires and billionaires who effectively select the candidates, by the Chief Executive Officers (CEOs) of its largest corporations who determine what gets done, and by the lobbyists who set the agenda and make it happen.

The leadership of the two major political parties, or political clubs if you prefer to call it that, keep our elected legislators in line so that they will execute the legislative mandates they receive from those who really wield the power.

All this might be somewhat of an overstatement, but it is essentially supportable. Supportable enough to encourage the people to take back their government by political activity that ignores the direction of the political leaders, the millionaires and billionaires, the CEOs and the lobbyists by striking out on their own to force petitions, legislation, constitutional amendments and the like.

This book provides no plan to accomplish this. This is basically a book of commentary on the present situation. It offers suggestions as to what can be done to change the current situation only as a starting point to facilitate thinking, not as guidance.

Lest something is done to stem the dysfunction in government and to reclaim true democracy, the decline of America will likely continue and eventually lead to chaos and failure.

Chapter 2

Anemic Economy

We still have the world's largest economy, but not for long. The trend has been downward since say the 1970s and accelerating.

China's larger population will eventually thrust its economy beyond ours, sooner instead of later. Chinese growth was materially aided by American corporate greed and misguided US tax incentives while America has largely stagnated. Reversing this is the major economic problem facing America.

American corporations taking advantage of lower Chinese wages at the expense of lost American jobs can be understood in economic terms and somewhat justified in that it provided lower cost products (like sneakers) for poorer Americans.

What cannot be understood and justified is the corporate greed that shifted cutting-edge American know-how abroad to such an extent that America no longer manufactures (and might no longer have the capacity to manufacture) the advanced products American ingenuity invented. What we call American made computers and i-products has become no more than the simple assembly of foreign manufactured components. American corporations are literally hocking America's future, creating competition that has already caused the stagnation of American wages in addition America's inability to keep its workers employed.

Even worse, the US government allows the continuation of the US tax loophole that induced American corporations to operate offshore in preference to operating domestically. As an exception to the long-standing US tax policy of taxing the worldwide income of Americans, corporations as well as individuals, the US government allowed American corporations to duck US taxes by operating offshore through foreign subsidiaries.

The foolishness of this is shown by American corporations including the earnings of their foreign subsidiaries in their Annual Reports to their shareholders and in SEC filings, but not in reports to the US tax collector. That gives the corporations the best of all possible worlds, reporting the foreign profits as earnings and not paying the US taxes on those profits. That allowed these corporations to accumulate trillions of dollars of untaxed profits abroad in vast cash hoards in addition to their taking advantage of lower foreign wages.

Closing this foolish US tax incentive for American corporations to operate abroad is probably the most important single thing we can do to stop America's stagnation, bring back jobs and collect trillions in taxes to help balance the budget. The trillions in accumulated cash American corporations have in their foreign subsidiaries speaks to still more foreign investment to come rather than domestic investment. America is essentially being sold out.

Much of the pressure America finds on its debt levels is a function of this foreign subsidiary tax loophole that foregoes US tax collections and hinders budget balancing. With a reluctance to increase US taxes on other taxpayers because of this shortfall in tax revenues, we have to curtail necessary domestic spending, even to the extent of sequester. We can no longer pay for the military we want, nor anything else. We had to institute across-the-board budgetary cuts.

American government debt goes up, and there are political battles about raising the US debt ceiling; battles that can and have closed down the government. Although there seems to be lack of constitutional authority for such a debt ceiling, the ceiling has proven useful to those who would force economic austerity as a means of debt reduction.

In the view of many economists, austerity has been discredited, here and abroad, as being counterproductive, while economic stimulus has been proven effective for economic growth. Others oppose stimulus as being handouts or unwarranted subsidies. Both sides are right to an extent, but compromise is not in sight.

And so it goes. There are a host of economic matters that must be re-examined lest debt levels, stagnation, inability to employ our workers or pay for our military accelerate the malaise America presently faces. The American public is losing its faith in America.[1] That malaise can accelerate into decline and ultimately failure of America.

Debt Levels, Tax Revenues & Spending

Simply put, America's debt level is a function of its tax revenues and spending. The budget matches spending and revenues, the difference being an addition or reduction in outstanding debt.

Congress controls debt levels by controlling both tax revenues and spending. As tax revenue collections are an estimate, and known by Congress to be an estimate, Congress presumably takes that into account when Congress authorizes the expenditure of funds.

However Congress reaches decisions authorizing spending, the government can only spend what Congress has in fact authorized and that could lead to the need to borrow to cover the authorized spending.

THE NON-EXISTENT DEBT CEILING

Why we need a "debt ceiling" that has to be raised by Congress is a simple and obvious question for it was Congress itself that voted for the spending and the taxing

---

[1] Bruni, Frank, "America the Shrunken," The New York Times, May 3, 2014.

levels that supports the spending. Thus Congress itself created the need to borrow to cover the shortfalls it authorized.

There is really no legal basis for a "debt ceiling" that has to be raised by a specific vote of Congress to accommodate an excess of spending over revenues. The constitution says that the public debt of the United States as authorized by law shall not be questioned.[1]

When Congress authorizes the expenditure of funds, it is automatically authorizing the payment of any debt incurred to make those expenditures. There is no other way to look at this. If Congress did not want to add to our debt when it authorized a new expenditure, it could have revoked some other expenditure it had authorized. Failing that, the possibility of government debt increasing had to be known and understood by Congress when it authorized the last expenditure.

The so-called debt ceiling was created by Congress itself in its never ending endeavor to arrogate power to itself at the expense of the executive branch. There is really no rationale justification or need for it. Congress just created for a bludgeon for itself to use to hammer the executive branch when the occasion created by Congress arose. Congress essentially created a mechanism for blaming the executive branch for the overspending it authorized.

The public (seeing the government debt exceed the ceiling) might well blame the executive branch (the President) for doing getting into that situation, not realizing Congress should be blamed. And blame should not be cast when the

---

[1] Amendment 14, Section 4.

ceiling is exceeded for that flows automatically from the time Congress authorized the expenditures. To make matters worse, the executive branch must choose the specific areas for spending curtailment (Congress deliberately keeping quiet about it) so the public would also blame the executive branch for that.

The existence of the debt ceiling has become a tool for extortion: Do this or that or we (Congress) won't raise the debt ceiling and you (the executive branch) will have to cutback spending. That would be a power gesture that could effectively shut-down parts of the government, and it did so in October 2013.

In 2013, the citizenry blamed the dysfunctional shut-downs on the Tea Party Republicans in the House for its refusal to increase the debt ceiling without an extortive pre-condition. The political fall-out was horrendous, likely to do away forever with extortive conditions if not do way with the debt ceiling itself. That was shown to be the case when the 2014 debt ceiling extension passed without any conditions.[1]

Tax revenue collections are an estimate that enter into the budget, but the expenditures authorized by Congress are firm, made with deliberation, clearing the way for the executive branch to spend the funds. If there is a revenue shortfall, deliberate or unintended, debt must be incurred to pay what Congress authorized to be paid. It is difficult if not ludicrous

---

[1] Weisman, Jonathan, and Parker, Ashley, "House Approves Higher Debt Limit Without Condition," The New York Times, February 11, 2014.
Weisman, Jonathan, "House Republicans Seek to Trade Debt Deal for Repeal on Military Pensions," The New York Times, February 10, 2014.

to maintain that that debt created under these circumstances wasn't authorized by law, which is all that the constitution requires.

Since all expenditures have to be, and have been, authorized by Congress, there is no authority for Congress to turn around and force curtailment of other expenditures Congress had previously authorized. Congress in fact authorizes all expenditures. The executive branch cannot spend what Congress has not authorized spent. If collected tax revenues happen to exceed estimates, the excess cannot automatically be spent by the executive branch as that spending would not have been authorized by Congress.

The so-called "debt ceiling" created by Congress has been put aside or modified by Congress from time to time as the need arose,[1] showing that there is no real ceiling.

Various schemes have been suggested to eliminate the debt ceiling formally, instead of merely disregarding it. One suggestion calls for authorizing the President to raise the debt ceiling unilaterally, with Congress having the power to reject the increase, with the President having the power to veto Congress's rejection, and with Congress needing an impossible to get $2/3^{rds}$ vote in each house to override the veto.[2] Such gyrations are unnecessary. Just repeal the ceiling itself as there is no need for it nor any constitutional requirement for it.

The short rejoinder to any suggestion that there be a limitation on the amount of debt the United States could issue

---

[1] Lowrey, Annie, "Lingering Confusion in Debt Ceiling Deal's Temporary Fix," The New York Times, October 17, 2013.

[2] Editorial, "How to Disarm the Debt-Ceiling Threat for Good," The New York Times, October 21, 2013.

is that Congress must control its spending authorizations. That is the only way to control debt levels. However, the budget process seems controlled by partisan politics, ingrained ideologies, and an inability to compromise other than on kicking matters down the road.¹

AUSTERITY versus STIMULUS

Whether to use austerity or stimulus is always at issue in both the annual budget process and in combatting an existing or expected economic slowdown. The alternate approaches become more crucial in times of outright recession, creating animosity because deep-seated, ideological principles are involved.²

Austerity is the byword of those who look to lower spending, lower debt, lower taxes, and reduce the size of government as the way to achieve economic growth and pay for what needs to be done.³ The austerity proponents point to stimulus programs as increasing government debt and crowding out job-producing private debt, as printing money

---

¹ Lowrey, Annie, "Budget Office Says Obama Plan Would Cut Deficit by $1 Trillion," The New York Times, May 17, 2013.
Peters, Jeremy W., and Weisman, Jonathan, "2 Parties' Budgets Show Big Rift as G.O.P. Renews 2012 Proposals," The New York Times, March 12, 2013.

² Swagel, Phillip, "Fiscal Collisions Ahead," The New York Times, September 4, 2013.
Rattner, Steven, "The Biggest Economy Killer: Our Government," The New York Times, October 23, 2013.

³ Stockman, David A., "State-Wrecked: The Corruption of Capitalism in America," The New York Times, March 30, 2013,
Reinhart, Carmen M., and Rogoff, Kenneth S., "Debt, Growth and the Austerity Debate," The New York Times, April 25, 2013.

that leads to bubbles, as crony capitalism and pork-barreling, and as bail-out gambles.

Proponents of stimulus look to stimulate economic growth by increasing spending.[1] They point to austerity programs as being a counter-productive restraint on economic growth, and as further reducing private-sector purchasing power while the economy sorely needed government spending to make up the private-sector purchasing power shortfall.

Both camps focus jobs,[2] infrastructure,[3] education,[4] research,[5] Social Security,[6] and the like but using different paths to get there.

---

[1] Solow, Robert M., "Our Debt, Ourselves," The New York Times, February 27, 2013.
Krugman, Paul, "Dwindling Deficit Disorder," The New York Times, March 10, 2013.
Krugman, Paul, "The Jobless Trap," The New York Times, April 21, 2013.
Krugman, Paul, 'The 1 Percent's Solution," The New York Times, April 25, 2013.
Krugman, Paul, "The Story of Our Time," The New York Times, April 28, 2013.
Krugman, Paul, "The Chutzpah Caucus," The New York Times, May 5, 2013.

[2] Bernstein, Jared, "Where Have All the Jobs Gone?" The New York Times, May 3, 2013.

[3] Semuels, Alana, "Across U.S., bridges crumble as repair funds fall short," Los Angeles Times, September 3, 2013.

[4] Editorial, "The United States, Falling Behind," The New York Times, October 23, 2013.

[5] Overbye, Dennis, "Particle Physicists in U.S. Worry About Being Left Behind," The New York Times, March 4, 2013.

[6] Editorial, "What's Next for Social Security?" The New York Times, June 9, 2013.

Fighting pollution,[1] and funding our courts,[2] are also involved in this battle. It sometimes seems like every area of life is impacted when there is a deficit accompanied by an economic downturn.

The European austerity programs curtailed economic activity and thereby increase deficits and debt levels. This has been repeatedly cited in support of the stimulus approach in America.[3]

Those who believe austerity programs depress economic growth would also believe that running budget surpluses during periods of weak economic activity would also depress growth,[4] the point being that additional spending is needed in times of weak economic activity.

It has been said that America would probably be close to full employment but for the austerity policies of the last three years.[5]

---

[1] Forrister, Dirk, and Bledsoe, Paul, "Pollution Economics," The New York Times, August 9, 2013.

[2] Viguerie, Richard A., "A Conservative Case for Prison Reform," The New York Times, June 9, 2013.

Liptak, Adam, "Budget Cuts Imperil Federal Court System, Roberts Says," The New York Times, December 31, 2013.

[3] Calmes, Jackie, and Weisman, Jonathan, "Economists See Deficit Emphasis as Impeding Recovery," The New York Times, May 8, 2013.

Povoledo, Elisabetta, "Italy's New Premier Puts Stimulus First," The New York Times, April 29, 2013

[4] Bradsher, Keith, "In Hong Kong, a Budget With a Surfeit of Surpluses," The New York Times, February 27, 2013.

Stuckler, David, and Basu, Sanjay, "How Austerity Kills," The New York Times, May 12, 2013.

[5] Krugman, Paul, "Fiscal Fever Breaks," The New York Times, December 29, 2013.

Many people feel that history clearly shows that forcing austerity is a formula for decline, while stimulus has been shown to work.[1]

Yet, other people are convinced that less government spending and less government debt will stimulate private sector growth and that stimulus programs cannot be trusted to produce results other than lining pockets.

With feelings being so strongly held in both camps, nothing gets done. Not even spending to restore our dangerous crumbling infrastructure (e.g., old gas lines blowing up and killing people) which would also serve to create jobs and boost the economy.[2]

Infrastructure rebuilding would have to be paid for by a combination of increased regressive as well as progressive taxes and user fees. However, the jobs created would increase purchasing power and spending, which increases tax revenues that more or less recoups the funds spent on the rebuilding projects. More important, it would create a safer society for all of us. But, alas, with strongly held views, agreement on infrastructure rebuilding proposals are unlikely.

But both the austerity and stimulus advocates would agree that a balanced budget should be the favored model if it can be achieved without dislocation. In normal times much

---

[1] Editorial, "What the Stimulus Accomplished," The New York Times, February 22, 2014.

Krugman, Paul, "The Stimulus Tragedy," The New York Times, February 20, 2014.

Krugman, Paul, "Why Economics Failed," The New York Times, May 1, 2014.

[2] Bittman, Mark, "A Cappuccino for Public Safety," The New York Times, April 8, 2014.

can be said about balancing budgets, and, in good times, it makes sense to use of budget surpluses to retire debt.[1]

Few persons would put all this aside in favor of using the "happiness index" of the United Nations to judge whether the needs being addressed would lead to personal happiness.[2]

Bottom-line, it would be best to cut through the rhetoric and economic jargon and merely agree that some things are simply worth going into debt for and that government debt should simply be kept from becoming permanent.

Dealing Out the Hand Unevenly

An unfortunate aspect about government is that there are always competing interests and that most if not all government actions will benefit or harm one interest group or another. All actions fall unevenly in one respect or another. It is just in the nature of living together and claiming the benefits of civilization.

A road built through one valley rather than an adjacent valley benefits one valley over the other, while both pay for it. Everyone in a community pays school taxes, even if some members of the community have no children going to school. A hospital is built at public expense to benefit everybody in the community, but by its nature the hospital confers more

---

[1] Medina, Jennifer, "In California, Governor Pushes a Rainy-Day Fund," The New York Times, April 30, 2014.
[2] Farrell, Paul B., "GDP will make a generation of Americans miserable," MarketWatch, May 11, 2013.

benefit on the elderly and others who have greater need for hospital services.

A recession is fought by dropping interest rates to extraordinary low levels so as to help increase production and produce jobs, which tends to benefit younger people while the elderly who have the bulk of the savings earn less interest on their investments.

Everything falls unevenly in one way or another. And that is also basic to the nature of things as some of us are stronger, faster, better looking, smarter, or richer than others and each of us reaps the special advantages and benefits our attributes lead to. On an economic level, we live in societies that support the common good, with both the support and the means of paying for it falling unevenly.

UNFAIRLY BURDENING THE NEXT GENERATION

"Burdening-the-next-generation" is the argument fielded against increasing long-term debt, whether that debt is caused by the now normal budgetary overspending, by spending to rebuild the infrastructure, or any other spending by government. It is essentially an argument that our government should not incur any long-term debt at all, because at any point in time there would be some debt outstanding that newborns will eventually have to pay.

The argument is used as a slogan by those who do not like big government or those who want to "starve the beast;"[1] the beast being our government and its tendency to spend whatever it gets its hands on. But, less extreme people also

---

[1] Hubbard, R. Glenn, and Kane, Tim, "Republicans and Democrats Both Miscalculated," The New York Times, August 11, 2013.

want to keep government debt down to what they consider acceptable levels, and also feel that it is unfair to saddle future generations with too much debt.

Out the outset, it must be conceded that existing government debt will burden the next generation to some extent. Debt does revolve. Some of the older debt is paid off currently. But new debt is also added currently, so that at any point in time there is always some amount outstanding that will fall on a future generation.

The way to avoid this is for each generation to fund its own way. Do what needs to be done currently and pay for it, leaving nothing to be paid by the next generation.

Yet, the current generation is currently paying for things that will benefit future generations. The entire infrastructure, paid for by the current and prior generations, will be left to future generations. This includes the city halls, police stations, schools, hospitals, parks, and housing that can still serve. The road system is also passed on to the next generation, including the interstates highways that were built with an eye to serving many future generations.

To be sure, many of the old roads have decayed, and many bridges need updating, showing that the current generation has been shirking part of its obligation to do what needs to be done, yet the cost of making the necessary repairs that will burden future generations would less of a burden than building it all anew. On balance, future generations probably owe a debt to prior generations for all that will be left to them.

We can quantify how much debt we are passing on to future generations. However, we don't know how much we are passing on to future generations. We don't know the value of the public assets bequeathed to them, although we do know that value is great. Whatever debt that might have been outstanding and left to be paid by the next generation would likely pail into insignificance when compared to the value of what the next generation will inherit.

Yet, a case has been made that our generation didn't do enough, spend enough, to limit climate change and damage to the ecology. And there is no way to quantify how much that would burden future generations.[1] This presents an interesting dilemma for all of us, particularly those who say that we shouldn't spend today and burden the next generation.

Fixing our and previous generations many ecological damages would cost a fortune, which, under present circumstances would necessitate the incurrence of massive debt that would burden future generations. But that would be justified as future generations would be the primary beneficiary of ecological improvement since this generation seems to accept ecological damage and living with it.

But, as was said, things do fall differently and there is no way to bean count who benefits more. It is what it is. "Burdening-the-next-generation" is no more than a specious slogan. Each generation leaves some debt and unfinished chores to the next generation, and so does the next generation, and so forth forever.

It is difficult to criticize the last generation, the generation of our parents/grandparents, for not having done enough and unfairly burdening us. To be sure, some burden was passed on to us, and we'll pass on some burden to the

---

[1] Gillis, Justin, "What Does Today Owe Tomorrow?" The New York Times, April 28, 2014.

next generation, but the issue is not whether we "burdened the next generation" but whether we unfairly burdened them. The issue essentially resolves back to debt levels and what our generation could reasonably have done about it.

Whether the outstanding government debt is too large depends on the circumstances, largely dependent on what society presently chooses through its duly elected legislators to spend and how that is funded. The current generation bears the interest expense on any debt it incurs, which theoretically measures the value of what it got from spending the borrowed money. But, still, however you cut it, the outstanding debt could appear insignificant compared to what the next generation inherits if ecological damage is excluded on the basis of their having to remedy it if they want to do so for their benefit.

We shouldn't make "burdening the next generation" into a slogan that automatically leads to the condemnation of current spending without thought and evaluation.

REDISTRIBUTION & CLASS WARFARE

Criticism about "redistribution" and "class warfare" is periodically heard when one group or another feels that the dealt hand has burdened them more than others. Most people in a democracy would look to see what is reasonable and justifiable depending on the individual circumstances, but some people would object to any differentials in burden.

In a democratic society, or in any other society for that matter, there will always be "redistribution." It is more obvious where money and taxes are involved, yet it permeates everything in one form or another. The "redistribution" might be from old to young, from rich to poor, from urban to rural, from the healthy to the sickly, and the like. Some of this "redistribution" was voluntary based on pitying the poor, which pity now seems to have disappeared and the poor are being blamed for being poor.[1] But "redistribution" also exists in reverse: from young to old, from poor to rich, and the like.

There has been "redistribution" from the days when those who could afford it gave alms to the poor in the streets. Or even further back when there were no streets and religious stricture required the edges of a field be left un-harvested so as to feed sojourners and the hungry.[2]

It would appear that religious law was first in requiring redistribution. The tithe was designed to use the funds of the rich to help the poor, without giving it a negative spin as the use of the word "redistribution" does today. Later civil law had some redistribution features. Today, those staunchly opposed to redistribution find it to exist in almost everything the government does or requires done.

"Class warfare" argumentation usually applies to the upper and lower classes as aliases for the rich and the poor. It is commonly viewed as the poor attacking the rich, a la the French revolution, but in a modern developed society the reverse is just as probable or more probable. Since the law is generally promulgated and enacted by the rich, the law is just as likely to favor the rich over the poor.

---

[1] Blow, Charles M., "A Town Without Pity," The New York Times, August 9, 2013.

[2] Old Testament/Hebrew Bible, Leviticus 23.22.

"Redistribution" has become a hot word,[1] best not used since so few people view things in a balanced way.[2] "Class warfare" has become fighting words even though things remain well-mannered without people going out into the streets and dragging out guillotines.

It is best to ignore these words as they have essentially become empty slogans, merely statements of a person's position as contrasted to an argument to be taken seriously. Let's forget the slogans and view things on the merits, which is what a democracy deserves.

FAIRNESS IS IN THE EYES OF THE BEHOLDER

No standards exist for the measurement of fairness.[3] Fairness, like beauty, must be in the eyes of the beholders. Concepts of beauty change from time to time and from place to place just as concepts of fairness change time to time and place to place. No standards and no rules account for the changes.

Looking at the merits of various policies, paths and programs, which is what citizens in a democracy should do, requires consideration of the surrounding circumstances. If the circumstances demand that a program be adopted for the benefit of society, it should be considered fair to raise the money from those who have the money.

---

[1] Harwood, John, "Don't Dare Call the Health Law 'Redistribution,'" The New York Times, November 23, 2013.

[2] Douthat, Ross, "Libertarian Populism and Its Critics," The New York Times, August 16, 2013.

[3] Bernstein, Jared, "On Tax Day: What's Fair?" The New York Times, April 15, 2014.

Levels of taxation are always at issue, and they have varied greatly. For the rich, the top tax rate has been over 90% and as low as an effective 10% overall rate, each being considered fair or unfair at the time depending on one's glasses. The level, the fairness, essentially depends on the surrounding economic, political and military circumstances and also the individual taxpayer's personal economic position.

When societal needs were greater, the tax rates went up. The highest tax rates came in the times of war when our society had to support the war machine. That is not considered unfair.

The same discernment applies to agreeing on the needs of society. We can all point to a need for this or that, again depending on how we see things through our glasses. The aggregate demands of everyone invariably exceed what is practically available under the prevailing circumstances. So difficult compromises based on the merits of the situation must be reached in culling out the less important. Casting out favored slogans won't do the job.

For example, it is reported that there will be a future shortfall in the Social Security fund which could be remedied by either cutting benefits or increasing Social Security or other taxes to bolster the funds. It is said that those who favor across-the-board benefit cuts are more interested in reducing the budget deficit than in strengthening the system.[1]

But, as pointed out, fairness might dictate an altogether different direction of reducing the benefits for upper-income retirees who statistically live longer and would normally

---

[1] Editorial, "What's Next for Social Security?" The New York Times, June 9, 2013.

collect more benefits. That makes sense because people who have a longer life expectancy normally have to pay more for an annuity or receive less. This is what emphasis on the merits yields, a vast improvement over obsessively sticking to old positions. We cannot avoid examining proposals on the merits, assembling the pros and cons and pursuing what seems best.

Not everything should skewered for the "greater good" of the great majority of people. If it were only that, government would have to continually favor only the great multitude, the poor and modest. Rather, concepts of fairness usually point to a need for balance.

Unfortunately, all this comes down to matters of judgment which so few of us care to use. It is easier to rely on pre-conceived views, on what we've been told by those we respect, and on slogans, rather than strain our minds and apply judgment.

In the end, we all arrive at our views, hopefully based on real information rather than misinformation, lies, or spins. Then it is a matter of compromise, where we really fall down.

We all want our own way. Yet we have to respect the other guy, the other view, and come to some sort of consensus. If not, we'll always have a dysfunctional government like we now have, and America will face further decline.

Subsidies

We all like to get something for nothing. When it comes from the government, it is called a subsidy. Somebody gets something for nothing and some other person or group pays for it. Unless there is a predominant public-policy purpose behind the subsidy, the subsidy is a handout that favors one party over others, and is paid for by somebody else. Subsidies are usually politically motivated and, if at all possible, surreptitiously paid in undiscoverable ways.

Getting free air waves (bandwidth) from the federal government was a wonderful subsidy until the government started to auction those rights off for billions of dollars. State and local governments continue to grant exclusive doing-business rights that represent outright giveaways. Local governments give variances that allow the building of more houses than their zoning laws allow, but do not yet recognize they are giving away valuable publically-owned rights and are not getting paid for yielding those rights. Subsidies take many forms, as many as the minds of mankind can conceive.

Many subsidies benefit specific individuals or specific business enterprises while others aid groups of individuals, businesses, or organizations of various types, including a multitude of charities. Some subsidies flow directly from the government in the form of cash to specific individuals, business or organizations or to anyone who qualifies under law (e.g., welfare and farm subsidies). Some subsidies flow in an around-about fashion as for instance in giving tax deductions for expenditures of various types (e.g., charitable donations and mortgage interest).

Many subsidies are not deliberately disguised and not deliberately hidden from public view, but yet can't be seen on first blush. For instance, all owners of real estate pay school taxes even though they have no children in the school system, thereby subsidizing the education of others. Tax-free municipal bonds operate as a federal subsidy indirectly paid to the states and cities because those bonds can be issued at less than prevailing interest rates (saving the states and cities money) while the interest earned on them by the purchaser of the bonds is exempt from federal tax (reducing federal tax collections).

Duly enacted laws on any level of government can function as a subsidy where those laws favor a group or industry.

This is not to say that all subsidies are nefarious hand-outs as many are justified by a sound public policy. The public-policy subsidies are usually debated in public forums, but we can never know what goes on behind the scene. Yet, unless or until we know better, we should accept public-policy subsidies as being justified and not merely being a raid on the treasury.

Subsidies are beguilingly vicious as the proponents invariably have some appealing argument for subsidizing this or that. Public-policy arguments can always be dredged-up for favoring this or that. The rub is cutting through all of the rhetoric.

Unjustifiable subsidies contribute to our inability to balance our budgets, allow the underserving to drive out the truly needy, motivate lifestyle decisions, distort economic decisions, impinge on our "free" market place, and, perhaps most important, lead to public malaise and dissatisfaction with the American system.

Thus, we face a situation where each and every subsidy proposal must be individually reviewed. Lines cannot be drawn in the sand. And sophistication must applied in determining whether a particular action on the federal, state or local level actually involves an unjustifiable subsidy.

We won't all agree on the public-policy aspects or on the granting of specific subsidies, but the important thing is that we identify and address the merits of each subsidy proposal. Determining that a subsidy lurks makes identification the more important part of the endeavor because so many are well hidden.

GIVING AWAY RIGHTS OWNED BY THE PUBLIC

It is so easy to gratuitously give away valuable public rights because there is no governmental expenditure that must be accounted for. That is, it escapes accounting scrutiny and doesn't get reflected in the budget.

This can happen on all levels of government, even the local level where someone is allowed to vary from a local requirement. Locally, it is called a variance, and a variance can be extremely valuable although most or many have limited or inconsequential value.

Once it is recognized that variances can give away very valuable public rights with the public receiving nothing in return for yielding it, mechanisms can be adopted to charge for the variance.

For instance, a local administrative body like a city planning commission must first determine what percentage of the value of various types of variance must be paid as a fee by the successful applicants (e.g., 50 percent) for the variance and a law enacted to that effect. The administrative body holds hearings to determine whether the variances are justifiable and should be granted, and another commission or committee (say the real estate assessors) estimate the value of the variance. The applicant for the variance would be given the option of accepting the variance and pay the fee, or walk away from the variance.

Some procedure like this, or one totally different, should be devised so that the public gets compensated for yielding the rights it owns. This would limit the windfall that normally arises from the granting of a variance, bolster municipal budgets and be equitable to everyone in the community.

To be sure, most local variances have little or no value, as for instance where a fence is inches over the line. But that too can be viewed as a taking of a neighbors or public land. A fence that is too high, impinges and public right to light and air. A public right looms in every variance.

Many are minor matters, minor to everyone except to the individuals involved, and those are not the focus here. The focus is on the giveaway of very valuable rights as the federal government discovered decades ago and started to auction off air waves.

A variance of the local zoning law to, say, allow greater density of building can have tremendous value that should be charged for, if not auctioned off so as to allow competition. The variance would represent a windfall profit to the party that obtained it, a windfall that society can justifiably share in.

For instance, a variance with respect to water rights can have enormous value. I recall one being valued at millions of dollars in a newspaper article. There should be no objection to granting such a variance if it was justified, and having society charge for it (at say 50% of the value) would be reasonable and help balance local budgets.

A recent Supreme Court 5 to 4 decision held that a community placing conditions on the granting of approval to develop a property is an appropriation of private property unless there is proportionality between the conditions imposed and the effects of the development (whatever that means).[1] The holding ultimately stands for the community only having the right to deny or approve, based on existing law. It cannot work out a deal.

This disregards the ability of the community to place conditions on granting its approval and the ability of the owner to agree with those conditions rather than take a denial. If the owner agrees to a deal, it would seem that there is no taking of property, but the court felt otherwise.

Because there can be no deal to allow the development go forward, this decisions created an incentive for the community to deny the application rather than allow an otherwise meritorious project go forward with the undesirable aspect (e.g., harmful environmental impact) put right.

This decision might well be reversed in time for it does seem to deter rather than aid development. It diminishes property rights rather than enhances them.

The federal government stopped giving away publically owned rights in the air waves when it started to hold auctions.

---

[1] Echeverria, John D., "A Legal Blow to Sustainable Development," The New York Times, June 26, 2013.

While a public auction is the perfect way to transfer public rights, auctions are not appropriate where there is limited interest or where the applicant should be rewarded to some extent for uncovering or creating the economic opportunity. In those cases it would be fair to deal only with the applicant, but charge a fair price for the rights granted.

The problem is identifying the existence of the public rights that needn't be given away for nothing, and establishing a system to charge for such rights. Most local politicians are not likely to favor such a proposal for it diminishes their influence, but the more publically spirited politicians could be more interested in balancing their local budgets.

GOVERNMENTS GRANTING EXCLUSIVE LICENSES

Another hidden subsidy would be the exclusive licenses that are given-away by governmental bodies without auction because only one party is seeking that license. This tends to create monopolies, frequently justified with the proposition that it is most efficient to have only one enterprise deliver the service or product (e.g., electricity or cable services).

We have seen the initial municipal grants of exclusivity expand in time into newly created areas (e.g., TV cable expanded into internet). We have also seen the initial marketplace grow to the extent of justifying multiple competing suppliers which would do away with monopoly pricing in the marketplace. Thus, the wisdom of never ending exclusive licenses becomes questionable.

Just like patents and copyrights have limited lives, so should government exclusivity grants. Business investments are usually justified on a payback period of say 10 to 20 years and something like that can be used for the period of exclusivity, with no renewals and no expansions being allowed. After that, the market should open to competition which still leaves the initiator in an enviable position, but limits its monopoly pricing potential.

Thus, there are ways to limit exclusivity that will in time do away with monopoly pricing. The rubric that it is more efficient for there to be only one supplier is belied when competition comes into a market and prices go down, and yet both make reasonable profits.

There is no reason for baring a competitor to try to enter the marketplace after the initial investor achieved a full payback. Neither the local government nor the local citizenry would be disadvantaged by allowing a competitor to compete in the local marketplace. Only the actual or potential monopolist faces disadvantage. If the single supplier is in fact more efficient, nobody could come into the market to compete with it -- so nothing would be lost by eliminating exclusivity after a reasonable, economic-payback period.

MATTERS OF PUBLIC POLICY

Legislation based on a valid public policy might operate to confer a subsidy to one group or another. A subsidy specifically addressed, openly debated and deliberately conferred by an aware legislature can be justified as being in the public interest.

Experts are need to evaluate how a proposed subsidy would fall, whether it would work, whether superior alternatives exist, and whether the cost is reasonable.

For instance, the International Monetary Fund economists published a study showing that energy subsidies that reduce energy prices charged consumers were expensive and counterproductive for the poor who would benefit more from spending the money on infrastructure, education and health care.[1] Also, the rich use more energy than the poor and it was estimated that they benefited up to six times more than the poor.

Studies like this are great, but would have been priceless if they could have been guestimated before the subsidies were enacted.

Expert reports by independent parties must be distinguished from apparently knowledgeable reports of interested parties. For example, an article (report or study) written by proponent of a tax subsidy and pointing out how good the tax subsidy was[2] should certainly be credited and take into account, but it is not the same as an independent study, and certainly not as creditable as a report by an honored institution like the IMF.

"Aware" legislatures should take all information into account, but legislatures being "aware" might well prove to be a fiction of our imagination. When it comes to subsidies, the legislature is subject to local political influence and the expectation of monetary contributions to future re-election campaigns and the merits of the matter might be secondary or irrelevant.

---

[1] Reuters, "Study Challenges Fuel Subsidies," The New York Times, March 27, 2013.

[2] Rubinger, Michael, "Two Tax Credits That Work," The New York Times, July 12, 2013.

It is perfectly possible, as has been recently seen, that members of the two political parties that could never agree on tax related matters would get together to provide "public policy" subsidies for those they favor.[1]

To disguise a hand-out to horse racing constituents (a faster tax write-offs for racehorses) the legislators buried it in a far ranging, important bill. And some legislators were hypocritical enough to disregard their basic principal of never enacting a tax cut without finding offsetting spending reductions. The length legislators will go to in order to provide subsidies to those they favor show how important subsidies are.

Unwarranted subsidies by unprincipled legislators burden our budgets and undermine our economy, contributing more and more to the decline of America. This is a function of the failure of our democracy to provide voters with effective ways to cast out unworthy legislators, which is addressed in the chapter *"Dysfunctional Democracy."*

UNINTENDED CONSEQUENCES

Unplanned adverse consequences can flow from perfectly justifiable public-policy subsidies. Being "unplanned" normally suggest that the adverse consequences hadn't been anticipated. Yet the potential adverse consequences could have been recognized and even explored, but not disclosed or mentioned as a possibility at the time the subsidy was enacted.

---

[1] Editorial, 'Hypocritical Tax Cuts," The New York Times, April 5, 2014.

Extreme care must be exercised in evaluating subsidy proposals because the dialogue is usually controlled by the proponents. Balanced, fully reasoned and all-encompassing presentations are rare since the moving parties are advocates, not evaluators.

The possibility, if not the probably, always exists that adverse consequences were anticipated and concealed when the subsidy was being considered. Once enacted, it is too late to unwind the matter and the public has to bear the consequences.

Thus, it is imperative for the public, legislators and administrators to identify, disclose and debate all the potential ramifications of a proposal. Cast sunshine on the potential negative aspects and forcing them into the open could lead to modifications or mitigations that makes the proposal fairer for all.

For instance, the Federal Reserve Bank (Fed) drastically lowered interest rates which would indirectly serve as a subsidy and stimulus to those who expand their businesses and provide jobs for the unemployed. There was no public mention or debate as to the lowered interest rates eroding the income of the elderly who depend on their CDs, Treasury bonds and other "safe" instruments our society councils the elderly to invest their savings in.

Thus, the recession was in part being fought on the backs of the elderly without public debate. It is not that the Fed shouldn't have reduced interest rates, but that there should have been a full and open debate which could have led to finding a way to mitigate the adverse impact on the elderly.

The severe reduction in interest rates also raised havoc with pension plans. In the last few decades, America went from defined benefit plans[1] to defined contribution plans.[2] Employees were counselled to be conservative in investing the defined contributions accumulated in their 401K accounts. US Treasury instruments and bank CDs are amongst the most conservative. With the Fed's brutal reduction in interest rates, these 401K accounts earned little, hardly enough to fund retirement.

In switching to defined contributions plans, corporate America fixed its pension cost by shifting the investment risk to employees while at the same time reducing its pension expense by just contributing less. Then the Fed comes along and, for the benefit of the economy in general, effectively does-in the 401K retirement accounts.

The government/Fed bears some responsibility in all of this because ways could have and should have been developed to mitigate the program's harm to the elderly and the 401K accounts in order to benefit others.

---

[1] The corporate employer promises to pay a monthly pension of say $4,000.00 upon an employee's retirement. It's up to the corporation to fund that liability, usually by setting aside and investing enough funds that will grow sufficiently to pay the defined $4,000 monthly benefit when it falls due. The employee is assured a known and fixed pension and the employer has the investment risk and an indeterminable cost.

[2] Every month while the employee is working, the corporate employer contributes a defined amount, say $500.00 to an account owned by the employee (called a 401K account). The employee is responsible for investing the funds in the account so that it will grow sufficiently to fund the employee's retirement, allowing monthly withdrawals from the account in an amount that cannot be known in advance because it depends on how well the account was managed over the years. The employer has a known and fixed cost while the employee takes the investment risk (or benefit) and will receive an indeterminable pension.

For instance, the Fed and the Treasury Department could have allowed the elderly and 401K accounts to invest in special, higher interest rate US Treasury instruments (akin to the old US savings and war bonds).

The point here is not to advance possible solutions but to point out the importance of comprehensive open debate with everything on the table.

USER FEES & CARBON TAXES

Nothing is fairer than getting the user to pay a fee for the use of public property. But user fees could merely be disguised taxes designed to burden specific persons or groups.

For instance, a superhighway funded by the issuance of bonds charges a toll (a user fee) aimed at paying off the bonds, yet the toll continues after the bonds are paid off. The New Jersey Turnpike is a case in point, being a major source of revenue for the State of New Jersey while the highway also carries a federal interstate designation (I-95) which is a toll-free highway on the entire East Coast except in New Jersey.

What a wonderful way to export the state's taxes (to the non-New Jersey travelers) under the guise of a user fee. What wonderful political chicanery must have been involved in achieving this.

Charging a fee for the use of the National Parks is perfectly justifiable, while at the same time it is perfectly justifiable to have no user fee for using a neighborhood park. There are valid public policy considerations behind both the user fee for the National Parks and the free use of local parks.

There are difficult considerations involved in deciding on a user fee aside from the possibility of it being a disguised tax. And the amounts involved can be large, humongous in the case of the proposed "user fee" or tax for placing carbon into the atmosphere. The primary purpose is said to be combatting pollution and global warming, with a secondary purpose of raising substantial tax revenues.[1]

A person could question the effectiveness of a domestic carbon tax since both pollution and global warming are worldwide, indicating a worldwide agreement is necessary. But proponents put aside the worldwide aspects and feel a domestic deterrent would still be useful although it might be necessary to increase domestic taxes dramatically so as to make it effective in the absence of international cooperation. But still, on any level, the tax would have to be significant to have an impact. A meaningful tax would produce so much revenue that the US income tax would have to be abolished.

Some people would say that getting rid of the US income tax is the driving purpose of some proponents of the carbon tax. As the income tax is progressive and the carbon tax is regressive, substituting the carbon tax for the income tax would likely benefit the wealthy and penalize the poor (class warfare in reverse). A political agreement on something like this would be impossible. Thus, substituting a carbon tax for the income tax would necessitate reaching a political deal to use the revenues for specific purposes that economically

---

[1] Tyson, Laura D'Andrea, "The Myriad Benefits of a Carbon Tax," The New York Times, June 28, 2013.

Friedman, Thomas L., "How to Put America Back Together Again," The New York Times, April 20, 2013.

Friedman, Thomas L., "It's Lose-Lose vs. Win-Win-Win-Win-Win," The New York Times, March 16, 2013.

preserve existing progressivities and regressivities, which would be equally impossible.

Instead of using the carbon tax as a revenue raiser, it could be structured to be revenue neutral by having those that do not reduce their pollution purchase "credits" from those who reduce their pollution. It would be a zero–sum game as those who reduce their carbon receive money from those who don't reduce their carbon.

Such a program promises to present a tremendous amount of controversy and conflict in setting pollution standards by industry, perhaps also by area, and perhaps even by company. The complexity involved in introducing such a program, policing it, and managing it is likely to be costly and overwhelming if not nightmarish. Policing the program would require the hiring people and probably invasive audits. Managing the day-to-day flow of funds would probably require the establishment of a new bureaucracy, with the entire program probably taking a decade implement.

All this within the context of the program possibly being unsuccessful in actually reducing pollution since inelastic demand in many polluting industries (e.g., coal utilities) could allow the carbon tax to merely be passed on to consumers. Electric bills could go up in some areas of the country and some business somewhere could earn a windfall profit by not passing-on to its customers the money it receives under the program, which is not a politically viable position.

Thus, the revenue-neutral carbon tax system may be too difficult to use and the impact too uncertain to even try. And this might well be the case with other user fee proposals.[1] User fee proposals are complex and should not be viewed as a panacea. Proponents of any form of carbon tax might be better off directing their time and attention to developing and advocating other approaches to reducing carbon in the atmosphere.

For example, solar panel costs have dropped over 75% in little more than half a decade.[2] With the various ways our society is fighting climate change, perhaps salvation is in sight without adoption of draconian measures not likely to work.

USING THE TAX LAWS TO PROVIDE SUBSIDIES

Voters, and the public generally, do not understand taxation and do not want to understand it. Consequently, the tax laws become a convenient way to obtain subsidies and to hide them from public scrutiny.

For example, companies buy and use equipment that last for more than one year. They are allowed depreciation expense deductions to spread the cost over the useful lives of the equipment so as to properly compute the annual earnings they report to shareholders. They are also allowed depreciation deductions in computing the taxable income they report to the tax authorities.

---

[1] For a discussion of the merits of airline user fees, see Stellin, Susan, "Tax Proposals Open a Debate on Airline Industry's Troubles," The New York Times, May 6, 2013.

[2] Krugman, Paul, "Salvation Gets Cheap," The New York Times, April 17, 2014.

As you would expect, depreciation deducted for tax purposes (which reduces taxes paid) turns out to be much higher than depreciation deducted in reporting earnings to shareholders (which results in more earnings being reported). Company managements maintain and the CPAs agree that the equipment actually last much longer than the tax rules assume so they feel it proper to reflect less depreciation in the accounting statements. It's the best of both worlds; higher income reported to shareholders and lower income reported to the tax authorities.

In the ended, the total depreciation deducted for both tax and accounting purposes has to equal the cost of the depreciable asset, so the net effect is that the government is making an interest-free loans to those who can take advantage of fast depreciation.

It is not just an accounting machination, but an indirect pass-through of actual cash. The government borrows funds because it collects less tax due to fast depreciation. Those who claim the fast depreciation save tax that would otherwise be paid and invest the savings, earning interest (perhaps on the very bonds the government had to issue). Thus, the government pays interest and the party claiming fast depreciation collects interest, in cash, perhaps in somewhat different amounts but there is still an effective pass-through of cash.

Eventually, the whole thing reverses as the interest-free loan is effectively repaid when the business runs out of tax depreciation to claim but is still depreciating the asset on its books for accounting purposes. But in the interim those claiming fast depreciation had received the largest "tax expenditure" the government makes to businesses because the dollar amounts involved are humongous.

Allowing faster depreciation for tax purposes is a subsidy justified by claims that it spurs investment and thus job creation, which has been proven to be specious. Businesses are not going to buy unneeded equipment just to get fast tax deductions. And if the equipment is needed, it would be bought anyway without the subsidy.

Even if some businesses cannot afford to buy the equipment they need, the fast depreciation deduction does not help them write a check for the purchase of the equipment. A loan program established by the government would do much more for these businesses and at a much lower cost.

The bulk of the money the government expends through fast depreciation goes to companies that have plenty of money, so the government is basically making interest-free loans to those that don't need it (but nevertheless seek it, for who can refuse an available subsidy?). Basically, fast tax depreciation is a hand-out to those who do not need hand-outs.

To make matters worse, it is a selective hand-out to the capital intensive industries. That effectively shifts the income tax burden to other industries that don't benefit from the subsidy, and those industries (e.g., the intellectual industries as compared to the hard assets industries) are at least equally important to America's future. Thus, this unjustifiable subsidy distorts the market place, as all subsidies do.

As though fast tax depreciation wasn't enough of a hand out, the current argument is to allow immediate tax expensing of depreciable assets. That is when a company buys a truck, it should get an immediate tax deduction for it. Of course, this would not be done for accounting purposes in reporting earnings to shareholders.

In order to eliminate the subsidy feature, tax depreciation should accord with accounting depreciation and there should be no immediate expensing. Going further, an argument could be made for not allowing any tax depreciation deductions, substituting a loss deduction when the equipment is no longer in service and is disposed of. Admittedly, this is pushy but no pushier than the proposals for immediate expensing of purchased equipment.

With recognition being given to depreciation being one of the government's biggest "tax expenditures" and likely to curtailed in a future effort to lower tax rates,[1] arguments for more tax depreciation subsidies have abated.

"Tax expenditures" are subsidies given by the government that the government recognizes as not being part of a fair income tax code. The subsidy is given in the form of reducing the income tax collected instead of subsidizing in the easily identifiable form of a US Treasury check. Whether the government is providing a bloated tax deduction or is instead writing a check, it is a subsidy. Subsidies in the form of a reduction in taxes otherwise due is shown as a "tax expenditure" in the list the government publishes every year.

The point in going through such detail on depreciation subsidies is to show that subsidy argumentation is very sophisticated and the public should not take these matters as they are presented for their consumption because there is usually much more to be said.

---

[1] Bartlett, Bruce, "Depreciation's Place in Tax Policy," The New York Times, September 10, 2013,

The best posture is to be against all subsidies no matter how well justified they seem when first broached, and await detailed and balanced review before forming a definitive opinion.

Subsidies for individuals are also in the government's tax expenditure list. The mortgage interest deduction for home owners is one of the largest. Like all other tax expenditures, this distorts the economic marketplace and provides a special advantage to one group and disadvantages another. Like fast depreciation especially benefits the capital intensive industry over other industries, the mortgage interest deduction operates to the disadvantage of renters.

Renters get no deduction for any part of the rentals paid even though the landlords pay mortgage interest on the rented properties and effectively pass-though the mortgage interest in the rental charged to the renter. Home owners get the tax deduction for the mortgage interest on the property, so the tax law winds up subsidizing home ownership and disadvantages renters.

Tax expenditures, because they do not arise from the normal give and take of a free marketplace, also provide the basis for tax fiddles. A person who has enough money to own a home outright without borrowing could nevertheless borrow on the home so as to deduct the mortgage interest at his or her high tax-rate and invest the borrowed funds borrowed in a fashion that subjects the earnings or appreciation thereon to tax at a low tax-rate or no tax at all.

The economic distortions created by tax expenditure subsidies are difficult to identify and could have telling consequences. For instance, the tax expenditure subsidy for deductible real estate taxes indirectly serves to subsidize schools in more affluent communities.[1] Real estate tax deductions are higher in more affluent communities, so more funds flow into those school systems. It makes for educational discrimination against those in less affluent communities, subsidized in part by the tax laws.

Some people would assert that the income tax laws should aim solely at raising revenues by taxing income, and should not include any public policy determinations that favor or penalize anything. That is, there should be no tax expenditures or subsidies at all. Yet, the tax law is riddled with provisions that have nothing to do with raising tax revenues but have everything to do with favoring, rewarding, or incenting something; basically subsidizing it.

The situation on the state and local tax levels is similar, except that the scope for tax subsidy initiatives is much broader. That is due to the states and cities having a greater variety of taxes, and local politics allows for more favoritism and special treatment.

For instance, a cut in the tax levied on serving mixed-beverage (cocktails) at live music clubs was proposed for Texas music clubs that would hold more concerts so as benefit unemployed musicians.[2] Serious money was involved, estimated at $60 to $80 million a year. Opponents felt the club owners would pocket the subsidy. Claims for subsidies can be never ending, and ingenious.

---

[1] Porter, Eduardo, "A Tax Subsidy for Richer Schools," The New York Times, November 7, 2013.
[2] Chammah, Maurice, "Law Would Halve Mixed-Drink Tax at Music Clubs and Promote More Concerts," Texas Tribune, May 2, 2013.

GOVERNMENT CHARGING FOR SERVICES

Where, for instance, a company shirks its duty or legal requirements and relies on the government to help when something goes wrong, the government should charge for its services. Not doing so is a hidden subsidy.

For instance, under the British salvage laws, in certain circumstances the British government could charge mariners who got into trouble for the cost of providing assistance to them, while the international norm is for nations to render help at sea without charge.

Recently, the world's largest cruise line operator "voluntarily" agreed to reimburse the US Coast Guard and Navy for helping two of their cruise liners that encountered trouble at sea.[1] The reimbursement followed pressure from a US Senator claiming the cruise line didn't adhere to the strict safety standards and thus shifted expense to the US government.

Although help at sea has been a longstanding US tradition, the US government incurring the expense of aiding shipping companies plying US waters while being exempt from US income tax may have raised the Senator's eyebrows.

A person might well ask why the US government enters into "reciprocal" tax exemption deals with foreign nations where there isn't really any reciprocity involved. Shipping companies register their ships in these nations which provides

---

[1] Palmeri, Christopher, "Carnival to Reimburse U.S. for Cruise Ship Incident Costs," Bloomberg, April 5, 2013.

Walker, Jim, "Under Pressure, Carnival Agrees to Reimburse U.S. ...," Cruise Law News, April 15, 2013.

Walker, Jim, "Cruise Lines Depend on U.S. Coast Guard for Safety and Security But Pay Nothing," Cruise Law News, April 9, 2013.

nothing other than a paper enrollment and a tax exemption, with the ship never even entering that nation's waters. The shipping exemption from US taxation does seem to operate as a subsidy for the shipping industry. Shipping companies might avoid paying any taxes.

Going on to another matter, the federal government got into the business of providing flood insurance back in 1968, largely subsidizing home ownership in the flood plains. In 2012, the subsidies were removed with some properties being grandfathered. Grandfathering ends this year and everyone who chooses to live along the shore will have to pay market rates for flood insurance, ending the subsidy.[1] Of course, those who benefit from the government's insurance subsidy are complaining and fighting for its re-instatement.[2]

The flood insurance subsidy emphasizes the issue of building in risky areas, which brings forth demands for additional government subsidies when the risks mature and government has to bear the cost of clean-up. The 2012 Hurricane Sandy which destroyed risky building areas near the Atlantic coast highlighted two remedial approaches, both of which cost the states plenty. New Jersey helped its residents reclaim their homes on the risky shores while New York favored incentives for its residents to move inland, while both states also bore the clean-up costs.[3]

---

[1] Alvarez, Lizette, and Robertson, Campbell, "Cost of Flood Insurance Rises, Along With Worries," The New York Times, October 12, 2013.
[2] Davenport, Coral, "Popular Flood Insurance Law Is Target of Both Political Parties," The New York Times, January 28, 2014.
[3] Schwartz, John, "No Easy Way to Restrict Construction in Risky Areas," The New York Times, March 28, 2014.

The 2014 landslide in the State of Washington promises a similar dichotomy in approach and emphasizes how much construction in risky areas costs governments.

While it might be difficult to get people to stop building in such areas, we can surely make certain they bear the economic risks through required insurance, higher real estate taxes and dropping governmental subsidies.

The pernicious thing about subsidies is that it destroys the normal give and take in a free marketplace. Risky area development should be governed by market forces which would put a lid on such development and keep it in economic bounds.

The absence of subsidies would force those who seek to develop in risky areas to match the expected pleasure against the pain of paying the full bill. That would put the expense of developing in risky area where it belongs, and put a lid on society accepting ever increasing risk.

The government's flood insurance policy led to overdevelopment and costly claims on the US Treasury after catastrophic events, placing an unwarranted and unfair burden on taxpayers. While the US government could charge market insurance rates, there is little justification for government to get involved in that or in any other business that can be handled in the free marketplace.

EXTORTING SUBSIDIES FROM STATES & CITIES

Large sophisticated corporations have found that they could negotiate for a subsidy from the state in which they are located for agreeing to remain in the state.[1] As long as there was no clear threat to move out of the state, it can't be called extortion, but some would say all such negotiations are extortive. However, more subsidies are obtained from other states wanting to attract business operations, but subsidies to prevent moving out of a state seems to be evolving.[2]

Most of the action is on getting subsidies for moving various types of operations into a state. Negotiating subsidies for locating office operations in a state probably plays a small part, but the trend might be accelerating as Toyota moves its headquarters from California to Texas, which Toyota says is to consolidate its headquarters near a manufacturing hub.[3]

Some people might believe the move was to obtain the Texas subsidies that will be given on both the Texas state and local levels. Some might believe the move was to escape California regulations without identifying the regulations that offend. Others might believe it was to save taxes.

Whatever Toyota's purpose, Toyota and any other company certainly has the right to move anything it wants for whatever business advantages it perceives in moving. It doesn't matter why Toyota chose to move and the reason given should be accepted at face value.

---

[1] Eder, Steve, "For ESPN, Millions to Remain in Connecticut," The New York Times, December 26, 2013.

[2] Knickerbocker, Brad, "Boeing machinists vote, with thousands of Seattle jobs on the line," The Christian Science Monitor, January 3, 2014.

[3] Hirsch, Jerry, "3,000 Toyota jobs to move to Texas from Torrance," Los Angeles Times, April 28, 2014.

Buss, Dale, "It's Not About Incentives: Toyota's Texas Move Is A Corporate-Culture Gambit," Forbes, April 29, 2014.

However, where government subsidies or corporate extortion are shown to be involved, the national interest should enter the picture. More on this later.

Film making is a big player in the subsidizing or extorting game.[1] Manufacturing operations dominate. But it is not just the companies that are seeking subsidies from the states since the states also pursue would-be subsidy seekers.[2] It has become a race to the bottom with the states seeking to bugger one another and industry raking in the spoils.

Manufacturing corporations negotiate subsidies for establishing new operations in a state even though they might have already decided to undertake operations in that state. The usual subsidies sought are cash grants, tax exemptions, land-use exemptions and special labor laws or in special treatment.

However, labor costs, transportation considerations, availability of raw materials and components are likely to be much more important to manufacturing companies than the subsidies that can be obtained.

Yet, the competition between states for jobs and between local politicians for bragging rights allows manufacturers to obtain subsidies for what they would have done anyway.

Providing financing assistance is another form of subsidy. The public might not be aware that corporations are able to issue tax-exempt bonds to finance the building of shopping malls, stores, golf courses, office buildings and

---

[1] Story, Louise, "Michigan Town Woos Hollywood, but Ends Up With a Bit Part," The New York Times, December 3, 2012.

[2] Story, Louise, "Lines Blur as Texas Gives Industries a Bonanza," The New York Times, December 2, 2012.

more, and some might also get sales tax exemptions and property tax reductions for doing so.[1]

Interest paid on these bonds are not subject to federal tax and thus the bond-issuing corporation pays a lower rate of interest, representing what is in fact a subsidy borne by the federal government.

The states and localities effectively dole out this federal subsidy at no expense to themselves so as to attract the construction projects that might otherwise go to other states and localities. Localities that do not normally attract non-resident shoppers would give sale tax exemptions to attract the building of retail stores in their community designed to attract shoppers from neighboring communities. Buggering one's neighbor has become a national sport.

Economists have begun to question whether the competition between the states is a zero sum game that benefits only the corporations receiving the subsidies.[2]

The subsidies are obviously unfair to those corporations not receiving subsidiaries, unfair to the states and cities that lose business activity; and also unfair to the states and cities that increase business activity if the economists are right in that the subsidies don't pay-off in the long-term.

However, remedial action is available. The unfair destructive behavior, which does not serve the national well, can be stopped. For instance, enactment of a federal statute perhaps based on the interstate commerce or equal treatment clauses of the constitution or on other grounds could forbid

---

[1] Walsh, Mary Williams, and Story, Louise, "A Stealth Tax Subsidy for Business Faces New Scrutiny," The New York Times, March 4, 2013.

[2] Story, Louise, "As Companies Seek Tax Deals, Governments Pay High Price," The New York Times, December 1, 2012.

states and cities from having any exceptions in their laws or from giving any exemptions or special benefits to anyone unless it is also extended to everyone already conducting business in the state.

Thus, a state can have lower tax-rates than other states but could not give a tax exemption or tax reduction in any form to any attract any industry or business unless the special treatment becomes applicable to every business already in the state. If an out-of-state business is attracted by providing a tax-free holiday, the tax-free holiday would apply to all businesses already in the state. Similarly, special treatment under the labor laws or modification of a regulation offered to attract an out-of-state corporation would have to apply across the board.

Companies would remain free to move anything anywhere and they would do so for business reasons, but both corporate extortion and state competition would be eliminated from the equation with a law like the one mentioned. A different type of law would be needed to keep corporations from gaming state corporate income and franchise taxes.

Many if not most states, including California, tax corporations doing business in the state using what is called the Massachusetts formula. Under that formula, the state corporate franchise tax is computed by taking the combined consolidated profits of the groups of companies (parent and subsidiaries) operating in the United States and allocating the profit among the states based on the average of the percentage of wages paid in the state to total wages paid, of sales receipts in the state to total revenues, and of the investment in property in the state (plants, buildings, inventories) to the total of property owned.

Toyota's move of its headquarters from California can be used to illustrate how the Massachusetts formula works without there being any intention to impinge Toyota's stated motive in moving. The California wage and property factors as a percentage of the totals would be reduced by the move, resulting in less of the consolidated income being allocate to and taxed in California. The Texas franchise tax is based on taxing capital employed in the state, using an allocation formula based on gross receipts in Texas to total gross receipts. Since the move of headquarters involves only wages and property, the Texas franchise tax is not increased. Thus, California franchise tax goes down while Texas franchise tax remains the same.

Dealing with interstate taxation is very difficult for each state can tax as they will. Each state can adopt any measurement of income that the state considers fair or equitable. There is nothing wrong with either the California or Texas formulas, but the formulas can be gamed.

The states should also be free to adopt any tax rate they want, including a lower rate so as to attract business operations to locate in the state. Tax-rate state competition is inherent in the system, influenced by how each state wants to grow, balance its budget and benefit its citizens.

An analogy might be local real estate tax rates which depend on how much services the community wants to offer its residents. Each community is aided or limited by the value of the real estate in the community, but within that context they can set their rates with whatever purpose they have in mind.

Although a more uniform way to tax across the many states would be useful to limit gaming, there might be no way to achieve it except perhaps by using only the sales revenue factor to allocate income. The wage factor can be manipulated by moving jobs place to place. The property factor can be manipulated by building offices, plants and warehouses in one place or another.

But sales revenues cannot or will not be manipulated because a business enterprise aims at increasing sales wherever the sales can be found. The sale factor would have to use sales to the ultimate consumer, disregarding intercompany sales, sales subsidiaries and the like which can operate as subterfuges.

States with heavy manufacturing, which benefits the state with more tax collections due to the higher wage and property factors, are the ones that are susceptible of losing jobs, plants and property as their corporations are romanced by states that don't use those factors. These states might counter potential raiders by dropping the wage and property factors, with the reduced tax collections recouped by increasing the franchise tax rate or in other ways. Of course, higher tax rates deter, but business operations are not likely to forgo sales and profits in a state so as to save a few dollars in state taxes. Populations and sales are where they are.

Subterfuges like using intercompany sales subsidiaries or sales representatives to avoid having sales in the state won't work for the consolidation rules and substance requirements would sweep all subsidiaries into one franchise tax return where the sales to the ultimate consumer are used. Not having any sales activities in the state and depending on an independently-owned distributor to handle sales in the state means taking in a partner, a very high price to pay in order to save some state tax, and it could endanger the business.

Thus, the formula that each states adopts to counter inter-state raiding depends on the states particular circumstances.

The adoption of uniform tax allocation rules or altering a state's tax allocation formula to stop corporate gaming does deserve consideration and study.

However, the time has come for stopping corporate extortion and unfair state competition. Coalitions of states or state governors might get it done. Broadly attacking the unequal treatment through litigating the matter in the courts would be more time consuming and less effective.

The Need for Good Accounting

Accounting will never be of general interest. There is nothing like the mention of accounting to cause a reader's eyes to glaze over.

Accounting crimes aren't comprehensible, sexy or violent enough to command attention, as gun crimes are. However, accounting crimes should be viewed more seriously, at least equally to gun crimes, because bad accounting can decimate the well-being of people and damage the economy more. That has even led to a suggestion that training in accounting should be included in the American educational curriculum.[1]

Readers should have a distinct interest in having our commercial enterprises, governments and non-profits adopt

---

[1] Soll, Jacob, "No Accounting Skills? No Moral Reckoning," The New York Times, April 27, 2014.

good accounting practices, lest the readers who are shareholders or taxpayers wind up holding the bag.

In general, we tend to leave accounting to the CPAs (the rule makers of the accounting profession) but, just as war is too important to leave to the generals, accounting is too important to leave to the accountants.

It is not that the CPAs cannot always be trusted a la Enron[1] type situations, but rather they are being forced to make public policy decisions they are not equipped to handle. And accounting clients, from profit-making businesses to non-profit organizations and governments, have been able to influence the accounting profession in different ways, so there is a large variation in accounting practice although accounting principles and fair presentations would appear to be applicable to all.

In one fashion or another, a person's savings are at risk since they must be invested somewhere and the losses emanating from something like Enron are likely to be widespread and material whether the investment is direct or indirect via pension plans.

Of course, there is always the inherent conflict of interest where the professional is paid by the client,[2] as it is the business enterprise or non-profit organization that selects and pays the accounting professional. For instance, accountants have more flexibility as to new matters arising from the

---

[1] Kahn, Joseph, and Glater, Jonathan D., "Enron Auditor Raises Specter of Crime," The New York Times, December 13, 2001.

Eichenwald, Kurt, and Brick, Michael, "ENRON'S COLLAPSE: THE STRATEGY; Deals That Helped Doom Enron Began to Form in the Early 90's," The New York Times, January 18, 2002.

[2] Norris, Floyd, "Accounting World, Still Resisting Sunlight," The New York Times, October 24, 2013.

constantly changing economic scene, and the accountant might be dissuaded from taking positions clients might not like. Some in the accounting profession accept "off balance-sheet" financing in the very face of the basic accounting principle that all assets and liabilities should be on the balance-sheet. This was the accounting issue at the core of the Enron situation.

The issue of auditor competence also arises. When a top organization is found to be talking about making a bogus accounting entry for fake income so as to fool the clueless auditors,[1] it shouldn't be viewed as a condemn all auditors. But it does show how knowledgeable, competent people sometimes view the accounting profession. In this instance it was a top law firm which allegedly wanted to borrow time to solve a problem financial problem they were facing.

With this allegedly taking place on the highest level in our society, a person can only wonder whether brazen accounting practices are widespread in the general economy.

Also in this context, a person might wonder how competent auditors actually are. Perhaps we should assume that auditors are basically competent, but ascribe any auditor cluelessness to overly tight audit schedules that miss uncovering accounting problems but maximize professional income.

---

[1] Goldstein, Matthew, "4 Accused in Law Firm Fraud Ignored a Maxim: Don't Email," The New York Times, March 6, 2014.

FAILURE TO RECORD ALL CURRENT EXPENSES

A commonplace accounting boondoggle relates to the failure to appropriately record in the current accounts all expenses related to the accounting period. If an organization currently incurs a contractual obligation that must be paid in the future, that obligation should be accounted for currently. The obligation should be recorded as a current operating cost and the future liability set up on the balance sheet as a payable. It's the only way to property compute current operating results and also satisfy the need to show all liabilities on the balance sheet.

The offenders in this are more likely to be non-profit organizations like state and local governments and charities, not the profit-making organizations. For instance, businesses had to give some accounting recognition to future pension costs arising from employee services rendered during the current year. Some businesses prefunded those costs (set aside cash that would grow sufficiently in time to pay the pensions), other businesses reflected the liability in their balance sheets (to show creditors and others the liability existed), while most businesses likely low-balled it so as to make current earnings look better.

States and municipalities frequently ignored future pension liabilities entirely. Pension issues would come to a head during the municipal bankruptcies seen in hard economic times, when it became a matter of the pensioners losing their pensions or the purchasers of the municipal bonds losing their savings.[1] Trillions of dollars are at stake, much more than robberies with guns.

The governors and mayors deliberately kicking the can down the road to their successors[2] knew what they weren't fulfilling their fiduciary responsibilities. They might have taken some solace in that the ultimate fault rested with the accounting profession, the assigned policemen who didn't police the accounts.

Years later, state and city voters find they face a horrendous tax bill because their governors and majors gleefully overspent since they were able to do so, because the true economic picture was being kept from the public.

Fortunately, readers (and the media) are able to do something about this even though they are not accountants and do not understand accounting. All they have to do at open forums is ask the mayor or governor how much cash the city or state pension plans distributed during the year to retirees and then ask how much was recorded during the year to cover the future pension liability of current employees. Or, if some significant mishap occurred during the year (e.g. a

---

[1] Davey, Monica, "Illinois Gives Plan Details for Bailout of Pensions," The New York Times, November 29, 2013.

Lyman, Rick, "Chicago Pursues Deal to Change Pension Funding," The New York Times, December 4, 2013.

Walsh, Mary Williams, "In Detroit Ruling, Threats to Promises and Assumptions," The New York Times, December 4, 2013.

Morgenson, Gretchen, "Playing Pension Games," The New York Times, December 7, 2013.

Lyman, Rick, and Walsh, Mary Williams, "Police Salaries and Pensions Push California City to Brink." The New York Times, December 27, 2013.

[2] Keller, Bill, "New York Is Not Detroit. But.," The New York Times, July 21, 2013.

bridge fell down), ask how much the city set aside last year for bridge repairs.

Even if the questioner doesn't understand the import of the response, someone will (perhaps a reporter) and their follow-up could cause sufficient political embarrassment as to force good accounting.

Like Judge Louis Brandeis once said, sunshine is a great disinfectant, and the citizenry should start asking what are essentially accounting questions.

NOT RESERVING FOR RISK

Many decades ago, banks invested massive amounts in less-developed country debt. They poured more and more money into these loans so as to earn the materially higher interest rates these loans paid, fully knowing those loans were much riskier.

They reported the higher earnings currently but did not establish accounting reserves for the country risk (the borrower's country could expropriate or refuse to allow repayment) and for the exchange risk (the country could lack dollars needed to repay the dollar loans).

There is always the credit risk that the borrower could default, but those cross-border loans faced these additional risks, and that is why they carried a higher rate of interest. The mere fact that these loans paid a higher interest rate showed that there was additional risk in them.

Lenders are paid to take risk, receiving a higher interest rate for accepting more risk. From the lending viewpoint, being paid adequately to accept additional risk is okay and it is reasonable to extend such loans. But the lender should not record as income all the interest earned currently without setting aside enough to cover the inherent risks the higher interest rate portends. This means that the investment in less-developed debt could have been decent investments, the problem being that the investments weren't being accounted for properly.

Few lenders made any accounting attempt to reserve for the losses that could be expected in the future. Setting up such reserves currently would depress currently reported earnings and provide a cushion to absorb the future losses when they arose. The lenders must have had a way to estimate those losses or they shouldn't have been making those loans. Even if they didn't make such estimates, the excess interest yield on those investment (or a significant portions thereof) could merely have been set aside to create the cushion for the losses as they matured.

For instance, assume the interest rate earned on domestic loans was 6% on average and the less-developed country loans paid 10% on average, with no great variance in the credit standing of the borrowers. It becomes obvious that something other than borrower credit risk is being covered by the higher interest rate paid abroad. Instead of reporting the extra 4% being received as current income, say half or 2% should not have been reported as income but set up as a reserve to absorb those other losses as they occurred. But the entire 4% spread was reported as current earning and the losses left for future accounting periods to absorb when those losses ultimately matured.

That was bad enough, but the accounting also served as an incentive to make more and more less-developed country loans. The ordinary year-to-year marketplace pressure to increase reported earnings caused managements to turn to making more and more less-developed country loans, resulting in building the huge, concentrated loan portfolios that such management would normally shun. Peers also investing in less developed country debt and reporting higher earnings reinforced the search for such loans.

Later, when the loans weren't being repaid, major losses were reported. Thus, it wasn't that the investment itself was bad, or that those who made the decision to invest who were at fault for making the investment; the fault rested with those who failed to account properly for the investment in less-developed country debt.

Decades later, the same thing happened with the subprime mortgage debt. Good accounting would have avoided the problem, and probably would have reduced the huge amounts invested in those instruments since the subprime debt would not have appeared to be so very profitable.

The higher interest rates being paid on the subprime debt showed that the knowledgeable knew about the inherent risks, otherwise the debt wouldn't have paid such high interest rates. In turn, the unusually high interest rates paid should have been the tip-off to the unwary that something was amiss.

To make matters worse, the vast amounts invested in the subprime mortgages directed ever more money into housing, which became a bubble, and tended to crowd-out other loans that would have bolstered other economic activity. Again, bad accounting precipitated greed and led to tremendous losses to those who bought the subprime debt, to those who sold the subprime debt, and to the economy.

In both instances, with the less-developed country debt decades ago and the subprime debt this decade, many managements failed to give accountants a seat at the table. Perhaps that was deliberate in the never ending quest to report maximum earning, or perhaps it was the dismal view managements and the general public have of accountants; the green-eyeshade, penny-pinching nerds who merely push numbers around.

Accountants clearly have an image problem which they should address. And managements should strive to have their internal accountants in the room and give them leave to speak up. And auditors and examiners should be especially wary of the most profitable loans in a portfolio.

ACCOUNTING FOR EXECUTIVE COMPENSATION

Not many, if any, businesses record as a current accounting expense an appropriate portion of the future liability to pay large amounts severance to top executives. As with other executive incentives like stock options, bad accounting breeds excessive executive compensation packages and exacerbates economic inequality.

One might speculate that currently accruing the cost (and disclosing it) of all the special benefits contractually committed when hiring top executives would place a damper on board of director generosity. Alas, there is no accounting rule to this effect.

All that might reasonably be done is for the accounting profession to review the need for such accounting rules taking into account that their existing rules harm America by nurturing ever greater economic inequality and other distortions.

The alternative, which America will likely have to face in time, would be statutory limitations on executive salaries, incentives and other compensation packages that the financial engineers and compensation consultants have devised (e.g., retirement, termination, retention, non-competition and more).

The Swiss experience with such limitations (discussed in the chapter "*Economic Inequality*") could be a model for this, except that American excessive executive compensation and economic inequality is much greater than in Switzerland.

A bill like this has already been introduced in California,[1] which was probably a bad idea since it could become a negative factor for California as other states try to induce California companies to move to their states. It is noted that the California Senate passed the bill only a few days before Toyota announced its decision to move its headquarters from California to Texas.[2] Bills like this should be pursued on the federal level so as not to add fodder to state competition for jobs and business operations.

ACCOUNTING FOR THE STOCK OPTION RIP-OFF

The accounting for stock options is interesting and happens to be correct as far as it goes. The accounting shows that there is no expense to the corporation because the

---

[1] Nash, James, "California Bill Boosts Corporate Taxes for High-Paid CEOs," Bloomberg, April 24, 2014.

[2] Hirsch, Jerry, "3,000 Toyota jobs to move to Texas from Torrance [California]," Los Angeles Times, April 28, 2014.

expense is essentially borne by the corporation's shareholders and represents a taking from them. That is, the corporation bears no accounting expense because the shareholders are essentially being fleeced through the dilution of their shares. This is fully explained in the chapter "*Economic Inequality*").

The absence of a recorded accounting expense for this type of stock option serves to hide the full impact of those grants and shield the board of directors from criticism for giving away such huge amounts as incentives for top executives. And it is hard to make the case that the high executive salaries did not already compensate top executives for superb performance. It is hard to make the case that a top executive truly needs additional incentives to do her or his best. And it is hard to make the case that increase in the market price of the corporate stock in the future would really be attributable to the executives' performance and not to other factors the executives do not control.

It would appear doubtful that most boards of directors would approve tens of millions of dollars of incentive compensation to a single executive if the corporation were to pay it in cash. The board is protected from criticism on granting these stock options for it never attached any corporate expense to the grant and the accounting for the grants keeps any expense from being recorded on the books.

The accounting could be changed to reflect the reality that the shareholders are paying the freight through the dilution of their stock holdings. The corporation could record on its accounting books a capital contribution from its shareholders in the amount the corporate executives made upon the exercise of the options, and then reflect that amount as an accounting expense of the period and so depress reported earnings to that extent. That is what really happened. Good accounting is a great disinfectant, or so Judge Brandeis would have said.

Better yet, the use of stock options should be barred as suggested in the chapter *"Economic Inequality."*

Hating the Internal Revenue Service

Hating the Internal Revenue Service is like hating the messenger. Both are irrational, but pervasive in our society.

The IRS has become a hateful symbol for people who are opposed to big spending and big government, apparently because the IRS provides the funds. Yet, it is Congress, not the IRS, which votes on and approves the collection of those funds and instructs the IRS to do so.

Being opposed to big spending and big government are perfectly fine political positions, but these people should direct their hatred and opposition to Congress, not to the IRS. The IRS is merely the messenger, the lackey who collects the taxes mandated by Congress.

The IRS haters do not realize that they help boost tax rates in America. Tax rates are higher than need be because the IRS is not adequately staffed to collect the mandated taxes due to the opposition of the IRS haters.

Collecting the taxes owed to the government under existing law would help keep tax rates down. It is known that Americans, individuals as well as corporations, cheat on their taxes. The fact that everybody doesn't cheat makes matters worse because those who pay their taxes bear the burden of paying more tax so as to cover the tax revenue shortfall from the tax cheats.

Hatred of the IRS has starved the IRS of the funds it needs to employ the people who collect the taxes. Public hatred of the IRS is mirrored by their congressional legislators who keep the IRS budget to a level materially below what is needed to collect the taxes owed. Low staff levels result in only a small percentage of filed tax returns being audited, which in turn induces more tax cheating by both individuals and businesses.

IRS auditors cover their salaries many-fold as their audit collections flow into the US Treasury. Increasing IRS staffing would result in increased tax collections in two ways; through their tax-assessment collections and by prompting less aggressive tax cheating due to the increased chance of being audited.

Other developed country societies have a more benign attitude toward their tax collectors, as explained in an article by a former editor-in-chief of the newspaper La Monde in France.[1] Since the French considers paying taxes a civic duty and favor big government providing many services that they are willing to pay for, France has a robust and effective tax collection arm employing some 120,000 people. Compare this to the approximate 100,000 employees of the IRS that deal with a much larger country.

Another objection to the IRS is more rational, but unfounded. People object to the complexity of the tax laws and resent the amount of time they have to spend in preparing

---

[1] Kauffmann, Sylvie, "Taxing Times for the Tax Collector," The New York Times, November 15, 2013.

their tax returns. Yet, the complexity is what creates the special features of the tax laws we all appreciate, like the tax deduction for charitable donations. The tax law would be much simpler if it didn't contain all those tax deductions. It is the complexity that make for equity in taxation, limiting what should be limited and granting goodies that should be granted.

IRS tax return forms merely require what Congress has mandated, and the IRS does attempt to keep it simple.[1] If you have a problem with say the medical deduction and the limitation thereon, address it to Congress and don't blame the IRS for it. The IRS is not at fault on this.

The IRS offers to help taxpayers file the required tax returns. However, the IRS had to curtail this because its budget has been decimated by Congress.[2] Again, the fault is not with the IRS but with Congress.

Perhaps the simple explanation to the hatred of taxes is that taxes naturally gravitate upward to the point of intolerance; that is, to the point where further tax increases to finance more spending will not be tolerated by the people or their representatives.

For some people, the point of intolerance has been reached some time ago. These people now want to "starve the beast" by limiting the funds that flow to the "beast," the beast being big government. They realize that the function of the IRS is to collect the taxes mandated by Congress, yet they

---

[1] Sunstein, Cass R., "Go Simple," The New York Times, April 13, 2013.
[2] Carrns, Ann, "Need Tax Help? I.R.S. May Not Be the Best Place to Go," The New York Times, January 31, 2013.

object to the collection of those funds so as to starve the government.

What they don't realize is that they are condoning cheating. Most of these people are law abiding and would not condone cheating in any other facet of life. The IRS catches cheats and these good people actually condone cheating by keeping the IRS from doing its job.

It is just their abiding or obsessive hatred of big spending and big government that colors their judgment and allows them to ignore the reality that others have to pay the taxes the tax cheats evade. The hatred they have developed for the IRS masks the realization that the IRS not collecting the taxes mandated by Congress only creates budgetary problems and pressure for increased or new taxes.

Studies have shown that "pure," "unreasoning" tax-hatred does exist. This was shown in how people go overboard to buy a sales-tax free product even though it costs them much more.[1] This anti-tax attitude is reflected in persistent IRS hatred. It is irrational, but it exists.

And it also exists in the halls of government where legislators of like mind starve the IRS by not allocating sufficient funds to the IRS to allow it to do its duty.

Legislators sometimes go further and publically applaud as legitimate tax minimization what some people view as tax evasion,[2] setting a very bad example for the population generally and compounding the IRS enforcement problem.

---

[1] Dunn, Elizabeth, and Norton, Michael, "Heavens, Not Havens," The New York Times, April 13, 2013.

[2] Shear, Michael D., "Torches and Pitchforks for I.R.S. but Cheers for Apple," The New York Times, May 22, 2013.

If we have a problem with big spending and big government, it should be faced directly in the halls of Congress which voted for it; not by undermining our government. We need to change attitudes and fight the real battles.

We should treat the IRS fairly and with respect, while at the same time condemning instances of IRS incompetence as we would do with incompetence anywhere else. But we don't treat the IRS fairly, and by so doing, we contribute to the decline of America. The degrading of an important arm of our government degrades America.

Competition & Industrial Policy

It didn't matter until about the 1970's.

America was running on all cylinders -- innovating, producing, building and raising living standards. America could afford it, so it had an open economic policy. Any foreign business could come here and undertake what they wanted as long as it was legal.

We wanted American businesses to have the same freedom abroad, but we knew and accepted that the rest of the world didn't view it that way. We were big and rich and we could afford putting up with the discrimination American businesses found abroad.

America favored globalization because it was the right thing to do. Globalization would help the growth of less-developed country economies to the obvious benefit of their citizens. America would also benefit through the creation of foreign markets for American goods, as if we weren't doing great without it and really needed it.

Business interests initially favored globalization as a way to expand their markets, not then appreciating that commencing foreign operation would also lead to their avoiding or evading American taxes. And, after all, the world was becoming smaller and becoming a global marketplace.

There were those who foresaw globalization coming back to bite America and that we shouldn't do too much to push it. But they were disregarded. Our good nature and our greed prevailed.

It wasn't open for American enterprises abroad. American movies became too popular, so France placed limits on American movies. It just incidentally happened to protect the French film industry, they maintained, as they were really aiming to protect their culture.

Europe didn't like the idea of being beholden to the American airplane industry, so a number of European governments got together to counter America by creating an airplane industry and subsidizing it.

Canada set up a board to vet foreign investments in Canada, protecting those industries or activities they wanted to protect. And so it went.

The less-developed countries were happy to welcome whatever America wanted to do. They weren't competing with America. They weren't competing with anyone. They were on their backs. Wage levels were low, ecology concerns were non-existent, and they became the contract manufacturers for America. But we had to teach them how to do things, effectively conveying our now-how.

China caught on early. At first the needle industries and the like served to provide Chinese jobs and feed Chinese mouths. It didn't take long for China to adopt an industrial policy aimed at enticing high-tech manufacturing with tax reductions. China allowed foreign automobile manufacturers to set up operations in China in to obtain know-how and the vehicles sorely needed.

But where they could go it alone, they did so. They effectively kept foreign internet and media interests[1] out of China so as to allow their companies to pirate their way in.

China was obvious in what it was doing, and the greed of American companies helped because the incentive bonuses American executives could earn by maximizing current profits was worth sticking their successors with fierce low-cost foreign competition and the ultimate loss of markets.

At the same time, American industry began to realize that the US government itself provided them with a US tax incentive to move operations aboard. All they had to do was to create a wholly-owned foreign subsidiary to house their foreign operations and that subsidiary wouldn't pay any US tax on its earnings.

US tax would be due on the dividends received from the foreign subsidiaries, but the foreign subsidiaries needn't pay dividends. It could have their foreign subsidiaries retain the

---

[1] Cieply, Michael, "Imax Faces a Threat in China," The New York Times, February 2, 2014.

profits earned and American businesses started to accumulate cash hoards in their foreign subsidiaries.

It was more advantageous to invest that cash offshore, so even more operations would be undertaken offshore instead of in America. The foreign profits became permanently invested aboard so America would never collect any tax.

Also, American business found that the foreign taxes that would normally fall on their foreign subsidies could be negotiated away by obtaining tax holidays or otherwise minimized, avoided, or evaded in the sophisticated ways the American companies discovered in time.

This became the best of all possible worlds. Profits accumulated abroad (largely untaxed) soon stripped the amounts needed to expand foreign operations, so cash started to be accumulated abroad (now amounting to trillions of dollars). The US government was reduced to taxing the domestic retail profits of the products brought back for sale here, while foreign sales were now conducted by the foreign subsidiaries.

At first, American jobs were shifted abroad with all the negative consequences of that. Later, when that ebbed after all that could be shifted abroad was shifted, America found it could no longer produce new jobs for its workers and American wages stagnated.[1]

---

[1] Schwartz, Nelson D., "Recovery in U.S. Is Lifting Profits, but Not Adding Jobs," The New York Times, March 3, 2013.

The standard of living of American workers actually declined,[1] while those of the foreign workers advanced astronomically.[2] There was even a suggestion that the 60% to 70% income growth in China and India in a decade may have taken place at the expense of the middle class in rich countries, especially the United States.[3]

Globalization had become de-Americanization of American industry. Globalization did operate to increase living standards abroad, creating new customers for American products. As the foreign manufacturing capabilities improved, the manufacture of more and more sophisticated products moved abroad. As the foreign markets developed, their governments demanded and obtained the transfer of more and more know-how and even the establishment of research facilities abroad.

Steve Jobs, the deceased co-founder of Apple, was probably the best product development executive known to mankind, but he had a very hard and perhaps unethical side to him. Some question whether he would be in jail if he were alive today.[4] He certainly pushed the envelope on all fronts, not too praiseworthy when it came to ethical conduct.

---

[1] Porter, Eduardo, "America's Sinking Middle Class," The New York Times, September 18, 2013.

[2] Leonhardt, David, and Quealy, Kevin, "The American Middle Class Is No Longer the World's Richest," The New York Times, April 22, 2014.

[3] Edsall, Thomas B., "Is the American Middle Class Losing Out to China and India?" The New York Times, April 1, 2014.

[4] Stewart, James B., "Steve Jobs Defied Convention, and Perhaps the Law," The New York Times, May 2, 2014.

He was accused of fermenting an illegal pack not to hire talent of other companies (which is a restraint of trade), of e-book price fixing, and of backdating stock options that would immediately profit himself by $20 million.

Perhaps his most egregious act was how he hurt America permanently in the manner and extent he went offshore to maximize profits. But, in a sense, it backfired.

Apple effectively wound up creating Samsung, which became Apple's major competitor.

And now Samsung, along with other foreign enterprises, are seeking to tap American research in America. For instance, Korean and Chinese companies are setting up in America "hiring experienced engineers and designers in an effort to soak up the talent and expertise of domestic automakers and their suppliers."[1] Large American companies now need Chinese partners to sell in Africa.[2]

After growing as contract manufacturers, some foreign manufacturers shed that business and developed their own products, going into competition with their former clients.[3]

Steve Jobs once blamed the lack of enough trained American engineers for not locating skilled manufacturing in the United States, suggesting the US government subsidize

---

[1] Vlasic, Bill, "Chinese Creating New Auto Niche Within Detroit," The New York Times, May 12, 2013.

[2] O'Brien, Kevin J., "Microsoft and Huawei of China to Unite to Sell Low-Cost Windows Smartphones in Africa," The New York Times, February 4, 2013.

[3] Yang, Lin, "Foxconn Tries to Move Past the iPhone," The New York Times, May 6, 3013.

Austen, Ian, "BlackBerry Staggers to a Deeper, $4.4 Billion Loss," The New York Times, December 20, 2013.

that,[1] as if Apple and other American companies could not have done so.

American universities would have graduated more engineers had American companies created American jobs requiring those skills rather than creating the jobs abroad in their quest for short-term profits. The fault does not rest with American higher-education institutions, but rests with American companies shifting manufacturing abroad and employing foreign trained engineers by using foreign contract manufacturers.

America would have been better off had Apple remained in the United States, and so too Apple's shareholders from the long-term viewpoint. Mr. Jobs obviously didn't think so, or was not concerned about it. His company took the most aggressive action around the world pushing the envelope on tax avoidance if not evasion with the infamous "Double Irish with a Dutch Sandwich," which apparently also had a Caribbean Twist to it, so as run profits around the world and pay little if any tax anywhere.[2]

Aside from the shortsightedness of America companies creating or accelerating the creation of formidable foreign competitors, they have stripped America of its manufacturing capacity for highly technical products. What we now call high-tech manufacturing in America is no more than the assembly of foreign made components.

---

[1] Duhigg, Charles, and Bradsher, Keith, "How the U.S. Lost Out on iPhone Work," The New York Times, January 21, 2012.

[2] Duhigg, Charles, and Kocieniewski, David, "How Apple Sidesteps Billions in Taxes," The New York Times, April 28, 2012.

Foreign competitors have done a better job than Americans in developing advances originated in America. For instance, America invented the internet and now America is 35th of 148 countries in bandwidth and at most 14th in connection speed.[1]

Preserving and enhancing the "made in U.S.A" label has become important to America as it still command a quality premium around the world. Yet existing policies continue to allow its degradation.

For example, America would be prostituting its "made in the U.S.A." label if America allows use of that label on the domestic assembly of industrial tools made in China.[2] Perhaps we should introduce an "assembled in U.S.A." label and require its use where most of the product's content was manufactured abroad.

America can no longer be as open and altruistic as it was. America can no longer afford it. America can't produce sufficient jobs for its workers. American wages have stagnated. The America standard of living is contracting, except at the top. America can't collect enough taxes to balance its budgets. America can no longer afford its military without cutting back on other vital needs. Americans can no longer be the gentlefolk we once were.

---

[1] Wyatt, Edward, "U.S. Struggles to Keep Pace in Delivering Broadband Service," The New York Times, December 29, 2013.
[2] Williams, Timothy, "In Blue-Collar Toledo, Ohio, a Windfall of Chinese Investments," The New York Times, December 26, 2013.

It is time for some hardball in formulating an industrial policy to stem the decline of America before it turns into a fall.

CREATING AN AMERICAN INDUSTRIAL POLICY

Aside from America closing the foreign subsidiary loophole that operates as an incentive for American companies to operate and expand aboard (which should be America's number 1 priority), the United States should develop an industrial policy that would govern what American companies can do domestically and abroad and what foreign companies can do in the United States.

Having let the genie out of the bottle with the American incentive for American businesses to operate offshore, in the last few years 50 American companies went whole-hog and completed mergers that allowed them to reincorporate offshore and save even more tax.[1]

The administration has a proposal that would effectively ban this, and it seems that it might have bipartisan support. Another proposal is to give up, end the U.S. corporate tax and instead tax the shareholders on corporate earnings (like a partnership) and increase other taxes.[2] This could have merit as we have already let the genie out of the bottle with our incentive for American companies to go offshore.

---

[1] Gelles, David, and De La Merced, Michael J., "Pfizer Proposes a Marriage With AstraZeneca, Easing Taxes in a Move to Britain," The New York Times, April 28, 2014.

[2] Rattner, Steven, "End Corporate Taxation," The New York Times, May 2, 2014.

Mergers and doing business restrictions should certainly be part of our industrial policy.

Trade policy, trade barriers and customs, and trade treaty negotiating authority (including fast-track) should be part of our industrial policy.[1]

So should domestic infrastructure repair and updating it where it impacts commerce and international trade.[2]

America's industrial policy should include laws governing foreign free-trade zones on American soil.[3]

Our industrial policy should also involve developing and enacting laws to stop the destructive interstate competition for jobs[4] and strengthen America's anti-trust enforcement.[5]

---

[1] Erlanger, Steven, "Conflicting Goals Complicate an Effort to Forge a Trans-Atlantic Trade Deal," The New York Times, June 12, 2013.

Lowrey, Annie, "House Stalls Trade Pact Momentum," The New York Times, November 12, 2013.

[2] Semuels, Alana, "Across U.S., bridges crumble as repair funds fall short," Los Angeles Times, September 3, 2013.

Robertson, Campbell, "Obama, Under Health Law Cloud, Hits Road to Push New Public Works," The New York Times, November 8, 2013.

[3] A country would use a free-trade zone to provide special exemptions to foreign corporations. They usually exempt the foreign corporation from that counties discriminatory laws deliberately aimed at foreign corporations. (E.g., see Editorial, "Reform With Chinese Characteristics," The New York Times, September 28, 2013.) America's foreign free-trade zones are not based on the avoidance of our discriminatory laws (we don't have many or any) but rather are used to facilitate the importation and re-export of goods without the foreign corporation being subject to regulations and taxes applicable to goods imported for use in America.

[4] Story, Louise, "As Companies Seek Tax Deals, Governments Pay High Price," The New York Times, December 1, 2013.

[5] Krugman, Paul, "Barons of Broadband," The New York Times, February 16, 2014.

Our industrial policy should enshrine our respect for the rule of law as it is a competitive component in attracting foreign corporations to undertake operations in America.[1]

America's anti-dumping and anti-subsidy laws[2] should be strengthened and made part of America's new industrial policy. There might even be a need for America to selectively increase its tariffs and provide subsidies for American businesses,[3] which should be reviewed in developing America's industrial policy.

One of the toughest issues to be faced in designing our industrial policy is deciding on the activities America wants to promote. Of course, providing American jobs is a major focus, but jobs in what occupations? In the current world scene, perhaps research should be favored over manufacturing.[4] Services, media, communications, education, security and a host of other activities enter into the picture.

America could emphasize its variety of skills in establishing industrial policy as contrasted to automatically focusing on manufacturing. Media, communications,

---

[1] Ewing, Jack, "Bet on U.S. Pays Off for Germany's Carmakers," The New York Times, February 4, 2013.

Nocera, Joe, "The Baby Formula Barometer," The New York Times, July 26, 2013.

[2] Bradsher, Keith, "U.S. and Europe Prepare to Settle Chinese Solar Panel Cases," The New York Times, May 20, 2013.

[3] Uchitelle, Louis, "Glassmaking Thrives Offshore, but Is Declining in U.S.," The New York Times, January 19, 2010.

Uchitelle, Louis, "Subsidies Aid Rebirth in U.S. Manufacturing," The New York Times, May 10, 2012.

[4] Lowrey, Annie, "Are Manufacturers Really Special?" The New York Times, February 22, 2012.

entertainment and other services are now extremely important. Innovation and the sciences have to be emphasized, giving our universities and colleges an enlarged role. Energy cannot be ignored. Every facet of American life is relevant.

Establishing industrial policy is bound to be extremely controversial and self-interest will create conflict. But there must be a way to establish priorities and tactics because the good old laissez-faire no longer works. We can no longer afford it. We must establish or at least suggest priority paths for the future and methods of implementing that without getting involved in detailed state planning.

If the government cannot do this, and it might not be able to do so because of dysfunctionality, suggesting America's industrial policy could be undertaken by any group formed to do so and having the financial backing to get it done by a good cross-section of knowledgeable individuals. We don't need government or corporate approval, nor even seek it, to come up with the first draft.

PROTECTING AMERICAN COMPANIES

Many foreign counties protect their companies from competition or otherwise limit nationals of other counties from undertaking certain activities or operations on their soil. They feel it to be in their national interest, while recognizing at times the conflict with their attracting foreign investment.[1]

---

[1] Barboza, David, and Buckley, Chris, "China Plans to Reduce the State's Role in the Economy," The New York Times, May 24, 2013.

America doesn't have state-run enterprises to be protected, but America does have an interest in protecting and bolstering American business enterprises when the national interest dictates that.

National security would be a prime motivator, but America should also protect embryo operations, protect American jobs, protect American ingenuity, and the like. America should also consider what foreign industrial activity it should attract or deter, what types of American enterprises could be acquired by foreign interests, and also address the activities American companies should not conduct or outsource abroad.

Domestically, America allows both American and foreign companies to prey on our states and cities by extorting cash and concessions for locating operations there. Both asking for and giving such special treatment should be made illegal so as to protect America companies placed at a disadvantage. Under the constitutional powers given the federal government, Congress should be able to forbid states and localities from providing special exemptions under their laws or grant other special assistances where the special treatment has or could have unfair interstate impact.

TRADE TREATIES AND TRADE POLICY

Trade policy deserves full coverage in our industrial policy as it has a significant bearing on where and how business is conducted.

For instance, in the past foreign carmakers invested heavily in manufacturing cars in America for the American market.[1] With the advent of America's free-trade agreement with Mexico, a number of foreign carmakers are going to build large new plants in Mexico as an export base, including exports to the United States.[2]

We should be very careful with trade policy, devoting the time and energy to get it right for America, as it is a driving force and very controversial.[3]

However, it should be said that it isn't at all clear that our trade policies and trade agreements have served America well, if at all. Perhaps there is so much controversy revolving around trade treaties because those trade deals can and have hurt America and the government isn't really capable of negotiating trade agreements that would be fair to all American business enterprises and their workers.

At times, it seems that America gives special dispensation to foreign enterprises operating or wanting to operate in the United States in exchange for whatever American enterprises want so as to conduct more business

---

[1] Ewing, Jack, "Bet on U.S. Pays Off for Germany's Carmakers," The New York Times, February 4, 2013.

[2] Klayman, Ben, "Auto industry love for Mexico grows with new Audi plant," Reuters, May 4, 2013.

[3] Editorial, "This Time, Get Global Trade Right," The New York Times, April 19, 2014.

Baker, Peter and Parker, Ashley, "Trade Issue Goes Untouched as Obama and Reid Meet," The New York Times, February 3, 2014.

Lowrey, Annie, "House Stalls Trade Pact Momentum," The New York Times, November 12, 2013.

Erlanger, Steven, "Conflicting Goals Complicate an Effort to Forge a Trans-Atlantic Trade Deal," The New York Times, June 12, 2013.

abroad. It is unlikely that the America companies that would compete domestically with the foreign entrants had a say in the deal.

Our government doesn't seem to know enough to restrain American businesses that go too far in promoting their own interests in trade negotiations. Besides, the government shouldn't even try to represent American industry when there is no clear unified industry view, which is frequently the case but cannot be ascertained because industry trade groups serve to muzzle members who disagree or are opposed to the powerful few in control.

And even if there is a solid industry view and a trade advantage to be gotten for them, on what ethical basis can the government offer concessions in the trade negotiations that would negatively impact another industry?

Because of this and other unclear and potentially unjust situations, our government cannot and does not allow the light of day enter into the trade treaty negotiations. Trade deals have to be negotiated behind scenes so the potential business opposition to the deal doesn't get the opportunity to investigate and involve itself.

And the government needs a special rule (the "fast track") to ram the negotiated trade treaties through Congress, for otherwise nothing will pass. Which is right because our country is too large, our interests are too diverse, and our industries too varied for there ever to be consensus in America if all the players knew what was going on.

So administration after administration has to finely hone its position in secret, working out special rules (effectively subsidies) that will never meet the light of day. It should be obvious that if trade treaties have to be finely honed on a sub-rosa basis, there is something very wrong with the whole process.

If America's business laws are good, just and fair to all, we should stick by them for all comers. If not, we should clean them up, not try to bypass that with a trade treaty which doesn't do the job and benefits only a few.

On the foreign end, if the foreign laws are adverse to American business, we should not reward that country for having such laws by making any concessions to that country or its industries. America cannot win in the trade treaty game and we should just refuse to play.

BOARD OF DIRECTORS RESPONSIBILITY

In the quest for short-term profits, American companies were committing long-term commercial suicide and sorely hurting America's domestic economy by flocking abroad for wage and tax benefits. Berating them for what is now water under the dam is of slight help as compared to Congress terminating of the US tax incentive to conduct operations abroad and collect the taxes due.

We should accept that the American manufacturing base has been diminished, but not accept the status quo. We should strive to re-establish an advanced manufacturing base so that we can keep American from utterly failing.

It is up to Congress to kill the foreign subsidiary loophole. It is up to the administration or some private group to start the endeavor to develop an industrial policy. And it is up to each members of a corporate board of directors to start having his or her voice heard[1] and stop being a rubber stamp for a management seeking short-term profits offshore that ultimately serves to create or accelerate the creation of formidable competitors and diminish America.

The board represents the owners of the corporation and the control of the company is in their hands, not management's hands. Management is the hired-hand, the subordinate, and should be under the control of the board, not the other way around.

The problem lies as much with the boards of directors as with corporate managements. Many managements have been proven to be short-sighted, going for immediate profits at the expense of the company's long-term position. It's a function of our incentive systems. It's up to the boards of directors, if they are not captives of management, to take the long-term view.

The boards consist of the elite of American society, people who no longer need to seek short-term advantage. For the good of America and their grandchildren, they should instill the long-range view in their managements. They can afford to do so, and they have the duty to do so.

---

[1] Nocera, Joe, "Buffett Bites Back," The New York Times, April 28, 2014.

Government Regulation

Regulation is basically the price of civilization. The philosopher John Locke said that purpose of government was essentially keeping people from harming each other and thus make them more secure. Regulation through law is the mechanism used, the simplest expression being the stop sign or traffic light.

I have an interest in you stopping at the stop sign and you have an interest in me stopping at the stop sign or we can harm each other. Such regulation is aimed at stopping harm.

As such, regulation should not be viewed negatively. We should try to keep regulation to a minimum, so as to maximize freedom, while deterring harm. With regulation as such being okay, the only question is what is right under the circumstances.

We should be suspicious of those who oppose or bombast regulation since they are likely to be the ones who pursue activities that can cause harm. On the same token, we must be vigilant against over-regulation by those who see harm in everything or who fail to balance the needs of society.

DOES AMERICA OVERREGULATE BUSINESS?

Claims are made that America overregulates, but like beauty, overregulation is in the eye of the beholder.

American companies moving their operations offshore, frequently to China, might say they doing that to escape American overregulation but it is more likely that their major focus is on taking advantage of lower foreign wages and benefiting from the American government's tax incentive to move operations abroad. Wage and tax reasons would far outweigh any regulatory reasons if any actually exist. Nevertheless, the claim that America overregulates should be explored.

While there are no generally accepted standards against which to measure, there have been reliable studies that show that America does not overregulate business.[1]

In World Bank studies conducted over nine years, the United States has consistently been high on the list of counties easiest to operate in. The Unites States was the 4th easiest country to operate in, while China was 91st on the list.

The World Economic Forum did a similar study where the United States ranked 5th while China ranked 26th.

Yet, American businesses have flocked to China speciously claiming that America overregulates business. It would appear that the claims of American overregulation is merely rhetoric, sloganism that should be ignored.

A business sponsored study effectively showed America to rank high in terms of overregulation, but upon examination it was found that the study relied on the visceral feelings of the business executives interviewed as there was no statistical data.[2] The visceral reaction to regulation by those who are being regulated is understandable, and that could be widespread, but it does not prove that there is overregulation. As in anything else, repeat something enough times and some people will begin to believe it.

---

[1] Rampell, Catherine, "Is Overregulation Driving U.S. Companies Offshore?" The New York Times, November 7, 2011.

[2] Mandelbaum, Robb, "In New Study, Entrepreneurs See the Glass Nearly Empty," The New York Times, September 3, 2013.

We should accept that business people can and will object to regulations they must comply with. Let them say that they don't like being regulated or that they feel their regulation is unwarranted (which would be correct statements from their viewpoint), but it is incorrect to say that America is overregulated.

IS MORE REGULATION NEEDED?

It seems as though each time America deals with a serious recession, business regulation increases so as to bar those being blamed for causing the recession from doing it again in the future.[1] This would indicate that America didn't have enough regulation in the first place.

The European Union, like America, had problems dealing with bank excesses. The EU's competition authorities had to resort to undesirable fines as a means of regulation since its banking regulators lacked authority to enforce actions it wanted the banks to undertake.[2] That exhibited EU's need for more or better regulation, while confirming that America had it right in that its bank regulators did have enforcement authority.

Decades ago America faced a severe recession and determined that its banks needed more regulation, resulting in

---

[1] Editorial, "Still Dangerous," The New York Times, November 9, 2013.
Eavis, Peter, "Treasury Chief to Declare Big Gains in Financial Reform," The New York Times, December 5, 2013.
Editorial, "Finally, the Volcker Rule," The New York Times, December 12, 2013.

[2] Bray, Chad, and Ewing, Jack, "Europe Sets Big Fines in Settling Libor Case," The New York Times, December 4, 2013.

the enactment of the Glass-Steagall Act of 1933. American came out of the recession and prospered, and the banks began to advance seemingly convincing arguments to lift existing regulations. The banks whittled away at Glass-Steagall until it was effectively dismantled. Another recession occurred, the banks were found to be major contributors to it, and re-regulation followed. The re-regulation included many features which can be viewed as reinstating Glass-Steagall. Deregulation followed by re-regulation like this suggests that America does not overregulate but rather tends to under-regulate.

Sometimes the devil you know is better than the one you don't know. California deregulated the energy industry only to encounter an energy crisis manufactured by "energy bandits" aimed at jacking-up prices.[1] However, this did not discourage California from deregulation where it makes sense because of changing conditions.[2]

Airlines were deregulated 35 years ago, which at first led to the creation of start-up airlines, more competition between airlines, and lower consumer airfares. But later it led to the vast consolidation we have today and much higher consumer airfares and less consumer choice.[3] That is in the nature of an oligopoly, which is what we have today in the airline industry with a few large players dominating the industry.

---

[1] King, Peter H., "State May Be Re-Energized, but Powerful Questions Remain," Los Angeles Times, January 20, 2002.

[2] Nagourney, Adam, "California Takes Steps to Ease Landmark Law Protecting Environment," The New York Times, September 10, 2013.

[3] Nocera, Joe, "Merge Is What Airlines Do," The New York Times, August 16, 2013.

It's too late to re-regulate the airline industry in order to block future mergers, so society has to rely on the anti-trust rules to stop mergers. Oligopoly pricing should lead to re-regulation in terms of fare limits, extra-charges limits, route rebalancing and the like may. And we see this in industry after industry.

A major cell-phone company tried to acquire a smaller one that would enhance its profit potential or rid itself of a competitor that had become a pain to them. The government block the acquisition so as to protect consumers from harm.[1]

Later, the smaller company turned the tables on the larger companies in its industry by lowering prices and changing a host of rules that disadvantaged customers. The smaller company became a fierce competitor, obtained customers from the larger companies and heaped credit on the United States government for blocking the acquisition.[2]

This turn-about showed how mistaken the owner of the smaller company was in first wanting to sell out instead of competing, but it did later give its subsidiary leave to fight it out. The turn-about demonstrated how successful a smaller company can be in an oligopolistic situation since, almost by definition, the oligopolist over-charges its customers.

This might be the best showing ever of how successful the anti-trust laws can be in protecting consumers and in highlighting the need for regulation. Never was it so clear that regulation works, works to the favor of the public and stops the overpricing and overreaching business practices of

---

[1] De La Merced, Michael, "Reactions to AT&T's Decision to Cancel Its T-Mobile Deal," The New York Times, December 19, 2011.
[2] Manjoo, Farhad, "T-Mobile Turns an Industry on Its Ear," The New York Times, February 26, 2014.

the regulated. What can't be understood is why so many members of the public are so blindly against regulation.

The acquisition action is now in media with the largest cable company in America trying to acquire the second largest and also with efforts to overturn the even playing-field provided by a free internet.

Perhaps cable companies should be treated as a utilities and regulated as such, being essentially fiber-optic funnels through which TV and internet signals are run just like electricity is run through the wire funnels owned by regulated electric utilities.

Again, oligopolists dominating internet access assures consumer overpricing as in any other area of oligopolist domination.

Regulation obviously has to be tailored to fit the specific situation and the surrounding circumstances, which requires great care. The American experience with regulation, deregulation and re-regulation shows that regulation in America had generally been well founded. This, in turn, could lead to suggestions for more regulation.

However, all biases for or against regulation should be put as aside in favor of carefully examining all regulatory proposals, not only from the point of view of the customer but also from the point of view of not unduly restricting businesses.

America needs neither more nor less regulation. It needs the right amount of regulation. Individuals shouldn't favor or oppose regulation in general, but be willing to look at each regulatory proposal on its merits.

PROTECTING THE PUBLIC AGAINST HARM

An American citizen goes to developed Europe, not to an inexpensive less-developed country, to have a hip replacement. That's because the cost of a hip replacement is 6 times greater in the United States.

In this instance, the hip implant's US list price would have been $13,000 and the hospital charges would have amounted to $65,000 excluding the surgeon's fee. That makes for a total exceeding $78,000, while the cost of having it done in Brussels was $13,660 including the surgeon's fee and round-trip transportation.[1]

The cost of manufacturing the hip implant in the United States was estimated to be $350 ($150 in Asia). Health economists pointed to inflated prices, multiple intermediaries, multiple mark-ups, and even charges of cartel as the causes of the exorbitant overpricing in the United States.

Much more than mere regulation seems warranted in such circumstances. Our trade policy of excluding foreign made implants should be re-examined, as should our laws that would allow or forbid the use of generic copies. We should investigate what can be done about multiple mark-ups in the health industry.

Price non-disclosure agreements, used in the medical device industry, should be barred and probably also forbidden in other areas of health care. Although most Americans would be against price controls, it should be considered where cartels are found to exist or non-competitive signals exist. A legislative path to accomplish this can be devised.

---

[1] Rosenthal, Elizabeth, "In Need of a New Hip, but Priced Out of the U.S.," The New York Times, August 3, 2013.

Short-term consumer loans (sometimes called payday loans) presents another situation where a segment of the population is subject to significant harm. Extremely high interest rates of up to 400 percent is being charged and there are also other predatory features that severely harm the poor who have to resort to such loans.

State usury caps are a form of regulation (like the New York interest rate cap of as little as 25%) that would ordinarily limit such predatory practices but they don't seem to work with payday loans. Payday lenders use avoidance practices that the state regulators are trying to stop.[1] Bank regulators, also being concerned with the harm to the needy being caused by somewhat similar lending by some banks, addressed the matter using their regulatory powers.[2]

And then there is the full galaxy of traffic and transportation regulations that protect lives of everyone on the roads and highways. Food regulations and inspectors protect our food supply. Air traffic controllers make flying safer. Licensing of medical and other professionals protects the public.

The list is endless, all un-objectionable except to those who can't comply or want to avoid the cost of complying. Keeping us (individuals and businesses) from harming each other is a basic function of government and regulation serves as an important tool. It is a price of civilization.

---

[1] Abrams, Rachel, and Silver-Greenberg, Jessica, "New York Subpoenas Websites in an Effort to Curb Payday Lenders," The New York Times, December 2, 2013.

[2] Editorial, "Banks as Payday Lenders," The New York Times, December 2, 2013.

DIFFERENT APPROACHES TO REGULATION

Another form of regulation, said to have a lighter touch, is the cap-and-trade approach suggested for use in regulating pollution in the production of electric energy. The cap-and-trade approach sets a regulatory standard for pollution producing facilities. The enterprises that better the standard are rewarded by effectively allowing them sell their surplus allowance to cash purchasers that can't meet their targets. Presumably, it's a zero sum game.

All the enterprises owning pollution producing facilities would have a significant incentive to reduce pollution based on the severity of the pollution standard. Utilities can be big polluters. But even in the worst cases, the bad utility polluters would be able to pass-on to their customers the cost of purchasing the pollution credits because these utilities are structured as monopolies without other sources of power being available to their customers.

On the other side of the coin, those earning and selling pollution allowances might pass on the cash received to their customers, but they might instead pocket it if their regulatory environment allows. While mathematically achieving a zero-sum game with cap-and-trade might be achievable, there is no certainty on how the program will fall on consumers or on other businesses.

America had a successful experience using the cap-and-trade approach to reduce acid rain, but ran into political problems in significantly scaling-up the approach to handle power plant emissions. The Chinese are now testing use of the approach to stem their egregious pollution levels.[1]

Chinese pollution is so bad that it forced the Chinese leadership to face the issue as to what good came of China's economic success if the Chinese people cannot live there healthily.[2] The same would appear applicable to parts of America. Thus, while the cap-and-trade approach will provide an incentive to reduce pollution in America, a significant program such as this could have consequences (known, unknown, unintended) that require careful exploration.

Pollution and global warming are worldwide phenomenon's having worldwide consequences, not problems that can be solved domestically. To be sure, domestic action helps but it wouldn't necessarily be as effective as a worldwide agreement, which should be the goal.

Setting cap-and-trade regulations (identifying what is good and bad and quantifying it for specific areas and atmospheric conditions, regions or even individual companies) is likely to be very complex, very controversial, very difficult to find consensus, and most difficult to enact. Administration and policing promise to be nightmares. With the effectiveness of such a program not being so clear due to the global aspects, trying cap-and-trade domestically might not be worth the effort.

On an ethical basis, some people would feel that cap-and-trade can put plants out of business and thus represent unfair

---

[1] Forrister, Dirk, and Bledsoe, Paul, "Pollution Economics," The New York Times, August 9, 2013.
[2] Friedman, Thomas L., "Too Big to Breathe?" The New York Times, November 5, 2013.

takings. In a sense that would be worse than a governmental taking where there is a claim for compensation. Forced bankruptcy leaves nothing for the shareholders and saddle the creditors with losses. The plants were perfectly legal when built and now the economics of cap-and-trade could put some of them out business.

There might well be calls for compensation for losses (as there is for instance in government taking of land for highways) forced by cap-and-trade regulation. As contrasted, other types of regulation, like bank regulation, normally applies prospectively to future operations, and don't operate to close down the enterprise.

One of the special problems presented by pollution control and gas emissions, climate control and global warming, and similar matters is that scientific advances can develop alternatives to regulation and potentially do away with the problems.

For instance, if a scientific way to clean coal is found, there would be less need or no need to regulate coal burning power plants in terms of pollution, but those plants would still add to global warming. Yet, scientists have tried to develop clean coal for decades to no avail. Other solutions or partial solutions are being investigated[1] but there is no telling what, if anything, will be found.

Also there might be other approaches to solving the problem, with some approaches being out of the box. For instance, the high public-health cost generated by coal burning power plants could justify a government funded operation to purchase all the coal burning plants at fair market

---

[1] Hamilton, Clive, "Geoengineering: Our Last Hope, or a False Promise?" The New York Times, May 26, 2013.

value and close them down. The health cost savings and selling off the franchises to build clean power plants could help pay for the program.

Yet, we cannot use the possibility of scientific, geoengineering or other solutions as an excuse to delay doing what needs to be done. Regulations can always be repealed when and if better alternatives are found.

As with all regulation, the need to do something about an egregious situation (which most people would agree with) leads to the exploration of ways to combat the problem (which is where disagreement arises). Thus, it's not the fact of regulation that generally troubles people, but whether the regulation would work and whether it is justifiable under the prevailing circumstances.

TAXATION AS REGULATION

Taxation can be a very effective form of regulation and also help in budget balancing. High taxes on tobacco and alcohol products were aimed at severely curtailing consumption, only to find that it had become more of a revenue raiser than a consumption depressant.

Yet, taxation remains as a potentially effective regulatory tool. It is a tool that could currently create conflict due to the opposition of a segment of the population to a tax-and-spend economy, to big government or to feeding the "beast."

The controversy might be mitigated by viewing taxation in the regulatory context as a user fee. User fees are good because they place the cost on those people who make use of the product or service, rather than have the general public bear the cost. Thus, we have National Park entrance fees.

We have gasoline taxes to provide the funds to build roads. We have tobacco taxes to help pay the health costs involved. And we can have a carbon tax, a form of carbon user-fee, for those who use pollution producing products.

Mexico recently imposed new taxes on food products considered unhealthy, primarily junk food and sugary drinks.[1] Mexico was able to overcome heavy lobbying by the industries opposed to the new tax.

The New York City Board of Heath approved a ban on the sale of large sized sodas, a favored project of Mayor Michael Bloomberg, only to find it overruled by a court.[2] The mayor obviously didn't use a tax on large size sodas, rather than the outright ban on sales by the NYC health board, because he would surely have found a negative reception in the state legislature that has to approve New York City taxes.

The tax approach, where available as it was in Mexico, might operate as an appropriate regulatory tool.

SAFETY ORIENTED REGULATIONS

Safety-oriented regulations come in many forms. All are aimed at avoiding physical harm to people and property.

Our traffic regulations are safety-oriented regulations we merely take in stride. We might disobey by speeding, and there might be pressure in some quarters to increase or

---

[1] Villegas, Paulina, "Mexico: Junk Food Tax Is Approved," The New York Times, October 31, 2013.

[2] Grynbaum, Michael M., "Health Panel Approves Restriction on Sale of Large Sugary Drinks," The New York Times, September 13, 2012.

Susman, Tina, "Mayor Bloomberg faces new setback in NYC super-sized soda ban," Los Angeles Times, July 30, 2014.

decrease speed limits depending on location, but nobody would seriously suggest repealing our traffic laws. So too, our child labor regulations. Or our car safety standards. Or, our building codes. And a host of other regulations that we don't even think about.

As a society, we even get upset when an offshore building used to contract manufacture products for an American company collapsed and killed people.[1] It was shoddy construction due to the absence of a building code that caused the building to collapse.

American public sentiment was that an American company using a foreign contract manufacturer should insist on the safety of foreign workers, even as far away as Bangladesh. As was implicit in the situation, Americans were willing to pay for a building code in Bangladesh through the higher prices they would have to pay for the products produced. The American public seemed focus only on saving lives.

But not so in Texas. Texas has the most workplace fatalities in America, but favors what it considers to be a free-market posture to attract jobs and businesses by not having fire codes. Texas even suggests that the absence of such safety regulations is a reason for companies to move to Texas.[2] Texan leadership claimed that fire codes wouldn't have made a difference as fires happen anyway, a surreal and self-serving position that experts would strongly dispute.

---

[1] Ali-Manik, Julfikar, and Yardley, Jim, "Building Collapse in Bangladesh Leaves Scores Dead," The New York Times, April 24, 2013.

[2] Urbina, Ian, and Fernandez, Manny, and Schwartz, John, "After Plant Explosion, Texas Remains Wary of Regulation," The New York Times, May 9, 2013.

More likely, it is that Texas does not want its companies to incur the cost of fire regulation as that would impinge on Texas's economic success, a position that would at least have some truth in it. A year later, Federal investigators confirmed that the lack of both oversight and regulation were contributing factors.[1] Thus it appears that Texans pay a great personal price in order to attract jobs and business.

China is fighting its problem with pollution, recognizing that China's economic success isn't worth much if the Chinese people can't live there healthily. So it might also be said of Texas's economic success if Texans can't live there safely. But that is their choice. Most if not all other states have fire codes so Texas cannot be said to present the American view on regulation.

Although Texas might be the extreme example, American businesses and political leaders have complained about the costs of regulation and its being a job killer. Yet a recent incident showed that complying with a regulation would have increased a parts cost by 57 cents and failure to follow the regulation resulted in many deaths.[2] This is, hopefully, an extreme case not likely to occur again, but it does serve to show that regulation serves a valid purpose and need not be burdensome.

Whether safety regulations can go too far will soon go before an administrative judge and perhaps the courts. The Consumer Product Safety Commission had a dangerous product recalled and is trying to hold the chief executive of

---

[1] Fernandez, Manny, "Lax Oversight Cited as Factor in Deadly Blast at Texas Plant," The New York Times, April 22, 2014.

[2] Kristof, Nicholas, "Job Crushing or Lifesaving?" The New York Times, April 30, 2014.

the now defunct corporation personally responsible for the recall cost estimated at $57 million.[1] The commission is using a criminal law doctrine that allows the "responsible corporate officer" to be prosecuted for corporate wrongdoing, the doctrine arising because corporations can't be put in jail and someone should to be held responsible for corporate crimes. However, extension of this doctrine to where no violation of law is claimed, or in administrative actions, is unprecedented and does seem un-called for.

DEBUNKING REGULATION

As is seen in Texas, people can be adverse to regulation because of the costs involved. Normally, it is the business interests who are adverse to regulation for it adds to their costs.

However, added costs can be passed on to consumers in the form of higher prices. If those higher prices could be charged and collected anyway without incurring the added regulatory cost, many business would chose to raise their prices, pocket the additional profits and not incur that regulatory cost. As most businesses already maximize profits by charging what the market will bear, the cost of added regulation would have to be absorbed and thus there is fierce business opposition to added regulation.

As was seen in the Bangladesh fire situation, American citizens were implicitly ready to pay a little more for the products produced in order to help assure the safety of the workers producing the products. In Texas, Texans seem

---

[1] Stout, Hilary, "Buckyball Recall Stirs a Wider Legal Campaign," The New York Times, October 31, 2013.

unconcerned about not having fire-codes and having the most workplace fatalities, or at least they seem to be doing nothing about it even though they are not likely to bear the cost of such regulation.

It is likely that Texas businesses, like businesses elsewhere, already maximize profits by charging what the market would bear with the result that any cost associated with fire-code regulation would come out of profits. These are the business men and women who generally debunk regulation at every turn.

They look at the absence of regulation as a competitive advantage, increasing profits. And state leaders of like mind would use the absence of regulation as a means of attracting businesses and jobs to the state. In a sense, both are being parasitic because there would be no advantage if others states also didn't have fire-codes and their businesses also didn't pay the cost of regulation.

The arguments against regulation are essentially business arguments aimed at increasing profits. Individuals tend take a more pragmatic and ethical look at regulation, favoring regulation where it is indicated without taking the next step of considering the possibility of the cost being passed on to them. More likely the cost of a new regulation will reduce profits and not be passed on to them, but the public is unlikely to consider this.

Nevertheless, if the public believed prices would go up, many would effectively view it as the price of civilization. These are the people who have the vote, so the business interests use whatever arguments they can dredge up to create a case against regulation.

Economic "interference" created by regulation is used as a pejorative label. All regulation can be viewed as "interfering," just as all laws of any type can be called "interference." It is only in a jungle that a person has complete freedom to do anything without interference (except by other predator animals).

Economic "uncertainty" created by regulation or the possibility of regulation is another negative label, as if everything else about business and economics were certain. Vague assertions of uncertainty without giving specifics shows such contentions to be empty debunking.

Regulation should be a neutral word. Regulation can be good or bad, depending on the circumstances. Blanket criticism just doesn't make any sense. In all instances where regulation exists, it is the product of careful consideration. The rhetoric against regulation is merely sloganism, aimed to deceive and achieve business advantage at the expense of the society that needs and seeks reasonable regulation.

The only issue as to regulation is whether the regulation is reasonable and appropriate to the circumstances, determined on the merits.

Innovation, R&D, Intellectual Property Rights

As seems to be the path of nations, new nations are initially copiers of another nation's technologies. America copied the British.

History has shown that innovation was associated more with wealth, or perhaps with leisure fostered by wealth, than anything else. England was the innovator of choice when America was a copier and it was a rich country.

Innovator nations change from time to time. When Islam was at its height in conquests, power and wealth in the 10th century, it became the "light of the world" in the arts and sciences and the foremost innovator of the age.

Perhaps it wasn't until the 1930s, on the eve of World War II, when vast amounts of money started to flow into research and development and American technological advances began to emerge. Government money funded a good part of this, although private enterprise also contributed. A lot of money flowed into R&D during the war years.

National embarrassment during the next war, the cold war, forced America to catch up to Russia's Sputnik. That was the late 1950s and America soon reached the top spot.

It was perhaps during the 1970s and 1980s that a functional America was as its zenith and the path of relative decline appeared. America was rich and other nations, not as rich but growing fast, first went on the path of coping American advances and later devoted more and more money to R&D and became newbie innovators.

In the first decade of the 21st century, Chinese R&D doubled while America R&D crept up in single digits. Patent filings by individual foreign companies began to exceed comparable American filings.

As a sign of American decline, American corporations were moving more and more of their operations offshore, soon followed by moving R&D efforts offshore. Lower foreign wages triggered that, made more appealing by the

American tax incentive (the foreign subsidiary tax loophole) for American companies to move operations offshore.

As can be seen from history, wealth funds technological gains. With the American government running out of funds and tightening its belt due to present inability to balance budgets, the American government no longer has the wealth to fund R&D as it was previously funded and should be funded. American companies, having the wealth, are funding more R&D offshore. The combination portends disaster.

With R&D holding the key to the future, the repeal of the US foreign subsidiary loophole is key to both balancing the budget and bringing R&D back to American soil. Repealing the tax loophole is the most important thing America can do to help stem the continuing decline of America.

After that, it is a question of what policies America should adopt to foster American based R&D and innovation. Improving American education on all levels is not covered in any detail in this chapter but is foremost on the long-range list of what can be done.

THE TWO FACETS OF INNOVATION

Innovation can be roughly broken-down into two basic segments. First, the ideas and fundamental research that leads to new or better technological paths, and, second, the development of that breakthrough technology into actual products that serve society and bolster the economy.

As the less-developed countries go through the copying stage, they would put their R&D efforts on development of products and the manufacturing technology to produce those products. Their products and manufacturing know-how, also copied, would become more and more sophisticated in time. Later, when they have all the manufacturing know-how that can be had and their economies are flourishing, fundamental research might be undertaken. This has been the path of East Asian success in recent decades,[1] as it had been the path of America in the past.

American fundamental R&D is mostly funded by the government and takes place in university and corporate laboratories and research facilities. Development R&D normally takes place in the private sector, building on what the American government started and made available to American corporations. Spending on the creation of military hardware has been a significant component of fundamental R&D it since the hardware is so cutting-edge.

R&D BUDGETARY CUTS

The continued curtailment of American fundamental research due to budgetary and political restraints will have the most adverse long-term impact on America, aside from the curtailment of education expenditures.

Yet it is the less exciting development R&D that drives the economy, produces tax revenues that pay for fundamental research, produces jobs that feed the population, and pays for the infrastructure and military America wants. Fundamental research has long-term impact while development R&D has both short and long-term impact. Hopefully, the curtailment of fundamental research won't last long.

---

[1] Fingleton, Eamonn, "America the Innovative?" The New York Times, March 30, 2013.

But is seems to have legs. In 1993 and again in 2011, the United States cancelled construction of powerful physics machines that would have been the tools for fundamental advances in particle physics, with the plans for the most advanced tool being turned over to a consortium that will build it in Japan with Japanese government funding.[1]

ANTI-AMERICAN COMMERCIAL ESPIONAGE

China has been pursuing the acquisition of advanced American technology in various ways, some of which can be called espionage.

Chinese scientists working in the United States are induced to turn over American technology when they return. Americans of Chinese ancestry are actively recruited to return to the homeland. American companies are induced to open research facilities in China. Chinese-American business associations in the United States are created to funnel technology to Chinese ministries and universities. American scientists are invited (and presumably paid) to lecture in China, all aimed at extracting information and technology sourced in America. China has even established technology-transfer centers (one staffed with 7,500 employees) to "convert" foreign technology.[2]

It appears that America has taken China under its tutelage in order to foster Chinese growth and development.

---

[1] Overbye, Dennis, "Particle Physicists in U.S. Worry About Being Left Behind," The New York Times, March 4, 2013.

[2] Wong, Edward, and Tatlow, Didi Kirsten, "China Seen in Push to Gain Technology Insights," The New York Times, June 5, 2013.

BUYING HIGH-TECH AMERICAN COMPANIES

In a particularly telling situation, a Chinese company purchased an American battery maker that the United States government had been funding for the development of batteries for electric vehicles.[1] The battery maker had received almost $250 million from the US government but couldn't hack it and went into bankruptcy.

The Chinese company outbid an American corporation, a Japanese corporation and a German corporation. The bankruptcy court and the US "Committee on Foreign Investment" approved the acquisition. The bankrupt company's military and government contracts are to be sold to a small domestic corporation, apparently satisfying security concerns even though the advanced technology went to the Chinese purchaser.

We should expect more of this as it basically represents some chickens coming home to roost. China has accumulated trillions of dollars of United States government debt from exporting Chinese made products to the United States. US dollars ultimately have to be spent in the United States buying American produced goods, properties and services and, as shown in this instance, American corporations. Let me explain how this works.

China wanted to sell its products in America, and American companies pay for all their purchases in US dollars. A US company could go out and use its US dollars to buy, say, German marks and use the marks to purchase sneakers (sneakers being used only for illustrative purposes) from China, but that added step has a cost and is pointless. Even

---

[1] Vlasic, Bill, "Chinese Firm Wins Bid for Auto Battery Maker," The New York Times, December 9, 2012.

though China did not at first have a use for the US dollars obtained for selling sneakers to American retailers, it continued to sell into America so as to keep its sneaker plants open and employ the workers coming into their cities from their far-flung fields. As physical dollars (the paper money) provides no yield, China invested the dollars it earned in US Treasury bonds.

It's not that China wanted the US bonds, but there was no practical alternative. It could sell the dollars to other counties (e.g. Germany) in exchange for their currency (marks) and buy their debt (German bonds), taking a haircut and being faced with the same problem of then being unable to use those currencies while taking on additional risk because the US Treasury bonds are considered the safest of investments.

Some people look at China owning so much American debt as giving China political leverage over America, but it actually works the other way. If China demanded to be paid, all China would get would be an ocean liner full of paper US dollars. The bonds only entitle the bondholders to repayment in dollars, physical dollars or by wire transfer. Thus, all China can really do with its hoard of US dollars is to buy American products, raw materials, real estate, businesses or other American assets, including American companies.

Thus, in exchange for our buying Chinese made sneakers, China can buy up America. But there is a catch. America can place limits and restrictions on the type of assets China can buy in the United States.

So, ultimately, it becomes a matter of co-operation, but only if America starts to effectively use its power to limit and restrict. Co-operation is in the interest of both countries and it is most likely that America and China would become closer, not further apart, over time. But only if America becomes tougher, doing things in China's face (limitation, restrictions) as China continue to do things (espionage) in our face.

INNOVATION IS NOT A JOB KILLER

Low-profile innovation is to be found in the relentless striving to become more efficient and increase productivity. In every endeavor, profit-oriented or not, people try to do what needs to be done faster and better, with the corollary being that the increased efficiency and productivity reduces available jobs.

High-power innovation that leads to significant technical advances has the potential displace even more workers. Nonetheless, it has been shown that over the longer-term technical innovation has increased the overall demand for labor by generating new products to be produced and new services to be rendered.

However, the assertion might be made that the process favors the abstract thinkers who can handle non-routine tasks and hurts those who can handle only routine tasks, presumably those lower-down in the income scale.[1] Statistics have shown that the quality of jobs have declined with technological change playing a role.[2]

---

[1] Autor, David H., and Dorn, David, "How Technology Wrecks the Middle Class," The New York Times, August 24, 2013.

[2] Tyson, Laura D'Andrea, "The Quality of Jobs: The New Normal and the Old Normal," The New York Times, September 20, 2013.

However, innovation also provides opportunities for workers to move up to better jobs that raise their status, their purchasing power and their well-being.

The children of print type-setters can no longer follow in the footsteps of parent displaced by linotype machines and digital computers, but can find employment in the digital world that provides a higher standard of living.

The unemployed type-setter can use inherent skills or obtain the education necessary to do less routine work or other work. Education can fill the holes. We should not oppose innovation and technical advances because some people cannot cope with change or transfer skills.

Innovation should not be viewed negatively as a job killer. We should not even think about stemming innovation in order to help the displaced workers unable to cope. We should help them by making general education and vocational training available.

Recently, factory apprenticeship programs to train highly skilled workers entered the American scene[1] and should lead to government programs of that nature to help workers displaced by innovation.

America's future rests with innovation and we should do what we can to foster it.

FOSTERING INNOVATION

To foster innovation, America needs an educational system that nurtures creativity, needs an economy that provides plenty of start-up capital, needs laws that protect

---

[1] Schwartz, Nelson D, "Where Factory Apprenticeship Is Latest Model From Germany," The New York Times, November 30, 2013.

intellectual property, needs a culture that preaches striving and provides gateways, and needs to celebrate risk-taking.[1] Some say our laws concerning the legal ownership of new ideas needs to an overhaul for that too has a bearing on innovation.[2]

Mostly, America needs out-of-the envelope breakthrough thinking. It could be called building visionary technologies.[3]

For instance, take the study of how fireflies make light with the aim of developing trees that glow in the night so as to light city streets and developing house plants that produce enough light to read by, while saving energy and reducing carbon.[4]

It is at the cutting edge where the most telling advances will be made, and the need to bolster government research funding becomes most apparent.

Personal opinions dominate the choice of basic paths available in our society. Fostering the "good life," however a person might define that, could be viewed as being selfish in contrast to emphasis being placed on serving society and innovating. Too much emphasis on sports in our schools could be viewed as being at the expense of academic excellence or displacing an emphasis on mathematics and sciences that leads to innovation.

---

[1] Keller, Bill, "Toy Story," The New York Times, November 17, 2013.

[2] Lobel, Orly, "My Ideas, My Boss's Property," The New York Times, April 13, 2014.

[3] Nocera, Joe, "Government Nurtures Innovation," The New York Times, May 2, 2014.

[4] Pollack, Andrew, "A Dream of Trees Aglow at Night," The New York Times, May 7, 2013.

Treating everybody alike in our schools could be a disservice to the brightest of the bright who have the greatest potential to do the most for society and do the most innovating. Some people would say the greater the talent the more it should be devoted to serving society rather than seeking monetary or good-life goals. Thus, the range of opinion varies widely and impacts America's potential for innovation in different ways.

America is behind much of the developed world when it comes to education, in particular in math and the sciences. American businesses decry the lack of engineers and scientists in the United States, using that as an argument to induce Congress to change the immigration laws to admit more foreign engineers and guest workers.[1]

Critics maintain that the push to hire from abroad is a business ruse for lowering wages in the United States and for avoiding the expense of training American college graduates.

If America lacks engineers and scientists, it would seem that the solution rests with improving American education, not in changing the immigration laws. And the fault could be that of the American companies who moved high-tech operations abroad and used foreign contract manufactures, whereas American universities would have graduated more American engineers and scientists had there been US jobs for them.

---

[1] Sengupta, Somini, "Tech Firms Push to Hire More Workers From Abroad," The New York Times, April 11, 2013.

EDUCATING AMERICAN ENGINEERS

Steve Jobs of Apple also seemed to blame the lack of American engineers as a reason for moving manufacturing offshore,[1] as if lower foreign wages and avoiding US taxes weren't reasons enough reason for his moving operations offshore. It is not as if Apple couldn't compete to hire the engineers America does graduate.

It seems logical that the more Apple and other corporations like Apple would compete for and actually employ American engineering graduates, the more engineers the American universities and colleges would graduate. It would be simple supply and demand, with the supply increasing as the demand goes up.

If this is the case, the lack of American engineers can be laid at the steps of Apple and others who effectively curtailed the education of American engineering graduates by moving operations abroad where foreign engineering graduates came into demand and foreign universities responded to the demand.

Graduating fewer engineers in America cannot be attributed to any deficiency in the teaching of math and science in the lower-education levels. If the demand for American engineering graduates actually existed, students in higher-education would strive for those jobs and prepare themselves by supplementing any lower-level deficiency they had in math and science.

By analogy, when jobs on Wall Street were attractive and available, Wall Street firms were able to find enough

---

[1] Duhigg, Charles, and Bradsher, Keith, "How the U.S. Lost Out on iPhone Work," The New York Times, January 21, 2012.

university graduates well-founded in mathematics and having the mathematical skills that are so important to that industry.

American corporations have the ability to induce the colleges and universities to accept more students who indicate a desire for a career in the sciences, engineering, and mathematics, as witness their successes in lobbying generally. The top schools now accept as little as 5 percent of the applications they receive,[1] so enough applicants can likely be found striving for careers in the sciences and math.

American corporations also have the wherewithal to contribute to the building or expansion of engineering schools at our universities and colleges instead of relying on cash-strapped federal, state and local governments to do so, or relying on retired billionaires to do so. There are just so many billionaires around like Irwin W. Jacobs, co-founder of Qualcomm (cell phone originator), who contributed $120 million the University of California at San Diego for what is now its Jacobs School of Engineering.[2]

With their need for engineering graduates, there would be more than enough justification for large American corporations to use some of the trillions in cash they have accumulated offshore to fund American engineering schools. But, of course, saving taxes takes priority.

American universities and colleges graduating more engineers is one thing. Training them would be the job of their employers. But how can newly graduated American

---

[1] Pérez-Peña, Richard, "Best, Brightest and Rejected: Elite Colleges Turn Away Up to 95%," The New York Times, April 8, 2014.

[2] Bell, Diane, "Irwin Jacobs strives to make lives better," The San Diego Union-Tribune, February 20, 2012.

engineers be hired and trained when American corporations prefer to move their operations abroad?

American corporations seeking to change the US immigration law so as to admit more foreign engineers to take the few available engineering jobs remaining in America because of the exodus of their operations from America does seem overbearing.

OUTSOURCING AMERICAN INNOVATION

America still happens to remain THE innovator amongst nations. For decades, the major scientific advances had originated in America. Yet, many innovations were copied and developed abroad so the innovation appears to be foreign based. Future innovation might actually be foreign sourced as American corporations establish R&D facilities abroad and train foreign nationals to do innovative work.

It is not known whether the establishment of foreign R&D facilities was voluntary on the part of the American corporations or was effectively forced on them by foreign governments. What is known is that foreign corporations are in fact seeking American talent.

The innovation edge that America had seems to be gradually moving offshore. American corporations outsource innovation from American soil while foreign corporations insource innovation to their home countries from facilities they set up on American soil for that purpose.

At first it was the needle trades that America outsourced, but only for contract manufacturing because of cheaper foreign labor; product innovation and design remained in America.

In the 1980s Japanese corporations (supported by their government) conquered the semiconductor market, particularly in memory chips, forcing the largest American manufacturer out of the business. About then, American corporations started to deliberately outsource technology jobs like computer programming.[1]

The movement abroad of back-office business processing followed with the technology that involved.[2] Electronic and computer manufacturing and information technology moved abroad as the outsourcing of manufacturing jobs continued.

The threat arose that the crown jewel pharmaceutical industry would move offshore with its heavy reliance on innovation.[3] The outsourcing of clinical trials followed[4] with whatever knowledge, know-how and technical innovation that involved.

American corporations outsourced in order to increase short-term profits, which is the focus of American management as induced by short-term American executive incentive practices. What would happen in the future to the American was of little or no concern as the profits of going offshore grew and executive bonuses blossomed. Also, those profits (now amounting to the trillions of dollars) did not come back to America due to the US tax incentive to keep and invest them offshore.

---

[1] Lohr, Steve, "New Economy; Offshore Jobs In Technology: Opportunity Or a Threat?" The New York Times, December 22, 2003.

[2] Lohr, Steve, "Offshore Outsourcing's Next Wave: How High?" The New York Times, February 14, 2008.

[3] Pollack, Andrew, "Medical Companies Joining Offshore Trend," The New York Times, February 24, 2005.

[4] Singer, Natasha, "Outsourcing of Drug Trials Is Faulted," The New York Times, February 19, 2009.

Having let the innovation genie out of the bottle, American corporations will face a new threat. American corporations, in their continual striving for more immediate profits whatever the long-term price, started to import lower-wage foreign talent for their domestic R&D operations and look to do more of that.

Perversely, opening the American immigration gates to allow the hiring of foreign talent at lower wages,[1] as American corporations are now striving for, would serve the interests of foreign counties rather than America.

The loyalties of foreign talent are likely to be thin. The foreign countries would gladly lure back their talented expatriates after being trained in America,[2] and the trained talent would be anxious to go as they would be in enviable positions back home.

The next shoe to drop is foreign corporations setting up operations in America so as to have a direct hand in outsourcing American innovation back to their countries. That is happening and it involves hiring experienced Americans "in an effort to soak up the talent and expertise" in an industry.[3]

According to samsung.com, "Samsung Semiconductor Incorporated, the world's largest designer and manufacturer of memory and logic semiconductors, storage and LCD panels, will build a 1.1 million square foot research and development

---

[1] Sengupta, Somini, "Tech Firms Push to Hire More Workers From Abroad," The New York Times, April 11, 2013.
[2] Sengupta, Somini, "Countries Seek Entrepreneurs From Silicon Valley," The New York Times, June 5, 2013.
[3] Vlasic, Bill, "Chinese Creating New Auto Niche Within Detroit," The New York Times, May 12, 2013.

(R&D) headquarters north of downtown San Jose." And foreign governments, particularly Korean and French (and indications of China and Japan) are also getting involved in seeking and buying American patents in quantity, launching patent-acquisition companies (derisively called "patent trolls").[1]

The trend is ominous. It does not speak of co-operation, but rather of raiding. America can no longer afford to let this continue.

CAN THE OMINOUS TRENDS REVERSE?

Gone are the pleasant days when an American company would conduct R&D on the French Riviera because the best American researchers and scientists could be attracted to work for the company in that paradise. Now national interests loom large in where and how R&D is conducted.

The importance of R&D in this day and age is recognized by governments around the world adopting competitive programs to attract or force the conduct of R&D activities within their boundaries.

China has a 25% tax-rate but offers a lower 15% tax-rate to attract new-tech and high-tech enterprises and certain integrated circuits production enterprises while the US tax system operates to induce US companies to go offshore and accept such offers. Together they dovetail beautifully, but neither is the American national interest.

It seems that all the developed countries, particularly the ones with good educational systems, have a variety of grants,

---

[1] Levine, Dan, and Kim, Miyoung, "Nation-states enter contentious patent-buying business," Reuters, March 10, 2013.

funding arrangements and other incentives for the R&D areas they consider important.

The poorer or lesser-developed countries don't have the money to do this and probably don't have the educated people needed in R&D, nor could they attract them. Their interest is in obtaining jobs currently for their unemployed workers. The larger, more developed nations can afford to look to the future more.

America has a tax-incentive for R&D, namely a meager and limited R&D credit against the US income tax of a company conducting business in the United States. Of course only profitable companies paying tax can benefit, not the start-up companies that have no taxable income. Besides, money is not well spent as there are too many definitional and accounting holes that lead to paying for research not actually done or for research in un-important areas.

Targeting important areas or providing incentives for much needed R&D can't be done through the tax code. Fostering research through the tax code is basically a hand-out, not the way to go and should be abandoned in favor of specific grants even though that requires the government to incur the cost of doing something to identify what research needs to be done and write checks.

Fortunately, America does fund some R&D through existing agencies like the National Institutes of Health and through grants to research universities, but the funds are drying up due economic stagnation and political dysfunction. However, wasteful R&D hand-outs through the tax code continue because they are hidden and protected from elimination by our dysfunctional political system.

As things develop, perhaps R&D competition might turn into to R&D co-operation. A large Swiss pharmaceutical company relocated its research headquarters from Switzerland to the United States to be near US universities and near American companies working in the same field. Perhaps this portends co-operation, perhaps not.

Perhaps America will do well in fostering foreign R&D so that it can rise to the level of American innovation and the world can look forward to innovative co-operation for the benefit of all. Maybe, but America probably has more to lose than gain in the interim. And it is a competitive world. Co-operation could be a form of raiding.

Maybe America's existing incentive to conduct operations in foreign countries would foster ever more activity offshore so that foreign wages rise to American levels and the wage incentive to outsource jobs will disappear in time. Perhaps. But another country with lower wages would step in before that happens.

Operations in or outsourcing to a foreign country where wages are going up could induce businesses to shift operations or outsourcing to other foreign countries where wages are still low.[1]

This, carried to an extreme, would indicate that wages throughout the world would have to approach American levels before the wage incentive to operate abroad disappears, which is not very likely to happen in the foreseeable future if things remain as they are. But things might be changing.

Workers in China, previously happy to come in from the fields and accept any job, are now striving for higher wages.

---

[1] Bradsher, Keith, "Wary of China, Companies Head to Cambodia," The New York Times, April 8, 2013.

It seems that they are aided by social media and smartphones, both American innovations that have become very popular in China. Social media and smartphones enabled sneaker workers to communicate, rally and strike to obtain higher wages, the government apparently going along in fear of social unrest.[1]

It seems that at least one American company is trying to reverse the outsourcing trend. The largest American retailer committed itself to buy more American made products.[2]

Perhaps the tipping point for some manufacturers to bring production back to the United States has been reached due to higher foreign wages, but that is doubtful as long as the American tax incentive to operate abroad continues.

Rather, it would seem that the US government should endeavor to get American corporations to return production to America, even to the extent of using force. Increasing customs duties might do the job and thus help American retailers help America by buying American made products.

Perhaps the ominous trend to go offshore will reverse in the very long-term, but a little gumption and hardball now could help us. Other nations have the trade surpluses and we have the trade deficits so some hardball shouldn't hurt us.

IGNORED EXPROPRIATION RISK

Tragic consequences can follow from the development of valuable property rights offshore. R&D conducted offshore

---

[1] Levin, Dan, "Plying Social Media, Chinese Workers Grow Bolder in Exerting Clout," The New York Times, May 2, 2014.

[2] Clifford, Stephanie, "Walmart Plans to Buy American More Often," The New York Times, January 15, 2013.

in foreign subsidiaries leads to patents and other intangibles property rights being owned by those subsidiaries. A foreign subsidiary of an American corporation would own the worldwide patent rights to any invention made by it, even the patent rights in the United States. And those foreign subsidiaries could be taken-over or expropriated by the foreign government.

This assumes that the foreign subsidiary bore the R&D costs, using the cash hoards accumulated abroad. Instead it might be possible for the American parent company to contract with its foreign subsidiaries to do R&D work for the American parent. The American company would pay the R&D cost plus a mark-up and becomes the owner of any intangible rights developed. By doing so, the American parent might be able to claim US tax deductions for its R&D expenditures and leave the foreign accumulated cash intact (enhanced by the mark-up) and also leave the potential for future innovation abroad. What is actually happening today in this regard is not known.

Foreign subsidiaries of American corporations are normally incorporated under the laws of the foreign country where the offshore operations are conducted. As such, the foreign subsidiary could be viewed as a national of that country, subject to whatever control and influence that foreign government would care to exercise over it.

The rule of law does not always prevail, and over the decades many things might transpire. The foreign government could take control of the foreign subsidiary and manage it and its patents, or interfere in any way it wants. It would be like a sovereign dealing with its national. There is always the risk of outright expropriation.

There is no telling what the ever changing world conditions might lead to. Bayer, the German pharmaceutical company, had to buy back the right to use its own name in the United States after it had been expropriated (along with its patents) during World War I. Jarring scenarios do arise from time to time.

The best place for a US company to conduct R&D and own the fruits of that R&D has to be the United States.

PROTECTING INTELLECTUAL PROPERTY RIGHTS

The United States government needs to induce foreign governments to protect intellectual property rights, but our government action seems to fall into the category of ineffective rhetoric. Once again, it is time for hardball.

It is amazing how many hurtful practices foreign governments pursue right in our face, but we remain reluctant to fight back, not only in-kind but by using any practices that would work. America the powerful is acting like a patsy by standing by and just using rhetoric.

Should we be cowered when American corporations in their self-interest insist on the status quo and suggest that our government would upset the apple-cart and create a trade war by fighting back?

Keep in mind, America can be selective in what it does. If one country stops sending us some electronics, another will and perhaps American companies might even be induced to establish domestic electronics manufacturing. The other country would be impacted by a trade war, so why is it always America that stands down?

Protection of intellectual property rights should be of prime importance to America, and in this we should put our foot down. Our trade experts can advise as to how this could be done with minimum abrogation of normal trade practices, but hardball requires some invasive tactics. It could be called tick-for-tack, equivalent retaliation, or perhaps a brutality cascade,[1] but does seem like fair turnaround.

Perhaps we are beginning to see something like this. Pending trade treaties with Asia and Europe were put on hold due to failure to obtain fast-track authority normally needed to ease the passage of trade bills through Congress.

In commenting on this, a top official took the hard line, noting that the American auto industry had only 1 percent market penetration in Japan,[2] presumably due to Japanese government restrictions, while Japanese auto manufacturers have a major presence in America.

It is about time we took the hard line, particularly on intellectual property rights because it protects innovation, America's future.

---

[1] Brooks, David, "The Brutality Cascade," The New York Times, March 4, 2013.

[2] Landler, Mark, and Weisman, Jonathan, "Trade Pact With Asia Faces Imposing Hurdle: Midterm Politics," The New York Times, February 14, 2014.

Chapter 3

Economic Inequality

Economic inequality is exhibited by simply comparing incomes at the top (the wealthy) and incomes at the bottom (the poor). Income amounts are important, but so are the possible reasons for incomes being so high and so low, the possible justifications for the divergence, whether discrimination is involved, and what we can do to mitigate the disparity.

Start with the proposition that America can only mitigate the disparity, not eliminate it, because economic inequality will always exist to some extent.[1] As individuals, we will never be equal in abilities, strengths and talents which underlie income potential. Inheritance and economic environments will also make for differences no matter how we are endowed.

Yet America has to seriously address economic inequality because "51 percent of all income earned went to

---

[1] Leonhardt, David, "Inequality Has Been Going On Forever ... but That Doesn't Mean It's Inevitable," The New York Times, May 2, 2014.

the wealthiest fifth of the population while only 3 percent went to the poorest fifth of the population ...."[1] This can lead to street riots or worse, something America has to head off.

Recent economic gains mostly benefited those at the top. Even with the expected economic recovery, future growth is likely to be lopsided, not broad.[2]

The constraint America once again faces is not to go overboard in the effort to mitigate economic inequality. We should strive to reduce economic inequality without overburdening the wealthier and without providing excessive assistance to the poorer.

We can sensibly believe that people should be able to earn as much as they can, which benefits our society and everyone in it. We can maintain that programs combating inequality will reduce economic growth, although the contrary appears more probable[3].

We can also rationally believe that nobody should live in poverty, that empathy is required in human relations,[4] and that those working a full-time job should earn a living wage.[5] We can also emphasize that it is in the tradition of all our

---

[1] Blow, Charles M., "The President, the Pope and the People," The New York Times, December 4, 2013.

Also see Lowrey, Annie, "The Rich Get Richer Through the Recovery," The New York Times, September 10, 2013.

[2] Editorial, "Recovery for Whom?" The New York Times, April 12, 2014.

[3] Krugman, Paul, "Liberty, Equality, Efficiency," The New York Times, March 9, 2014.

[4] Kristof, Nicholas D., "Where Is the Love?" The New York Times, November 27, 2013.

[5] Blow, Charles M. "Minimum Wage, Maximum Outrage," The New York Times, April 16, 2014.

religions to help the poor and thereby combat economic inequality.[1]

To some extent, all these positions are valid, good, virtuous and honorable, so we should stop casting our absolutist slogans against one another and work together toward a reasonable resolution. We should look to the merits of all mitigation proposals, consider fairness within our own perspectives, and not go overboard in any direction.

Nor should we fail to correct the aspects of our society that are shown to be illegal, blatantly or ethically wrong, or just plain unconscionable. For example, we should view excessive executive compensation and stock option thievery to be unconscionable and strive to correct it. We should not tolerate fraud in our public assistance programs and strive to provide obvious shirkers with jobs, or force work or training in some fashion.

Economic inequality exists throughout the world, with one Nobel Prize laureate pointing out that the perpetuation of inequality in some counties is a matter of choice, the choice belonging to the wealthy[2] and, in America, discrimination against the poor and particularly against blacks contribute to the inequality.[3] Another Nobel Prize laureate would point to representatives of wealthy Americans as actually wanting to

---

[1] Goodstein, Laurie, and Povoledo, Elisabetta, "Pope Sets Down Goals for an Inclusive Church, Reaching Out 'on the Streets,'" The New York Times, November 26, 2013.

[2] Stiglitz, Joseph E., "Inequality Is a Choice," The New York Times, October 13, 2013.

[3] Stiglitz, Joseph E., "How Dr. King Shaped My Work in Economics," The New York Times, August 27, 2013.

hurt the poor,[1] and that job creation isn't on the corporate agenda because corporate America is doing just fine and high unemployment allows corporations to take advantage of workers.[2] These are high-powered voices, not to be ignored.

Nor should we ignore voices that go the other way. The growing affluence of the rich is not causing the economic immobility of the poor and proposed solutions like an increase in the minimum wage targets the wrong things -- low wages are a human capital problem, where bipartisan consensus on opportunity, mobility and aspiration enhancement is possible without polarizing the debate with erroneous class warfare rhetoric about inequality.[3] The issue does not revolve around spending, but instead revolves around family instability which we can and should address.[4]

Let us put aside all the generalizations, rhetoric and criticism, and discuss what makes sense in mitigating economic disparity.

---

[1] Krugman, Paul, "Enemies of the Poor," The New York Times, January 12, 2014.

[2] Krugman, Paul, "The Fear Economy," The New York Times, December 26, 2013.

[3] Brooks, David, "The Inequality Problem," The New York Times, January 16, 2014.

[4] Douthat, Ross, "More Imperfect Unions," The New York Times, January 25, 2014.

What Can be Done on the Low-Income End?

America already has a host of governmental programs and laws aimed at helping the poor and reducing economic inequality.

As suggested in the chapter *"Government Programs & Laws,"* all government programs and associated laws should be reviewed periodically to determine whether they are still serving their stated purposes, whether their costs were as anticipated, and whether the ease of fraud or abuse has destroyed their utility. Fraud would have to be meaningful if not pervasive to do-in a program, not like the modest 5% abuse level in the food stamp program.[1]

Programs aimed at helping the poor should be subject to rigorous review as should the programs and laws helping the rich.[2] We might be more familiar with the programs helping the poor because they tend to be better known by the general public, but there are other programs that are designed to help the rich or happen to work that way.

Nor should government programs that aid the poor be automatically extended and endlessly expanded because they do "good." All government programs do "good" for someone, and all have costs that must be borne by someone. Theories about fighting programs before they take hold and

---

[1] Severson, Kim, "Food Stamp Fraud, Rare but Troubling," The New York Times, December 18, 2013.
[2] Kristof, Nicholas, "A Nation of Takers?" The New York Times, March 26, 2014.

automatically expand[1] would be sidestepped with a program requiring periodic review and justification of all programs. Both prudence and good government should require periodic reviews of all government programs under current conditions.

It has been established that various government programs have worked to improve conditions and elevate the poor.[2] Yet it has been shown that America is not the land of opportunity it once was in terms of American children moving up the social ladder.[3] This alone indicates that, for all we do, things are not working as well as they should.

So let's critically review all existing programs and let the chips fall where they may. Eliminating faulty programs that don't work will open the door to adopting programs that work. But this promises to be difficult in this era of budget shortfall and sequestration where programs are likely to be cut for lack of funds rather than ineffectiveness, and new programs run into budgetary constraints.

For instance, a New York City program of limited rental subsidies tied to working or job training got 75% of the participants on their feet, but the state and federal funding ran out.[4]

---

[1] Harwood, John, "Fighting to Stop an Entitlement Before It Takes Hold, and Expands," The New York Times, November 12, 2013.

[2] Kristof, Nicholas, "Progress in the War on Poverty," The New York Times, January 8, 2014.

[3] Calmes, Jackie, "Obama Presses Case for Health Law and Wage Increase," The New York Times, December 4, 2013.

[4] Editorial, "Battling Homelessness in New York City," The New York Times, December 13, 2013.

ENHANCING FAMILY LIFE

It has been pointed out that programs aimed at enhancing and stabilizing family life of the poor would be more effective than calling for more spending to combat economic inequality.[1]

How family life can be enhanced and stabilized is a matter best left to social scientists. That would be a superb addition to the roster of programs that could be undertaken to combat the vicious cycle of poverty and inequality.

Such endeavors will call for more spending but, if and when successful, they are likely to produce offsetting cost reductions in other programs for the poor. The same might be said for programs aimed at bolstering education and training for the poor.

LONG AND SHORT-TERM PROGRAMS

Thus, there can and should be two approaches in combatting economic inequality. One approach would be aimed at the long-term by addressing the underlying causes of poverty and the lack of social mobility and other fundamental causes of inequality. The other approach would aim at putting food on the plate today, taking care of immediate needs.

The latter would include programs like increasing the minimum wage and also updating overtime pay

---

[1] Douthat, Ross, "More Imperfect Unions," The New York Times, January 25, 2014.

Kristof, Nicholas, "Where the G.O.P. Gets It Right," The New York Times, April 9, 2014.

requirements.¹ Both can be done at the same time, with smarter spending being the key, not necessarily more spending. This could involve the curtailment of some programs that have not been successful or have gotten too costly for the benefits they produce.

Obviously, curtailments will be opposed by those receiving the benefits as will expansion of programs be opposed by those who feel that they would be negatively impacted.

There will be something to be said in support of both camps. We should draw conclusions based only on the merits, being very careful because incomplete or specious argumentation will abound.

INCREASING THE MINIMUM WAGE

For instance, increasing the minimum wage would directly help those who have to rely on public assistance even though they have jobs and are earning wages.²

Cities pursue minimum wage increases because they don't have the taxing power to fund other programs that combat economic inequality.³

---

[1] Eisenbrey, Ross, "It's Time to Update Overtime," The New York Times, January 10, 2014.

Gabriel, Trip, "Fleeing to Next Town, Bosses May Find Minimum Wage Is Rising There, Too," The New York Times, December 6, 2013.

[2] Editorial, "Work and Rewards," The New York Times, December 6, 2013.

[3] Lowrey, Annie, "Cities Are Fighting Income Inequality," The New York Times, April 6, 2014.

Increasing the minimum wage would appear to be a worthy endeavor, yet the opponents (read the fast-food providers) maintain it would cost jobs.

But it would cost jobs only if sales are reduced. If sales remain the same, the jobs will remain. Thus, there is no merit to the argument that such workers will automatically lose jobs. Lost jobs depends solely on the level of future sales, as to which there is no certainty.

If prices were already set at the maximum the marketplace would bear, which is likely to have been the case, profits will go down, not sales.

Also, looking at the other side of the coin, greater purchasing power in the hands of the minimum-wage workers will increase overall spending[1] and increase someone else's sales and profits, with a multiplier effect as that goes through the economy. It can even flow back to the fast-food providers and increase their sales.

Like most other changes to the status-quo, things fall differently on different parties. Some initially benefit, some lose immediate advantage, but if the change is fair, it usually serves to benefit everyone in the society.

The minimum-wage battle necessarily involves the exercise of economic power, with the employers having all the power, and the workers relying on the goodwill of others to help them.

Economic fairness is involved when people working hard are not able to earn a living. That sends very bad messages to others we want to encourage to work and send bad messages abroad about America's ability to take care of its people.

---

[1] Editorial, "The Campaign for a Bigger Paycheck," The New York Times, January 1, 2014.

Forecasting the economic effects of a proposed program or change in a program is most difficult, to say nothing of quantifying the costs and benefits.[1] With all our modelling and forecasting talents, it has been shown time and time again that forecasted disasters just don't occur.

It seems like economic forecasting is invariably consistent with the views and attitudes of the forecasters, so it might be best to cast it all aside and apply plain old common sense.

The President pointed out that his extension of health care and his proposal to increase the minimum wage will help address economic inequality.[2] While there is no agreement on the health care side, there does seem to be agreement on the minimum wage.

Polling shows that increasing the minimum wage is favored by most Republicans, Democrats, and independents, but House Republican leaders are opposed it[3] for political reasons. Thus, the position of our society on the equities is clear and it favors increasing the minimum wage.

What is un-understandable is why other industries who would benefit from more consumer purchasing power in

---

[1] Greenhouse, Steven, "$15 Wage in Fast Food Stirs Debate on Effects," The New York Times, December 4, 2013.

Mankiw, N. Gregory, "Help the Working Poor, but Share the Burden," The New York Times, January 4, 2014.

Lowrey, Annie, "Minimum Wage Increase Would Have Mixed Effects, C.B.O. Report Says," The New York Times, February 18, 2014.

[2] Editorial, "The President on Inequality," The New York Times, December 4, 2013.

[3] Martin, Jonathan, and Shear, Michael D., "Democrats Turn to Minimum Wage as 2014 Strategy," The New York Times, December 29, 2013.

America do not stand up and vote their interest as does the industries striving to continue paying the low wages.

Pure power politics seems to play an outsized role when it comes to the minimum wage, and it is not all about economics, what is good for our society, or common sense.

JOB CREATION

Job creation should be first on the roster of endeavors to combat inequality. If it is true that corporate America favors more widespread unemployment (since that keeps wages down and facilitates filling any open jobs[1]), corporate America cannot be expected to participate in endeavors aimed at reducing unemployment.

Some people argue that unemployment benefits serve only to reduce the incentive to search for- jobs (which it does to a modest extent) while eliminating such benefits would force more competition between workers that would reduce wages and encourage hiring. Others point out that the argument is fallacious.[2] While the disagreements between economists could be mind boggling, the practicalities of the situation are clear.

More vocational training and apprenticeship programs would be of great help in combating inequality through job creation. Hopefully, corporate America would at least join in this effort as it would directly and indirect benefit its bottom line.

---

[1] Krugman, Paul, "The Fear Economy," The New York Times, December 26, 2013.

[2] Krugman, Paul, "The Punishment Cure," The New York Times, December 8, 2013.

Without the full backing of corporate American, if that should be the case, it would have to fall to government to take on the effort to create jobs. Devoting time, attention and treasure to improving America's decaying infrastructure would do just that.

The underlying issue here, as it is in many but not all of the ways to combat inequality, is one of providing enough tax revenues to do the job, a matter addressed separately below.

The particular value in devoting tax revenues to infrastructure rebuilding is that it improves the lifestyles of everyone and produces economic benefits that offset or cover the cost involved and effectively recoups the funds expended.

Yet our society seems to devote more time and attention to projects that contribute little to society but increase profits of the wealthy.

This was seen in the rejection of a needed rail tunnel between New Jersey and New York, which was no more than a political gesture of the New Jersey Governor to show he was tough on spending. It was known that traffic between New Jersey and New York was horrendous, as that was subsequently used for another political gesture, but that didn't matter. Only politics and vote getting mattered.

But building of a tunnel through the mountains of Pennsylvania went ahead with extraordinary speed even though there would be no net benefit to society since the tunnel would just shift profits from one group of traders to other traders. The tunnel shaved three milliseconds of communications time between the Chicago and New York financial markets in order to allow some high-frequency traders to profit at the expense of other traders.[1] The priority was obviously to pursue every more profits at the top and not bother with the infrastructure that benefits everyone.

Only the voters can put a stop to the political antics, and only regulation can limit the unbridled laissez-faire gouging that serves only a few. For instance, if the Pennsylvania tunnel is a good idea, it should be restructured to benefit the customers whose orders go through the tunnel and not to benefit traders.

Allied to infrastructure rebuilding would be endeavors to rejuvenate failing cities and to restructure economically segregated communities.

INCREASING WORKER MOBILITY

Aside from the greater availability of jobs in wealthier as compared to poorer communities, statistics have also shown that inhabitants of the wealthier communities have much longer average life expectancies.[2]

As the economically segregated poorer communities steal years from human lives, it is important that America deal with it.

Social Security, health care, social services, jobs, and work force issues are intertwined in this, along with economic considerations that can lead the poorer, economically segregated communities into bankruptcy.[3]

---

[1] Krugman, Paul, "Three Expensive Milliseconds," The New York Times, April 13, 2014.

[2] Lowrey, Annie, "Income Gap, Meet the Longevity Gap," The New York Times, March 15, 2014.

[3] Stiglitz, Joseph E., "The Wrong Lesson From Detroit's Bankruptcy," The New York Times, August 11, 2013.

Instituting programs that increase the mobility of the poor so as to allow them to move nearer to communities that are more likely to provide work or provide appropriate daily transportation would help diminish inequality.

So would modifying "place-based" anti-poverty programs available only to local recipients because those programs deter the poor from moving to find work.[1] Once they lose their local residence status, they'd be left in limbo if the move doesn't work out.

Perhaps some transitional period, or a temporary trial period, can be devised to avoid this counter-productive aspect of the "place-based" programs.

SOCIAL PROGRAMS

In addition to the endeavors that directly combat inequality though increasing the wages of the poor (minimum wage increases, extension or enforcement of overtime pay rules) and the indirect job-creation endeavors, there are a number of social programs that indirectly combat inequality.

Such a program was already mentioned; the one aimed at enhancing the family life of the poor,[2] which should help stabilize poor families and foster values that would improve life in economically segregated communities.

Instilling respect for education and self-improvement would also serve to influence poor young people to pursue

---

[1] Lehrer, Eli, and Sanders, Lori, "Moving to Work," National Affairs, Issue 18, Winter 2014.

[2] Douthat, Ross, "More Imperfect Unions," The New York Times, January 25, 2014.

Kristof, Nicholas, "Where the G.O.P. Gets It Right," The New York Times, April 9, 2014.

educational opportunities. Such a program has been elevated as an approach to rival affirmative action programs in education. Affirmative action programs have drawbacks while instilling respect for education at an early stage has no drawbacks.

Affirmative action programs based on race served to elevate the poor and thus they did combat economic inequality. However, the Supreme Court banned race-based preferences, but allowed the promotion of diversity by other means[1] that can be more directly targeted to the economically deprived.

Much is already being done to help the poor participate in higher education opportunities, like the Pell grants, and even more as to secondary schools. The action has now shifted to pre-school programs that have been shown to also combat inequality.

Focusing on and providing "opportunities," instead of spending more on existing programs, are now being emphasized.[2] Perhaps it is only a matter of semantics with "providing opportunities" being the same as "combating inequality," but it does seem to place more emphasis on self-determination and self-help and de-emphasizes the use of expensive governmental programs.

---

[1] Lewin, Tamar, "Colleges Seek New Paths to Diversity After Court Ruling," The New York Times, April 22, 2014.

Liptak, Adam, "Court Backs Michigan on Affirmative Action," The New York Times, April 22, 2014.

Editorial, "Racial Equality Loses at the Court," The New York Times, April 22, 2014.

[2] Calmes, Jackie, "In Talk of Economy, Obama Turns to 'Opportunity' Over 'Inequality,'" The New York Times, February 3, 2014.

No governmental expenditure is involved in a unique idea that surfaced to combat economic inequality. The idea was that the United States Postal Service, which still operates in poor neighborhoods where the commercial banks have fled because of the lack of business, should undertake to offer postal banking services to the local population.[1]

This would not violate of our economic system's taboo on government or quasi-governmental units like the USPS going into business to compete with private enterprise. The commercial banks justifiably left these communities by closing their unprofitable branches, so it is not a competitive matter.

USPS would be providing a service needed by the inhabitants of the communities (save them time and expense of going elsewhere, improve their lifestyle, and instil the virtues of thrift) while making a profit because USPS already has facilities there.

While this makes economic sense on a number of levels aside from combating inequality, opposition by commercial banks might be expected. Opposition can be understood whenever one's commercial bailiwick appears invaded.

The problem would be limiting the program's roll-out to only the poor communities, as the program could possibly expand to wealthier communities if the public demanded it. Yet, there are countries that do offer postal banking to all their citizens even though these counties are loaded with prosperous commercial banks offering services to all.

---

[1] Baradaran, Mehrsa, "The Post Office Banks on the Poor," The New York Times, February 7, 2014.

LOWER PRODUCT PRICES FOR THE POOR

The poor obviously benefit from lower prices as is seen by the expansion of discount retailers that either cater to the poor or attract the poor. However, the point has been made that some laws serve to increase prices in the market place. For instance, it has been shown that protecting intellectual property rights results in higher costs to the poor who have to pay more for protected products.[1]

Any suggestions that America should change its basic laws in this regard should be opposed. It is one thing to help the poor and quite another to alter valid public policies that best serves our economic system.

What Can be Done on the High-Income End?

On the high-income end, combatting economic injustice necessarily involves either reducing the income of the wealthy (the rich, the so-called 1%, and the excessively compensated corporate executives) or increasing the tax rates in the higher income brackets.

These approaches immediately bring forth "redistribution" and "class warfare" arguments from opponents.

---

[1] Stiglitz, Joseph E., "How Intellectual Property Reinforces Inequality," The New York Times, July 14, 2013.

REDISTRIBUTION ARGUMENTATION

Redistribution from the rich to the poor has been with us from the most ancient of times. The rich gave alms to beggars, gave a tithe or other required payment to their religious organization which helped the poor, and also gave directly to charity. All this giving, some voluntary and some mandated by religious law, represented redistribution from the rich to the poor.

This continues, supplemented nowadays by taxes collected by governments from the rich and used in part for the poor. All members of society benefit directly or indirectly from the charitable work funded by tax revenues. Charity has never been view negatively as the present day ranting against redistribution would have it.

Some would argue that it is not the wealthy who somehow caused the problems faced by the poor. This leads to a seemingly equitable, but somewhat selfish, position that the wealthy shouldn't have to bear the burden of helping the poor. While some of the wealthy are not totally free of blame for the existence of the poor, most of the wealthy undoubtedly bear no responsibility.

Yet, civilized society serves the wealthy in untold ways. Legions of people who are not wealthy prop-up the society in which the wealthy live, and protect that society. The rich could view their helping the poor as the price of living in civilized society.

There is no issue as to redistribution actually existing; it has existed from ancient biblical times and will continue to exist.

The word "redistribution" should not be used as a fighting pejorative slogan. The only issue as to redistribution is whether the extent of redistribution currently taking place is fair under existing circumstances viewed solely on the merits.

CLASS WARFARE ARGUMENTATION

Class warfare appears to be used as a defensive slogan by or on behalf of the upper-class claiming to be attacked by the lower-classes.[1] Yet, it has been shown that there as many instance where it is the upper-class that is waging a class war against the lower-classes.[2]

Allegations of reverse class-warfare have gotten to the point where those who represent the wealthy are being accused of actually pursing and having pursued policies to advantage the affluent at the expense of everyone else.[3]

It has also been pointed out that inherited wealth ("patrimonial capitalism") is becoming more prevalent than self-made wealth (amongst the 10 wealthiest in America, 6 are heirs and only 4 are self-made), which represents a drift in America toward oligarchy.[4] In this regard we are beginning to look like Russia, known for its oligarchic society since it left communism.

---

[1] Opinion, "Class Warfare in Switzerland," The Wall Street Journal, November 19, 2013.

[2] Kristof, Nicholas, "A Nation of Takers?" The New York Times, March 26, 2014.

Krugman, Paul, "The Undeserving Rich," The New York Times, January 19, 2014.

Krugman, Paul, "Free to Be Hungry," The New York Times, September 22, 2013.

[3] Krugman, Paul, "Wealth Over Work," The New York Times, March 23, 2014.

[4] Ibid.

Yet, for all the talk of class warfare, it all comes back to the issue of fairness. Each group accuses the other of class warfare when a proposal contradicts their perception of fairness.

References to class warfare are meaningless slogans that only serve to divert discussion of a proposal's merits. Again, we have to start looking at the heart of proposals being advanced and consider them on the merits as compared to burying thought by casting about slogans.

Subjecting the higher income groups to higher tax rates is frequently ascribe to class warfare. Yet, it is normally expected that the tax rates in the upper tax brackets will be higher, with the sole issue being whether the tax rates are fair considering the surrounding circumstances.

The collected taxes serve many purposes like budget balancing, educating society, and supporting the military that protects everybody in our society as well as combatting economic inequality, while at the same time creating the environment that nurtured the earning of the wealth being taxed.

If anything, the various "classes" benefit and need one another.

EXCESSIVE EXECUTIVE COMPENSATION

The huge differential in compensation levels in America has already lead to street protests aimed at the upper 1% of our society, but hasn't led to violence and hopefully never will.

Yet, there is little resentment against Bill Gates (founder of Microsoft) and other entrepreneurs who took risks and

ECONOMIC INEQUALITY

became wealthy. We all want the do the same. Nor is there much resentment against celebrities (movie stars, athletes and others), who have individually proven themselves to be particularly unique.[1]

But there is widespread resentment against business executives who generally command high if not unreasonable salaries (plus all sorts of sign-on and termination packages) and then insist on receiving handsome incentive compensation in order to induce them to do excellent work, as if that were not already contemplated in the high salaries they receive.

It has been said that "when pay setters set their own pay, there is no limit,"[2] the French economist Thomas Piketty being concerned how rampart free market capitalism can worsen inequality and threaten democratic societies.

America fought and won the capitalist battle against socialism, but socialism is now coming back as witness an avowed socialist being recently elected to the City Council of a major American city.[3] Excessive executive compensation is an important contributor to this.

Poverty levels in America go up to say a $50,000 income level for a large family. Middle/upper-middle incomes go up to say $200,000 (or 4-fold the poverty level) with little resentment.

It appears that public resentment starts when incomes go up to the $1 million range (20-fold the poverty level),

---

[1] Nutting, Rex, "Why the Super Rich Get Richer – And You Don't," MarketWatch, February 23, 2014

[2] Edsall, Thomas B., "Capitalism vs. Democracy," The New York Times, January 28, 2014.

[3] Johnson, Kirk, "A Rare Elected Voice for Socialism Pledges to Be Heard in Seattle," The New York Times, December 28, 2013.

intensifies against executives who claim income in the $10 million range (200-fold the poverty level) and explodes at the $100 million level (2000-fold the poverty level).

LIMITING VARIOUS EXECUTIVE PACKAGES

On March 3, 2013, the Swiss voted to curb executive pay by a two-to-one majority; that is 68% of the voters favored the curb.[1]

Switzerland, the international banking paradise, has a strict capitalist bent and a flourishing democracy with per-capita income about 50% greater than per-capita income in America. A person could hardly argue that Switzerland is a nation of malcontents that employ class warfare.

Class warfare was not an argument used in Switzerland by the Swiss. It was Americans who suggested class warfare as a cause of the Swiss revolt against excessive executive compensation.[2]

Switzerland has a history of being concerned with its economic success, its competitive position and its status as a good place to conduct business. Corporate Switzerland argued that dire consequences would flow from the proposed curbs on executive compensation, argued that the curbs would restrict future growth and drive away talent. But, a huge majority of the Swiss people would not stand for the widening gap between the rich and poor and the curbs were enacted.

---

[1] BBC News, Europe, "Swiss Referendum Backs Executive Pay Curbs," March 3, 2013.

[2] Opinion, "Class Warfare In Switzerland," The Wall Street Journal, November 19, 2013.

In this vote, Switzerland barred a Swiss company from giving sign-on and exit bonuses to executives. In America, we call a sign-on bonus a "golden handshake" to induce a chief executive to join a company and we compensate a chief executive for exiting the company with a "golden parachute." It is "golden" for it is usually in the magnitude of millions of dollars.

It is particularly troubling that these golden parachutes are given to failed executives so as to get them out of the company, where a person would have thought that the hiring contract could specify removal for poor performance. But the top executives write their own contracts, accepted by compliant boards of directors.

The top executives are aided by well-paid corporate compensation consultants who earn their livings by kowtowing to the top executives and striving to ever increase compensations levels. It is to be noted that executives one rung down the ladder usually have no written contracts and yet are willing to accept the jobs for the opportunities the jobs present without demanding golden handouts.

How companies ever got to offer such excessive compensation packages and offer huge amounts of incentive compensation is beyond contemplation. One would have thought that the prestige, perks and power conferred by the top position or positions in a corporation make those positions so desirable that the competition for them could actually have resulted in lower salaries and no bonuses.

Perhaps these bonuses and huge pay packages were indeed the creatures of the so-called "professional" compensation consultants whose economic interests and increasing fees are essentially based on corporate comparisons of ever-escalating compensation packages that they and their industry compatriots created.

The Swiss voters were also concerned with the amount of wages (cash salaries) these executives are paid. These wages were on average 56 times the wages of the lowest paid corporate employee. The wages were so high that the concerned voters wanted shareholders to expressly approve them. The approved wages would include the so-called annual "bonuses" a company pays its executives, presumably for work done beyond the level of excellence contemplated in the high wages being paid.

Again, a person has to wonder how any society ever got to justify those huge bonuses paid year after year to all top executives, as if the executives really required incentives to perform -- or as if all executives needed to be rewarded for being above average, just like the all the children in Lake Wobegon are above average.

A recent study shows these payments to be ineffective[1] in incenting anything.

The European Union had become concerned with the excessive executive compensation being paid by the banking enterprises it has oversight over. As a result, the EU decided to limit bonuses to one year's salary, or two years' salary with explicit approval of shareholders.

Requiring shareholder approval makes sense since board of directors are rarely independent of the executives who appointed them or work with them, and are usually influenced by the "professional" compensation consultants they

---

[1] Morgenson, Gretchen, "Pay for Performance? It Depends on the Measuring Stick," The New York Times, April 12, 2014.

invariably employ so as to take compensation responsibility off their shoulders.

Limiting the size of the bonuses shareholders can approve makes sense because shareholders (at least in America) normally rubberstamp their consent to any matter presented for their approval.

Some American companies allow shareholders to vote on executive compensation but only in an advisory way not binding on the board of directors.

The shareholders invariably rubberstamp approval, but in the one disclosed situation where shareholders disapproved the executive compensation in two consecutive years, it made no difference.[1] In that case, the executive earned about $80 million in one year, about $580 million over eight years.

It seems that advisory votes are just a sop, possibly dreamed up by compensation consultants to create the aura of legitimacy.

The American version of the Swiss limitation would entail an act of Congress applicable to corporations traded publicly. The only compensation to be paid by such listed corporations to executives should be limited to salaries in whatever amounts the board of directors specify, with accounting disclosure. Except for salaries, expense account reimbursements and a limited annual bonus, the corporation should not be allowed to make payments of any kind to executives. That would include incentive payments, parachutes, termination payments, non-competition payments, or payments for damages of any kind unless granted in actual litigation. No employment agreement should provide for any

---

[1] Streitfeld, David, "Still No. 1, and Doing What He Wants," The New York Times, April 12, 2014.

payments of these genres or other such payments. Employee stock options are separately covered below.

The limited annual bonus paid to employees (including executives) who are selected to receive a bonus by the board of directors should not exceed one year's salary. The bonuses should be included as a charge to fourth quarter earnings, with the press release disclosing the aggregate amount of bonuses and the individual bonuses of the named top executives.

Doing it this way would bring sunshine to the relationship between the bonuses paid and the earnings for that very year. It would force the board to face reality and not make any bonus determinations or estimates until the results for the entire year are in.

Shareholders and the financial community seeing the annual results and the bonus payments will have time to react as the bonuses cannot be paid until approved by shareholders voting in the annual meeting. This would allow the board to yield to criticism and reduce the bonuses.

Is this draconian? It's not draconian in the context of today's friendly boards of directors chosen by the top executives themselves. Not draconian in the context of rubber stamping shareholders. And not draconian in the context of the role runaway compensation consultants play today.

Other proposals would should certainly be sought, but they should have teeth because the excessive executive compensation problem has been publically condemned for decades with nothing getting done. And the excessive compensation grows excessively year upon year.

LIMITING EXECUTIVE SALARIES

A half-year later, the Swiss decided to have a referendum on limiting executive wages; that is, limiting the annual salary paid currently in cash to an executive.

A 2012 study showed that executive wages, on average, were 56 times that of the lowest paid employee. The referendum would limit executive wages to 12 times the wages of the lowest paid employee, a very severe cutback that seems to be aimed at punishment rather than reform.

In November 2013, the Swiss voters turned down this referendum.[1] It would appear that this was too extreme even for the voters who were shown by opinion polls to be upset by huge executive salaries.

The reformation might have attracted a more favorable vote if the comparison base wasn't at the extreme (the lowest paid employee, the janitor); it could have been average wages of all employees, the average of executive pay at the bottom rung or some other measure. The multiple of 12 also seemed very low.

Actually, the average top executive salary in Switzerland being only 56-fold that of the lowest paid employee seems very low in comparison to American executive salaries which could be higher. Median compensation in 2013 for top executives of the 100 largest publically traded American corporations was about $14 million, with the highest close to $80 million,[2] but that includes incentive bonuses and stock

---

[1] Ewing, Jack, "Swiss Voters Decisively Reject a Measure to Put Limits on Executive Pay," The New York Times, November 24, 2013.

[2] Nocera, Joe, "C.E.O. Pay Goes Up, Up and Away!" The New York Times, April 14, 2014.

Eavis, Peter, "Executive Pay: Invasion of the Supersalaries," The New York Times, April 12, 2014.

profits in addition to salaries. Salary comparisons were not shown.

However, it would also appear that the Swiss voters could have rejected any numerical limitation whatever the base and multiple. A definitive multiple could be viewed as too invasive, too difficult to set and enforce and too easy to get around. Yet, they were the same voters that disposed of golden handshakes and parachutes and got shareholders involved in approving executive salaries.

Considering that ballot initiatives rarely succeed in Switzerland (merely 110 made it to a vote in 32 years and only 20 passed[1]), the rage against economic inequality must have been deeply felt by the Swiss. Economic inequality had triggered two ballot initiatives, and the matter might not be over.

Shortly after the second Swiss vote, but surely not related to it, the Pope added his voice in denouncing "a free market that perpetuates inequality."[2] In Switzerland, the explicit public concern may have put a damper on excessive Swiss executive compensation. Probably not so in America.

In France, the government got a go-ahead to levy a special "millionaire tax" on corporations paying a yearly salary of more than 1 million euros.[3]

In America, nothing has come of attempts to limit excessive executive compensation. The "Occupy Movement"

---

[1] Stamm, Peter, "Why the Swiss Scorn the Superrich," The New York Times, November 22, 2013.

[2] Goodstein, Laurie, and Povoledo, Elisabetta, "Pope Sets Down Goals for an Inclusive Church, Reaching Out 'on the Streets,'" The New York Times, November 26, 2013.

[3] Reuters, "French 'Millionaire Tax' Cleared," The New York Times, December 29, 2013.

of youths claiming to represent 99% of American society started public demonstrations in 2011 on Wall Street in New York City, primarily protesting against economic inequality. Interestingly, the Swiss movement to curtail inequality was also largely a youth movement.

The Occupy demonstrators were nonviolent, as the movement was meant to be, but yet militants appeared. Some say the militants were planted there by opponents of the Occupy Movement. Conflicts with the police arose throughout America and hostile feelings resulted.

The establishment argued that the Occupy Movement was class warfare against the wealthy while the movement argued that the 1% was waging class warfare against the 99% with their extreme economic inequality. The Occupy Movement largely dissipated, luckily this time, with limited public damage.

Curtailing excessive compensation in America is both desirable and necessary to keep our society functioning. Limitations must be placed by law on all publicly held corporations as it has been shown time and again that boards of directors cannot and will not rein-in excessive compensation. After all, the boards are selected and appointed by those who expect to receive excessive compensation and shareholders usually rubberstamp proposals. But not Warren Buffett who deliberately withheld approval of a giant company's executive compensation plan, and then spoke out against it.[1]

The special bonuses and exit packages are particularly offensive. Any incentive compensation at the top executive

---

[1] Nocera, Joe, "Buffett Bites Back," The New York Times, April 28, 2014.

levels is just plain bullshit[1] as if those executives weren't already being paid on a level that assumes excellence and as if they needed incentives to perform.

Proposals to limit all executive compensation other than salaries should take priority. Attempting to limit salaries would be premature and, if done, should be on the federal level instead of the state level.[2] It is the compensation other than salaries that is the greater problem and should be addressed first. Limiting excessive executive corporate salaries should be given more time, but not forgotten.

EXECUTIVES OF NON-PROFIT ORGANIZATIONS

Excessive executive compensation is also being seen in non-profit organizations like private colleges making incentive payments to recognize the achievements or to ensure continued service of their Presidents.[3] The three top earners had compensation packages in the $3 million range.

As with profit-making businesses, it is possible that friendly college boards of trustees are beholden to the college administrators. Board members could have been suggested by or actually chosen by the college Presidents and would probably be reluctant to object to excessive compensation because of the normal camaraderie found on boards. And the boards might well defer to the "professional" compensation

---

[1] See Frankfurt, Harry G., "On Bullshit," Princeton University Press, 2005.
[2] Nash, James, "California Bill Boosts Corporate Taxes for High-Paid CEOs," Bloomberg, April 24, 2014.
[3] Lewin, Tamar, "Pay for U.S. College Presidents Continues to Grow," The New York Times, December 15, 2013.

consultants who have an interest in ever increasing compensation levels.

The college administrators are surely competent. They have done well by their institutions, but that is reflected in their salaries that are many times that earned by the best professors.

Like their counterparts running large corporations, they should not need incentives to do excellent work. Nor should they receive other types of special payments that not offered to professors. The rationales for such payments are specious and contribute to the high cost of education.

Where compensation paid by a non-profit organization appears out of line, concerned members, ordinary citizens, or Attorney's General should deliberately file breach of fiduciary duty lawsuits so as to publicize the excessive compensation and cast as much mud as possible on the elite members of the boards/trustees who probably didn't think or think it wrong to pay so much.

What must be said should be said publically and loudly with the aim of embarrassing the trustees or board members for only that will bring restraint. Such lawsuits, even if not fully pursued and ultimately successful, would not be lost on the board members.

For profit-making corporations, excessive executive compensation is compounded by the stock option profits that unconscionably increase executive compensation and unfairly get the individual stockholders to unknowingly pay the expense.

FORBIDDING USE OF STOCK OPTIONS

Stock options operate as a rip-off on shareholders, an unjust taking that should be made illegal. Stock options serve as a cost-free give away to corporate executives and are a terrible form of incentive. Corporate use of stock options should be forbidden. This necessitates a complex explanation, but first the easy aspects.

Because stock prices do fluctuate over time, fluctuate widely for some companies, and stock option grants are frequently given year after year, stock option grantees are almost guaranteed a profit by timing the exercise of their options (which history has shown is most often immediately followed by open market sales of the stock acquired).

Over a period of time the stock market price of a company might wind up being flat. However, even with a stogy corporation there are fluctuations in market price due to varying market conditions. An executive who times the option exercise and stock sale can still realize substantial profits even where a stogy corporation is involved.

Yet, there is no necessary relationship between executive performance and stock price. Over time, stocks do tend to go up almost assuring a future bonus; a bonus granted at a time when the executive's future performance is unknown.

Moreover, executive performance could be poor or mediocre and the stock price go up due to general economic conditions, stock market conditions, or because the company's industry is doing well even though the company itself is mediocre. A company and its stock market price can be doing well with no thanks to the CEO who could be a turkey going along for the ride.

The point here is that stock options are probably the poorest way to structure an incentive bonus.[1] There are better alternatives, if incentives are actually warranted, as will be described.

In addition, nobody knows how much money is being given away when the stock options are granted. It is like Alice in Wonderland as the options could prove to be worthless or provide fantastic wealth. Thus, the board of directors really doesn't know the extent of its largesse when it grants stock options, knowing less and less as the term of the option increases to 10 years.

To be sure, the paid compensation consultants will provide all sorts of statistics proving anything they want to prove, but that doesn't even qualify as guesswork because those consultants cater to top management who hired them and it is in their interest to benefit the person who pays the tab.

The worst cut of all is that the individual stockholders in the corporation are being had. They bear the economic cost of the stock options through the dilution in the value of the stock they hold.

The profit the executives make upon exercising the options is reflected in the dilution of the stock value due to issuing stock below the then market value. Thus, if the option price is $5 (per share) and the value is $50 when the option is exercised, the executive has a $45 profit while the stockholders effectively bear the $45 dilution caused by the corporation issuing stock as less than fair value. When the fair market value of the stock was $50, the corporation could

---

[1] *Also see* Morgenson, Gretchen, "When the Stock Price Hides Trouble," The New York Times, October 12, 2013.

presumably have issued shares for $50. Issuance for less than $50 creates dilution.

The law should look at the unissued shares of the corporation as being owned by the stockholders, not the corporation. The law effectively does this, as the shareholders have to approve the stock option plan and, of course, in this esoteric area they would approve anything dressed up for them by the compensation consultants.

It should be a breach of fiduciary duty to issue shares for any purpose for less than fair value and requesting shareholders to approve that should be forbidden. The tax laws even treat stock options as having been paid for by the shareholders, not the corporation.

The corporation gets no tax deduction when it issues the option shares for $45 less than its value, and the executive does not have to treat the $45 profit as taxable compensation. Should the executive later sell the shares, the profit would be taxes at capital gains rates.

Thus the stock option is a means of compensating executives at the lower capital gain rate while neither the corporation nor its shareholders get any tax deduction for compensation expense. Actually, the executive need never pay tax on the $45 profit if she or he holds it until death, at which time the heirs get a step-up in tax basis. In the meantime the $45 increase in the executive's net worth allows use of that money though borrowing on the stock.

If the accounting for stock options reflected the reality of the situation it would be obvious that the shareholders are actually paying the bill. For instance, if the executive had a $45 profit on the exercise of the option, the corporation should have recorded the receipt of a $45 capital contribution from the shareholders and recorded a $45 compensation expense.

In that case, the corporation would have had a $45 tax deduction and saved some tax which is the normal situation with compensation paid by the corporation.

Congress was somehow convinced to go along with the situation, probably justifying it because the IRS didn't have to give either the corporation or the shareholders a tax deduction for the $45. Yet, had it allowed the tax deduction it would have collected a tax from the executive who made the $45 profit, perhaps of a comparable amount. Normally, the IRS wouldn't cotton such round-about deals, but then the entire stock option house of cards would have collapsed. Congress accepted the deal, probably at the behest of the business community which would then be able to pay huge amounts of compensation without reducing earnings reported to shareholders.

This is the situation with qualified stock options that meet Congress's requirements. Stock options can also be issued in non-qualified forms with different tax and accounting ramifications but still having the feature that some, if not most, of the economic compensation expense could still be borne by the unsuspecting individual shareholders.

There is no public policy justification for allowing stock options. Perhaps the unjust taking from the shareholders and the corporate breach of fiduciary duty in issuing shares for less than fair value are the lesser evils when compared to the imbalances created as those stock options exacerbate economic inequality in America.

Yes, it is a breach of fiduciary because the taking is known to management and the board, as is the lack of shareholding understanding in their rubberstamping approval.

Allowing corporations to use stock options provides a vehicle for CEO friendly boards of directors make huge giveaways without having appeared to have done so. It is so easy and apparently innocuous to grant executives 100s of thousands of shares in stock options which doesn't appear on the books of account as an expense and which could eventually amount to $100,000,000 in compensation for a single executive. It is most difficult to imagine that any board of directors would authorize the payment a bonus check for $100,000,000 in cash, but it is so easy and hidden to do so with stock options.

In addition, there are alternatives to stock options that are more effective as incentives (again, as if incentives were really needed) and would cost the corporation and shareholders much less (with corporate tax deductions).

Bonuses can be paid in cash, or in corporate stock if there isn't enough cash in the corporate coffers as would be the case with young or start-up companies. Paying a bonus in shares of stock is just like issuing the stock at fair market value and giving the cash received as cash compensation.

Paying a bonus in in shares of stock has the great advantage of knowing how much is being given away. If the stock is selling for $50 a share and 1,000 share are given as a stock bonus, the bonus clearly amounts to $50,000. Such a grant would be based on the executives meritorious performance during the year just ended which would be known to the board and thus have some logic behind it.

Or, if the incentive is to be a future one (so as to keep the executive from leaving), a bonus paid in shares of stock could be designed to vest years later if the recipient is still employed at that time or designed to vest pro-rata over a stated number of years. As corporate stock is unlikely to become worthless, the recipient of a stock bonus will always be in-the-money, while a stock option is no more than a gamble as the option might wind-up being worthless.

The stock bonus is a much better form of incentive than the stock option in any circumstances, and it doesn't fleece the individual shareholders. Because there is a charge to earnings upon granting stock bonuses, board of directors are likely be more conservative in granting such bonuses. Can anyone even imagine a board granting a $100,000,000 stock bonus to one executive?

With reported earnings being charged for stock bonuses, it is unlikely that the board would make the unconscionably high grants as they do with stock options.

Bottom line, the simple remedy is for Congress to bar the use of stock options by publically traded corporations.

TAX THE HIGHER INCOME GROUP

Increasing tax rates in the higher tax brackets serves to directly reduce economic inequality. It reduces the net take-home income at the top, and also serves to supply funds that could be used to fund inequality combatting programs or for budget balancing purposes.

The issue to be faced is not whether it is acceptable to subject the upper-income tax brackets to higher tax rates than the lower-income tax brackets. The issue is whether the proposed differential in tax rates is fair under the surrounding circumstance.

Fairness is always in the eyes of the beholder and there are no standards for determining fairness. The federal income tax rate has been as high as 94% in the top bracket. The top tax brackets have always been need-driven, the 94% being necessary to finance World War II and thus fair at the time.

For 2014, the top income tax rate rounds to 40% on taxable incomes over $457,000 (married) and the bottom income tax rate is 10% and that wasn't enough to finance the military and avoid sequester.

It has repeatedly been pointed out that because of exemptions and the like, many if not most of the poor pay no federal income tax. Others point to the very rich effectively paying only 10% of their income in federal income tax. Those in the middle tax brackets pay federal income tax at the highest effective rate.

Billionaire Warren Buffet complained that the richest Americans generally pay a lower percentage of their income in federal taxes than do those in the middle tax brackets,[1] which he considers unfair and points to his inclination to pay more in tax.

These are the generally cited statistics and while these statistics are accurate they do not tell the whole Federal tax-burden story.

Actually, these statistics distort the story because they consist only of the federal income tax. The federal government levies a number of other taxes that are very

---

[1] Calmes, Jackie, "Obama Tax Plan Would Ask More of Millionaires," The New York Times, September 17, 2011.

substantial and burden the different income groups differently.

The very productive federal payroll tax falls primarily on the lower income groups as does many of the excise taxes. And, there are also the federal taxes paid by businesses that have to worked into the determination of who actually pays how much of the total federal tax bill.

A reliable, bi-partisan report[1] took on the chore of attributing the business taxes to the real people who effectively pay those taxes using esoteric methodologies. The report did that in order to figure out what real people pay in federal taxes. Thus the report includes the federal income, payroll, excise and other taxes, including the hypothetical distribution of the federal business taxes (which didn't change the statistics very much).

The report broke the numbers down to each of the tax brackets used for the income tax, but I combined and rounded them so as to show the net result in a simple fashion:

Tax Bracket	Income	Tax Liability	Tax Rate	% of Total Tax
0 to $50,000	2,072	187	9%	8%
$50,000 to $100,000	2,963	450	15%	20%
$100,000 to $500,000	5,012	1,122	22%	49%
Over $500,000	1,670	523	32%	23%
Total/Average	11,719	2,284	20%	100%
	($Billions)	($Billions)	(Average)	(Average)

---

[1] Joint Committee on Taxation, "Modeling the Distribution of Taxes on Business," (JCX-14-13), October 16, 2013.

Thus, instead of it being bandied around that the poor pay no tax (that is, no federal income tax), they actually pay 9% of their income in federal taxes. Instead of the rich paying tax at a 40% rate (that is, at the top federal income tax bracket), the effective tax rate is 32%. However, at the top of the top, the effective tax rate for the 400 richest Americans was between 15% and 20% during the years 2002 and 2009 because they had large amounts of tax favored dividends and capital gains.[1]

The foregoing table presents the basic information necessary to address tax fairness. On average, the poor pay a little less that 10% of their income in a variety of federal taxes, which might be considered a heavy tax load since their income is so low.

The rich pay between 15% and 32% of their income in federal taxes, a relatively low burden compared to what the rich paid in prior decades and what the rich pay in other countries.

The tax paid by the poorest Americans, the people actually considered to be in the poverty group, does seem excessive; and even at that, there is not enough tax revenue to avoid sequester.

As the poor are already paying too much in tax and the middle income group pay the highest rate of tax (more than the wealthy), only the taxes of wealthy should be increased to in order to avoid disasters like sequester.

---

[1] Business Day, "How The Richest Have Fared," The New York Times, November 1, 2013.
Stewart, James B., "High Income, Low Taxes and Never a Bad Year," The New York Times, November 1, 2013.

Some of that is already happening as there have been some increases in taxes in the higher brackets.[1] The superrich and the merely rich had effective tax rates under 25% in 2011 and the 2013 increases did not boost the effective tax rates much. The point needing emphasis is that changes in the top tax rates do not move the overall effective tax rates very much, and Americas still bear a lower tax burden than most developed countries.

All that concerned citizens should really conclude from this discussion of tax burdens is that the surrounding economic circumstances should have a strong bearing on tax rates and on how the federal tax burden should be split up amongst the various tax brackets.

It would seem that there is room for a moderate increase in the top federal income tax rates so as to alleviate the current and near-term budgetary constraints and make a dent in economic inequality by providing the funds necessary to pursue new socially oriented programs (opportunity programs rather than increased cash payments or lowering payroll taxes).

The more aggressive of that mind would not only advocate increased tax-rates in the upper tax brackets, but also advocate reducing the payroll taxes.

With the rapidly rising inequality, a proposal has surfaced to index tax rates to income inequality so that the tax rates at the top automatically increase as income inequality gets worse.[2]

---

[1] Norris, Floyd, "Merely Rich and Superrich: The Tax Gap Is Narrowing," The New York Times, April 17, 2014.

[2] Shiller, Robert J., "Better Insurance Against Inequality," The New York Times, April 12, 2014.

But, clearly, everyone of all mind-sets should band together to induce Congress to allocate more funds to the Internal Revenue Service to catch the tax cheats so they too can also contribute to combating economic inequality.

Changes of attitude are beginning to appear. A staunch supporter of the proposition that lower taxes promise greater growth now acknowledges that Americans already have a lower tax burden than in most developed countries; and also acknowledges that in the last decade the promise of lower taxes creating growth and improving the well-being of Americans hasn't been fulfilled, conceding that the argument for higher taxes looks stronger.[1]

America can't afford to wait another decade before increasing taxes on the higher income groups. Besides, as the wealth at the top has grown so much over the last decade, only confirmed scrooges would be concerned with a moderate increase in tax.

FUNDING THE INTERNAL REVENUE SERVICE

Collecting the taxes due under the current tax laws and current tax-rates will help in combatting economic inequality. Much of the collections would fall on the wealthy and the funds collected would alleviate budgetary pressures, including the pressure on existing programs aimed at reducing economic inequality.

It is difficult to argue against enforcing the tax laws already enacted as that would be tantamount to condoning

---

[1] Douthat, Ross, "The Case Against Higher Taxes," The New York Times, April 15, 2014.

cheating. Tax cheating serves to shift the tax burden from the dishonest to the honest, an unjustifiable state of affairs.

Congress has been depriving the IRS of the funds it needs to hire the staff necessary to fulfill its function of collecting America's taxes. Perhaps the legislators reflect an inherent hatred of the IRS. Perhaps they feel that tax collections go to keeping government oversized, something that they are very opposed to. Perhaps they favor the wealthy in their class war against the less fortunate.[1]

A small fraction of filed tax returns is audited by the IRS due to its skeleton staff. If Congress allocated the funds the IRS needs, the IRS auditors would collect many times their salaries from the tax cheats.

And more audits would lead to greater compliance in the future, with the collection of still more tax revenues. It would be a win-win for everybody but the tax cheats.

CLOSING THE TAX HAVENS

Concomitant with funding the IRS so as to allow it to enforce our existing tax laws, America should enact laws that would effectively put the tax havens out of business. By one estimate, wealthy individuals around the world do not report at least $21 trillion to their governments.[2]

Wealthy Americans also partake but the IRS has failed in curbing the tax drain from the US Treasury because the US government has diplomatically bombed in combatting tax

---

[1] Krugman, Paul, "Enemies of the Poor," The New York Times, January 12, 2014.
[2] Higgins, Andrew, "Europe Pushes to Shed Stigma of a Tax Haven," The New York Times, May 22, 2013.

havens. However, the European Union has had some degree of success in having its own member nations, Austria and Luxembourg, curtail their tax-haven operations.[1]

Many American lawyers, accountants, bankers, financial institutions, financial engineers, and politicians benefit from the existence of the tax havens in addition to the wealthy. It is about time Congress recognized that it is being forced to increase the tax burden on honest Americans by allowing the dishonest evade our tax laws. Small business has recognized that.[2]

The tax haven counties needn't have extended their bank secrecy laws to citizens of other countries. Their having done so shows that they had no concern or regard for the other countries, including America. The tax havens were knowingly and deliberately helping the world's drug cartels, terrorists and wealthy tax cheats avoid taxes and launder money.

Multinational efforts to stem the tax havens have failed. America, to its shame, had pulled out of such an effort[3] obviously at the behest of those Americans who benefit from the existence of tax havens.

The lack of American bank support in combating tax havens is puzzling. As far back as 1983, the staff of a Senate subcommittee found that tax havens undermine the integrity

---

[1] Higgins, Andrew, "Europe Pushes to Shed Stigma of a Tax Haven," The New York Times, May 22, 2013.

[2] Browning, Lynnley, "Small Businesses Go After Offshore Tax Havens," The New York Times, July 20, 2010.

[3] "A Retreat on Tax Havens," The New York Times, May 26, 2001.
"Backing Sought for Offshore Tax Initiative," The New York Times, June 14, 2001.

of American banks.[1] Also, a person might wonder why the American banks ever allowed the tax haven banks to become such big and formidable competitors for their natural American customer base.[2]

We should not deal with tax haven countries like we deal with friendly countries. As pleasant as it might be on a beach in a rock in the middle of ocean, the tax haven countries operate right in our face. Their laws are aimed at helping American citizens and American corporations evade American taxes. They produce little and basically contribute nothing the world economy. Yet, their gun sights, in the form of their local banking laws, are aimed directly at us.

The solution is simple. Congress should pass a law forbidding all American financial institutions, including banks, from dealing with specified tax-haven countries including baring all transfers of fund to or from these countries. That should serve to close tax haven operations.

Terminating all banking activity with specified tax haven countries would be hard ball, deservedly so. We should keep in mind that the nations that extended their bank secrecy laws to Americans did it in America's face. It's almost akin to an act of war as they knowingly harm us in full realization that the American Treasury would be raided. America can and should reciprocate, particularly now, in our years of decline, as we can no longer afford the tax haven drain.

---

[1] Gerth, Jeff, "Offshore Banking Perils Cited In A Senate Study," The New York Times, March 15, 1983.

[2] Scott, Mark, "Tax Haven Crackdown Creates Opportunities for Bankers," The New York Times, April 5, 2012.

KEEPING AND EXTENDING THE ESTATE TAX

Only about one hundredth of 1% of the estates of the dying pay the estate tax because it exempts $5 million of asset value.

The exemption was justified on the basis that it would exempt small farms and family business from tax and thus allow those assets to remain in family hands. However, the application of the exemption is much wider than that and most people do not consider $5 million to be small.

Although the exemption should be viewed as being very generous, fairness would indicate that indexing for inflation is appropriate.

The estate tax is amongst the least costly to collect, and potentially raises a great deal of revenue. It a tax on property, not "double taxation" of income as the critics would label it. Just like the real estate taxes that most of us pay annually are not considered "double taxation," neither should the estate tax be labeled "double taxation."

Calling it "double taxation' would be a false label just like calling the estate tax a "death tax." It can't be a "death tax" because it exempts a huge percentage of estates. With almost all of the estates of dying being exempt, it is clearly not a tax on death but rather a tax on the transfer of huge blocks of wealth. It is a tax on the transfer of property.

Taxes on the transfer of property are commonplace, whether in the form of real property transfer taxes or everyday sales taxes. The estate tax is merely another type of tax on the transfer of property that not only produces needed revenues but has a number of valid social purposes behind it.

The heirs to an estate get an increased tax basis for the inherited property, reducing the future income tax they would otherwise have to on the sale of the inherited property. Some people would view this as being unjust.

There is an argument that there should be no increase in tax basis on death for income tax purposes while the full fair market value of assets should still be used for estate tax valuation purposes. By analogy, this is the case with the annual real estate tax we pay on our residences -- the real estate tax is based on the fair market value of residence and there is no increase in the income tax basis of the residence because a real estate tax had been paid on it.

However, there is justification for increasing the tax basis upon death lest a tremendous clerical burden be put on heirs to preserve inter-generational records that might be difficult to find. Yet, the increase in tax basis of assets in exempt estates under $5 million in value begins to look like a tax loophole. All the tax avoider need do is to hold on to vastly appreciated assets, like corporate stock or heirloom real estate, so that the tax basis would be increased in the hands of heirs.

This serves to make property immobile (keeps it off the market), which is not economically desirable. And, at the extreme, a step-up in tax basis of $5 million could save the heirs say $1 million in income tax while no estate tax is paid, which seems unwarranted.

This matter deserves study and perhaps development of a way to dispose with inter-generational records and yet collect some tax on the step-up.

Arguments fabricated against the income tax are also used against the estate tax. Taxes are said to punish work, achievement, and success (with the greater the tax, the greater the punishment), with the result that the estate tax creates an incentive for people to work less.

Yet, it is just as likely that the incentive created by taxation would be for people to work harder to make up for the taxes paid. But, most rationally, it would seem that whatever the tax rate (unless it is virtual confiscation of a 100% tax rate or close to it) people will strive to earn as much as they can. Only the idle rich in our society have an incentive to work less.

Another fabricated argument is that taxes reduce the savings society needs for investment, while the government would spend what is collected in taxes. Yet, the government is invariably borrowing in the market place to make up for budget shortfalls. With the government reducing its need to borrow because of additional tax collections, there is an inherent offset and the estate tax has no net-effect on the accumulated savings available in the marketplace.

The so-called detriments flowing from estate tax just don't exist, but the benefits of the estate tax are real.

Obviously, the estate tax supplies funds for the needs of our civilized society as reflected in the congressionally approved budgets and spending authorizations. And the funds supplied through an estate tax come from those who would not face deprivation in paying the tax.

When a concentrated effort to repeal the estate tax was being made by the rich scrooges of America, more than 900 of the richest Americans, including Bill Gates and Warren Buffett, sent a letter to Congress opposing repeal of the estate tax, which they view as a constructive part of the American tax system.[1]

Those subject to the estate tax, the rich amongst us, were particularly benefited by our government nurturing and protecting business interests that provided for the earning of wealth, by our government guarding the transfer of wealth to heirs, and by our government preserving our society and its infrastructure for future generations.

STEEPLY PROGRESSIVE ESTATE TAXES

A new and telling justification for the imposition of heavy progressive estate taxes on the very biggest of estates has evolved. Six of the ten wealthiest Americans got their wealth through inheritance,[2] rather than working like Bill Gates and Warren Buffett did, and much more of that can be expected in the future.

America is in danger of becoming an oligarchy, where business concentration in a few hands drives out the competition that makes a capitalist society work. Russia is a good example of an oligarchy.

More important, contributing millions of dollars to political candidates or used to otherwise influence the legislative process is small change to the very wealthy. American democracy is being sidetracked from being of, by, and for the people to being of, by, and for the very wealthy. Our democracy is being destroyed.

---

[1] Nichols, John, "Responsible Wealth Trumps Irresponsible Estate Tax Repeal," The Nation, June 13, 2012.

[2] Krugman, Paul, "Wealth Over Work," The New York Times, March 23, 2014.

Huge disparities in wealth destabilize our society. It is in the national interest to stem the growth of very large fortunes.

Thus, what is needed is a steeply progressive estate tax. Teddy Roosevelt favored it in 1910 and, if nothing changes, we're now headed toward a society with a hereditary aristocracy of wealth,[1] indicating even more need for a steep progression in the estate tax.

The French economist Piketty looks at a progressive wealth tax as a means of limiting the concentration of wealth and brings out critics crying Marxism.[2] With Teddy Roosevelt having favored higher estate tax rate, it can hardly be called Marxist. It's just sloganism that raises tempers and diverts discussion on the merits.

Aside from limiting the concentration of wealth and fighting the trend toward an oligarchy, a steeply progressive estate tax would provide the more tax revenues to help balance the budget, avoid sequestration pressures, and help reduce economic inequality.

But much more important, it would help preserve our capitalist economic system and restore a democracy of, by, and for the people.

CUTTING THROUGH THE NOISE

The economist Thomas Piketty has become very popular in America and has triggered a good deal of controversy. A

---

[1] Krugman, Paul, "America's Taxation Tradition," The New York Times, March 27, 2014.

[2] Krugman, Paul, "The Piketty Panic," The New York Times, April 24, 2014.

backlash against Piketty's views has started and thankfully so.[1]

Piketty's view is said to maintain that free markets enrich the owners of capital at everybody else's expense. That is an indictment of the capitalist system which other economists would say has served us well, and it has done so.

But all that is beside the point when it comes to economic inequality since Piketty's view drives the discussion in unnecessary and undesirable directions.

The salient point is that economic inequality has in fact increased and something need be done about it lest we do have Marxist type class warfare in our midst. The last decade has clearly shown a diminution of the lower income groups and heightened growth at the top, which is intolerable when it is as continual and accelerating as it is.

Lest we wind up with movements more effective than the Occupy Movement, which can rip the nation apart and ruin the economic system that has generally served us well, we have to stem the accelerating inequality. Only that will allow our capitalistic system achieve the ideals rightfully attributable to it.

The varies steps advanced in these pages, and certainly countess more to be advanced by others, is not inconsistent with our capitalistic system but is actually in support of it.

---

[1] Douthat, Ross, "Marx Rises Again," The New York Times, April 19, 2014.

Brooks, David, "The Piketty Phenomenon," The New York Times, April 24, 2014.

Douthat, Ross, "The Diminishing American Edge," The New York Times, April 22, 2014.

Douthat, Ross, "Piketty, Doom Loops and Haymarket," The New York Times, April 22, 2014.

Unless we fix our system, it could crash and take America along with it.

We must tinker with the system as it is very clear that it no longer serves all the people. We don't need to abandon the system, which Piketty's view could lead to, but make some changes that would preserve it. Unless the system is tinkered with, the system could crash no matter how it is described.

What is so objectionable about the suggestions offered to combat economic inequality, and others that will surely appear in time, that we should even take a chance of the system crashing?

Chapter 4

Government Programs & Laws

America and Americans tend to take good things too far. What was initially good can become excessive, unwarranted, too costly and sometimes counter-productive. This is seen in the laws our legislatures pass, in our government programs, and in the decisions our courts reach.

Once a program or law becomes generally accepted by the public as a good thing, our legislators and courts tend to extend it further and further with insufficient thought being devoted to whether the extension is a good thing. Perhaps it is our lawyers and adversarial system that induces all sides to push for more of this or that, without considering whether the pushed for expansion is good for America. The favorable aura surrounding a good program or law stymies thought and limitation.

The focus in this chapter is only those situations where it is time for a roll back where a law or program has been taken too far.

In each instance, readers might be disturbed because good laws and programs appear to be criticized and desecrated but that is not the case. It is just the counterproductive or harmful aspects of the laws and programs that are explored in these pages.

Going too far with good things can and does hurt America, diminishes it, and would continue to do so and possible accelerate unless something is done about it. Taking a law or program too far wastes our time and treasure and diverts attention from what might help stem the decline of America.

To illustrate how we tend to go too far in our laws and how these matters are tackled in this book, the laws concerning the so-called "corporate veil" are the first addressed.

EXTENDING THE CORPORATE VEIL

The corporate veil protects corporate shareholders from being sued for the debts or actions of the corporation. If the corporation fails, or the corporate assets explode causing immense damage, those harmed in the process cannot go after the shareholders to recoup their losses.

The persons who had been harmed can look only to the assets of the corporation and, if that is insufficient, they have to bear the loss. Thus, when enormous adversity strikes, the corporate veil effectively shifts the risk of loss from the owners to others.

Stated another way, the corollary of protecting the shareholders from losses is shifting those losses to others.

Somebody has to bear the loss. The assets of the corporation have been depleted and there is nothing left to take care of those not yet compensated. The public policy question was whether it is to be the shareholder or the victims.

The public policy behind the corporate veil is easily understood if you focus on the individual who wants to enter business without potentially losing his or her home if the business fails.

It can be appreciated that society wants individuals to take risk and enter into businesses that serve the general good. But risking the loss of one's home or other personal assets if the business is unsuccessful, or if something goes wrong, is a major deterrent to such risk taking.

Thus, society created a law to allow the risk-taker to limit the risk of loss to only the assets the risk-taker devotes to the business, thereby protecting the home and other personal assets from loss.

The individual is allowed to form a corporation and transfer to the corporation the assets to be used in the business. The individual becomes the investor in the corporation, owing the corporation's stock. The investor conducts the business by working for the corporation or by having the board of directors hire executive managers.

Then, if there is a loss exceeding the value of the corporate assets, the investor is protected. The loss has to be borne by somebody else who had dealt with the corporation or was harmed by it. This is the public policy rationale behind what has come to be called the corporate veil.

Thus, shifting the risk of loss arose from a balancing of the public interest, from an implicit trade-off society entered into for the greater good.

However, like other good things, the corporate veil has been taken too far. The law now allows a corporation to limit its risk by forming a subsidiary corporation that has its own corporate veil. Thus, if the subsidiary fails in its business or its activities result in damaging others in excess of amounts that its assets can cover, the parent company cannot be sued for the losses sustained. The parent corporation is protected from losing more than its investment in the subsidiary.

This is not the same as protecting the individuals who invested in the parent corporation from losing their homes or other personal assets if the parent corporation's business failed or its assets exploded and destroyed surrounding properties.

The parent's corporate veil protects the investor from losing more than she or he placed at risk in the parent corporation. With the expansion of the corporate veil to a subsidiary of the parent corporation, the parent corporation protects the assets already placed at risk in the parent corporation from risk exceeding what it had contributed to the subsidiary. There is no public policy justification for providing a second layer of risk protection and shifting still more risk to others.

All that the extension accomplishes is to create an incentive for parent corporations to invest as little as possible in a subsidiary and have the subsidiary conduct risky businesses. If the risk materializes and there is a major loss, the parent can only lose what it contributed to the subsidiary and any greater loss is shifted to others.

We see this in most large corporations having thousands of subsidiaries. I do not know the circumstances under which British Petroleum paid for the Gulf of Mexico oil spill, so I speculate. I would suspect that BP, the parent corporation, was protected from liability for the mishap caused by its subsidiary company because of the subsidiary's corporate veil. This would mean that those hurt could collect only from the subsidiary and what it owned (which was probably just enough to conduct the activities assigned to it) and could not go after BP, the parent company.

Yet, to its credit BP appears not to have claimed the corporate veil protection, perhaps prompted by business and public relations reasons because BP and its other subsidiaries had significant operations in the United States subject to public backlash. Others might not have chosen to do that and would have claimed the corporate veil protection extended to subsidiaries, resulting in the public being saddled with the gulf losses.

America went too far in extending the corporate veil to subsidiaries and the law should be changed. There is no reason to protect the assets put at risk in the corporate parent by recognizing the corporate veil of subsidiaries. The investors in the corporate parent are already protected, as was the original purpose in having a corporate veil, and there is no reason to multiply that protection by extending it to subsidiaries of the parent, potentially expending it a thousand fold depending on how many subsidiaries the parent formed.

Parent corporations could argue that they too need protection to go into a risky business, but that goes too far. If the business expansion entails ordinary risk a corporation would encounter, as would be the usual case, the corporate parent company should be at risk. If the risk is too great for the corporate parent to take, as in the case of entering into a new industry with unknown risks (like drilling in deep waters or mining the deep seas), the risk would also be too great to shift to the public or to the victims.

Compare that with say a retailer with multiple stores, each placed in a subsidiary corporation which has the protection of the corporate veil. Using a separate subsidiary for each store many have been primarily done for convenience of administration which is just fine, but protection of the corporate veil presently goes along with that. If the roof of a store falls down on customers, there is probably insurance to cover it. But if not, it would not appear to be too much to hold the parent liable to the victims if the subsidiary assets are insufficient to cover the losses. The investors in the parent corporation have their protection and there is no reason to protect the parent company from the risks in its business whether conducted directly or through subsidiaries it formed.

It is in the marine area (and potentially in some cutting-edge scientific endeavors) where risks abound because so much remains unknown. While the marine scientists grapple with protecting the ecology, the oceans, and the life within for future generations, more and more marine risks are exposed.[1]

But nothing is said addressing the legal issues. The matter is particularly difficult in that tuna don't sue when they get poisoned, and fisherman might find it impossible to prove personal damage even if they should be able to use class-action suits. We are beginning to learn the risks of deep-sea oil drilling, and we have no idea what risks will be exposed when deep-sea mining commences.

In situations where there is so much potential risk that corporations would be reluctant to undertake the risk without being able to limit it to an undercapitalized subsidiary protected by the corporate veil, society should find a way to set up a "superfund" to handle the industry risk for all players, perhaps also having the government share in the cost as the public contribution.

With the elimination of the corporate veil for subsidiaries, the potential players would go forward by contributing to the superfund. Each player can then estimate the potential profit and the superfund contribution and go forward or not.

The corporation going forward, other players, and society itself would be protected by the superfund, and the accountants will be pleased because the cost of protection will be placed where it belongs.

This, or similar arrangements, might be found to handle risk. But any possible arrangement should not detract from

---

[1] Birnbaum, Elizabeth, and Savitz, Jacqueline, "The Deepwater Horizon Threat," The New York Times, April 16, 2014.

society now limiting the corporate veil to only the parent corporation and baring all subsidiaries from having corporate veils.

Corporations dealing with other corporations can be expected to protect themselves. But corporations that harm the ecology, which cannot protect itself, should not able to hide behind the corporate veil of their subsidiaries. Nor should subsidiaries be able to protect their parent corporations from liability where they are at fault in causing damage that their assets are not sufficient to cover.

If a proposed venture is worthwhile enough, it would be undertaken with superfund insurance to protect the ecology and people being hurt. If the proposed venture fails because insurance is too expense, it would only serve to illustrate that society would be picking up too much risk by allowing continued subsidiary corporate veil protection. Forcing superfund insurance to protect against large risk is not too much to ask for. All of us as individuals do it as we insure against people getting hurt in our homes or as we drive cars.

PERPETUATING GOVERNMENT PROGRAMS

In the normal course of things, governments enact a variety programs for valid policy reasons. They are all considered valid in the sense that the programs were openly debated, faced legislative scrutiny and were approved by the legislature. Over time, new features are added to the good programs; the good programs being the ones that the public favors. Some programs die; the ones that lose public favor and the legislature repeals them.

Some people maintain that certain types of programs, particularly entitlement programs, take on a life of their own and are automatically expand in time.[1] Of course, this could be expected of any program that becomes popular and the legislatively approved expansion can be viewed as validation of the program.

Non-entitlement programs are also expanded in time, as for instance farm programs. And both Republicans and Democrats do it, as witness the Republicans under George W. Bush expanding Medicare to include prescription drugs, which were not included when the Democrats under Lyndon Johnson expanded health care by creating Medicare.

Expansions are not automatic because there must be reason and rationale behind them to convince the legislature to adopt the expansion. Expansions do not just grow on trees. The automatic expansion argument is used by those who dislike a new or expanded program and aim to derail it.

We should not be averse to adopting a new program because it might possibly be expanded in time. Such an argument really suggests that America cannot control what it does legislatively; that is, it suggests we are unable to set limits. The argument is also foolish in that, if carried to the extreme, America could never do anything for everything might possibly be expanded in time.

---

[1] Harwood, John, "Fighting to Stop an Entitlement Before It Takes Hold, and Expands," The New York Times, November 12, 2013.

Nor should we be adverse to curtailing or terminating a program that is not doing what was expected of it. However, we should be careful to distinguish between programs that didn't work at all and programs that did in fact work as billed but not well enough because they were cut back in the political give and take before enactment[1] or the initial implementation was faulty. But whatever created the problem, if a program doesn't work, it should be made to work, cut-back or eliminated.

All programs should be viewed periodically on the merits, particularly the ones that seem to be politically driven handouts for the poor or for the rich.[2]

Economic conditions and societal needs do change over time, costs can go up or down, loopholes and fraud opportunities might have appeared, and new ways of achieving the policy goals might have evolved. While our legislature remains dysfunctional and can't even handle urgent day-to-day business, such periodic reviews aren't very likely. But, this too will change in time.

A useful example of such a change comes from what is now one of the most functional state legislatures in the nation since it changed it electoral laws a few years ago. California had been most aggressive over the decades in its environmental protection policies which limited development, but the legislature changed materially and began considering

---

[1] Editorial, "What the Stimulus Accomplished," The New York Times, February 22, 2014.

[2] Kristof, Nicholas, "A Nation of Takers?" The New York Times, March 26, 2014.

revisions because changing conditions deterred legitimate development.[1]

In normal course, significant programs go through a period of de-bugging after getting started. After the bugs have been take out, the programs should operate reasonably as designed. If not, review and tune-up or termination is in order.

As an automatic rotational system for legislative review of government programs is unlikely in the present environment, all that can be expected is ad hoc reviews when something dramatic happens or some legislator happens to get stirred up. A legislators might become aware of problems, of run-away costs, of abuses or of fraud and be motivated to file corrective bills. Failing that, it is up to an alert public or media to push for reviews.

Or it might fall to a judge or court to review a government program. Whether a government safety regulation can go too far will soon go before an administrative judge and perhaps the courts.

The Consumer Product Safety Commission had a dangerous product recalled and the commission is trying to hold the chief executive of the now defunct corporation personally responsible for the recall cost estimated at $57 million.[2] The commission is using a criminal law doctrine that allows the "responsible corporate officer" to be

---

[1] Nagourney, Adam, "California Takes Steps to Ease Landmark Law Protecting Environment," The New York Times, 2013.

[2] Stout, Hilary, "Buckyball Recall Stirs a Wider Legal Campaign," The New York Times, October 31, 2013.

prosecuted for corporate wrongdoing, the doctrine arising because corporations can't be put in jail and someone should to be held responsible for corporate crimes. However, the use of this doctrine where no violation of law is claimed and its use in administrative actions is unprecedented and does seem to go too far. It clearly deserves judicial review.

COUNTER-PRODUCTIVE INCENTIVES

If it can be shown that an otherwise good program creates counter-productive incentives, we should feel obliged to eliminate the adverse aspects or eliminate the program.

Unemployment benefits reducing the incentive to look for a new job is being debated[1] as is the possible incentive to game the system by those who do not really want to work. Better information is needed to determine whether these counter-productive incentives are meaningful enough to seek and build-in fixes to the system. Just as a new system might have unintended and unanticipated consequences so might changing the system.[2]

Any program or law that is shown to produce counter-productive incentives or have adverse consequences should be reviewed, not just assistance programs. Where the adverse aspects of a program are overshadowed by the good the program does, elimination of the program would not be a

---

[1] Krugman, Paul, "The Punishment Cure," The New York Times, December 8, 2013.
[2] Mulligan, Casey B., "Policies That Discourage Full-Time Work," The New York Times, January 8, 2014.

remedy and fixes should be sought. But where no good comes of program, like the US tax incentive for American companies to move operations offshore, the program or incentive should be eliminated.

Examples abound. Discovering that a pattern exists of working just so long as to qualify for a new round of unemployment benefits, should disqualify the applicant. A person with a seasonal job should not be able to claim unemployment benefits off-season, but should be required to take any other type of employment during the off-season. A person laid off under circumstances that indicate the particular job is gone forever should not receive unemployment benefits while seeking those non-existent jobs; retraining for other jobs should be required or the unemployment benefits denied.

In each situation, knowledgeable persons working with the program should shoulder the responsibility for improving the program, for making it more efficient, for making it less costly and for ridding the program of the bad aspects. If not them, who?

Such knowledgeable persons (e.g., former administrators, lawyers dealing with the program, administrative judges and the like) should seek each other, form appropriate groups to pursue change or write articles proposing fixes.[1]

---

[1] E.g., Frye, D. Randall, "Fixing Disability Courts," The New York Times, January 19, 2014.

PERPETUATING FRAUD-PRONE PROGRAMS

America has to curtail or eliminate otherwise good programs that have become un-administrable or fraud ridden, rather than continuing to pay the freight. We seem to go too far in trying to make such programs work instead of just closing them down. As a nation, we cannot and should not devote our time, energy and treasure to make something work that is inherently unworkable. But we must be certain that the program is in fact unworkable.

For example, the plotters and schemers have found ways to get claims for disability approved when disability does not exist. Social media photographs of healthy claimants had provided false-claim alerts, but the foolish postings probably dried up. Normally, it is difficult, expensive or impossible to prove that someone does not have a back-ache or other aliment.

Lawyers even advertise that they have doctors who are familiar with disability claims. It could just be a friendly offer of assistance, but it could also refer to friendly doctors having extensive records of getting claims approved. It has become a virtual certainly that anyone who spends the time and effort to pursue a disability claim would be successful irrespective of whether the person actually qualifies.

In one scheme as many as 1,000 people (including many retired and pensioned New York City police officers and firefighters) were suspected of bilking $400 million from the Social Security disability system.[1]

One alternative is to improve the system,[2] throwing more money at the verification process but doomed to failure unless a new system to evaluate disability is found. And that will not be found unless it is in the form of inappropriate star-chamber medical trials conducted at an enormous cost.

No matter how well-meaning such programs might have been, the programs should be terminated with the money saved devoted to other programs or approaches.

Many of the truly disabled collect for their injuries from their employers or from lawsuits they file. Other disable workers have pensions that provide adequate support when they retire.

It would not be unhuman to eliminate benefits for those who already had a monetary recover or have adequate support in terms of pensions or personal wealth. Means testing claimants could reasonably be mandated.

Which, in turn, suggests that the entire disability program could be abandoned with the people needing support being handled by the welfare system. Eliminating the wasteful and superfluous disability component of the Social Security System might help preserve the rest of the system, but it wouldn't be a free-ride as the welfare system might need help.

---

[1] Rashbaum, William K., and McKinley Jr., James C., "Charges for 106 in Huge Fraud Over Disability," The New York Times, January 7, 2014.
[2] Frye, D. Randall, "Fixing Disability Courts," The New York Times, January 19, 2014.

This approach, and others that make sense (perhaps like retraining the disabled for jobs they are able to handle), deserve study because it does seem wasteful to perpetuate expensive programs so susceptible to fraud. We should be able to find better and more economical ways to provide assistance to those who need it.

In other situations where abuses are showing up, we should stop paying for the abused procedure or activity even though some people might be deprived of legitimately needed care. Although potentially severe on those with legitimate needs, approaches like this could help preserve of the overall program for the greater good and alternative or secondary procedures adopted were necessary.

For instance, media exposés have recently shown that some doctors and physical therapists have billed Medicare for multi-millions of dollars <u>each</u> even though they are single practitioners. This enrages, gives the entire Medicare program a black-eye, and suggests that program administrators have to be inept to allow it.

If those practices or procedures cannot be instantly controlled, and it seems that they can't, those practices and procedure should be eliminated immediately, with the chips falling where they may, and forcing alternate treatments that aren't or can't be abuse.

Our society can no longer afford the largesse of the past. We know that there is no free lunch, so what we waste on the one hand keeps us from benefiting elsewhere. As we can't do everything, we are constantly drawing a line. In all instances, we should draw against abuse and fraud. We can try to do the best we can with any adverse consequences, but we should still let the chips fall where they may in realization that greater good will be served elsewhere.

Should America stem its decline and become rich again, we can reverse this. But for now, it is necessary.

GAMING CONTRACT LAW

When it comes to contracts, the overwhelming economic power belongs to large business enterprises doing business with the general public.

An explicit or implicit contract is considered struck between the parties when products or services are sold. The business enterprise offers to sell its product or provide its services at a price and under the stated conditions and the customer accepts (the contract is entered into at this point) or walks way.

Normally, there is no written contract when products are being sold at a stated price in a store. The warranty that might be included in the product packaging appears to be a formal agreement or contract, but the customer seldom reads the warranty before buying the product. A customer buying the product is stuck with the warranty as written.

Besides there is no way a customer could get the warranty altered. Product manufacturers write warranties they want to write within what the law allows, and competing manufacturers are likely to have the same language. The only option the customer has is to walk away and that accomplishes nothing.

In some industries, like automobile, warranties have become a competitive matter and are prominently disclosed if not specifically advertised, but still it is a take-it-or-leave it proposition.

Service industries usually use written signed contracts (or, if digital, signing by checking a box) that describe the scope of the service and the conditions under which those services are rendered, with the time-term included. Again it is a take-it-or-leave it proposition, with the customer having no option to change it and basically no alternative since all the vendor would essentially have the same terms.

To be sure, prices vary, time-terms vary, and service speeds or other aspects might vary and be disclosed if not emphasized, but there is no way to change the fine print. And very few customers have the time, inclination or stamina to read the extensive fine print, to say nothing about understanding it.

As a result, businesses are in a position to take advantage of their customers and they do so.

For instance, the stock-brokerage industry requires the customer to yield rights given by law by requiring customers to sign mandatory arbitration agreements. This means that the customer cannot sue individually or in a class action group but has to accept what an arbitrator decides based on what the contract defined as wrongdoing.

Sometimes the contract bars the customer from publically disclosing her or his claim against the company (as a lawsuit would) even if the company deliberately mislead, lied or used fraud. This allows predators to continue to find new victims, while society should demand or at least allow disclosure and dissemination. The wolves of Wall Street thrive on such practices.

This is a set-up for abuse, and abuses have taken place. The fault rests with contract law as the courts have interpreted for centuries, not adjusting to modern society. It is another instance of the taking a good thing, this time contract law, and going too far with it. Some would stay that society cannot go too far with a rule of law, but that should not be a valid argument where the law is being used to abuse.

Of course, the courts should enforce the normal provisions found in contracts, like forcing the customer to pay the agreed price for the agreed term. It is generally a good thing to hold a person to other provisions agreed to in a contract, provisions that are reasonable and pertinent to the rendering of the services.

But that should not extend to provisions that are extraneous to the services being rendered. The companies know the customers do not read the contracts, and the judges would also know it, perhaps by their not reading the fine print when they sign for services. Just looking at the length of the contacts written by a company, by an army of lawyers, and it becomes obvious that customers (even judicial customers) would not read it.

Our contract law emanates from bygone centuries, when contracts were negotiated face to face between parties who basically knew what they were doing. Today, the contracts are pre-printed and are of such length and detail that it is known to all (the business enterprises, lawyers and judges) that they are not read by the person who <u>presumably</u> agree with the terms of the contract when he or she signs it.

The presumption is wrong, and known to be wrong by all, including judges. Yet, using century old contract law precedents, judges persist on basing their holdings on a meeting-of-the-minds agreement known by the judges to not exist.

All that can reasonably be said, and should be held by judges today, is that the customer agreed to reasonable terms that could be expected in that type of commercial transaction, with the content covering only the elements necessary to such a contract. Let me explain this.

The customer should be bound by any stated price for the product or service and any stated term of service, and be implicitly bound by reasonable terms and other provisions necessarily found in such contracts.

For instance, fine print requiring the customer to make public appearances demonstrating the product should not be enforced by the courts even though the customer signed the contract. The customer would not ordinary anticipate that the agreement would contain such a provision. Judges would or should reasonably believe that the customer would not have read the contract, and also reasonably believe the seller would know this. The judge should, in equity, disregard the extraneous provision. And, there should also be a law requiring the judge to do so.

The same should apply to forced arbitration provisions and the like, which are not normally known to the public, not understood, and not expected when the customer is merely buying a product or services.

A standard of reasonableness should prevail in enforcing implicit contracts. An implicit contract arises, for instance, where a customer, client or patient agrees to buy or engage services without price or any other terms being mentions.

Assume a doctor charges a $1,000 fee for a procedure done in the office in ten minutes, and no price had been mentioned to the patient. It is the doctors "normal" fee as stated in a price list the doctors maintains in the office, but not specifically brought to the attention of the patient. Assume that patients with insurance pay only $100 and the doctor has many of them.

It can logically be said that the patient implicitly agreed to pay the doctor a reasonable fee, not any amount the doctor choses to charge. If it were the latter, the doctor could charge $10,000 or $100,000 or even a million dollars.

Thus, reasonableness must be the controlling standard -- not what's on the doctor's fee list, not what an organization of like doctors have on its list, but rather what is being accepted by the doctor when true negotiation and agreement was involved. That would be the $100 fee the doctor agreed to accept from by insurance companies (perhaps adjusted somewhat for volume). Perhaps, $150 might be reasonable fee instead of the $1,000 charged, but not more.

Thus, the proposition advanced here is that public policy, equity concepts, and perhaps economic duress considerations should allow, and probably require, the courts to disregard abusive "contractual" provisions.

These would be provisions in the non-negotiated contracts prepared by one party and required to be signed by the other party without alteration. These would be the provisions that work to the advantage of the party that prepared the agreement and to the disadvantage of the other party. These would be the provisions that weren't likely to be read or understood by the customers who were asked to sign the contract. These would be the provisions that operate to have the signing customer yield a right, privilege or the benefit of any law favoring or available to the customer.

There is no way to know how far contractual abuse of customers in the marketplace extend. Based on a recently uncovered situations, the abuse might be much greater than anybody could anticipate.

For instance, a particularly clever lawyer found a way to effectively create a digital contract with customers who download coupons to buy the company's products. By downloading the coupon, the customer agreed to a contract with the company. There were also other things, not relevant here, the customer could do online in the website which would also be deemed to have created a contract.

The contract created online by downloading the coupon had the customer yield the right to sue the manufacturer. It forced arbitration. The company apparently preferred the online coupon approach to placing a statement on product packaging stating the company couldn't be sued. That would not have gone across very well with customers.

And it didn't go across very well when a newspaper disclosed that customers who downloaded coupons to buy

Cheerios agreed by doing the download to yield the right to sue General Mills and instead were forced into informal email proceedings or binding arbitration.[1] Three days after the publication of the newspaper article, and the immense criticism it triggered in social media, General Mills reversed its position and gave up its legal stratagem.[2]

This indirectly suggest that there is much more going on in the marketplace to contractually bind or abuse customers. Perhaps the best example of how the scope of this abuse can expand was a restaurant hanging a sign on its door making entry into the restaurant into an agreement to settle any dispute (e.g., getting poisoned) through arbitration.

Unreadable or unread non-negotiated contracts could also allow a product producer to take certain advantages, perhaps evading laws specially designed to stop that.

A recent newspaper article explained how Tesla, the electric car manufacturer, sold directly to customers instead of selling the usual way through car dealerships.

A Wisconsin purchaser bought a Tesla which was out of service 66 days during the first year for repairs. Wisconsin's lemon-automobile law allowed the filing of lawsuits and barred purchasers from waiving that right through forced arbitration. The customer discovered that the five page purchase contract he signed required all disputes to be settled

---

[1] Strom, Stephanie, "When 'Liking' a Brand Online Voids the Right to Sue," The New York Times, April 16, 2014.

[2] Strom, Stephanie, "General Mills Reverses Itself on Consumers' Right to Sue," The New York Times, April 20, 2014.

in arbitration in California, but notwithstanding that he sued Tesla.[1]

The State of Wisconsin had addressed the never ending controversies between car dealerships and customers by establishing lemon standards and allowing customers to return lemons for refunds. It also voided any waiver of the rights granted by the law. Using local dealerships was the national standard way of sells cars until Tesla started to sell direct.

It is not clear whether Tesla isn't subject to such lemon laws because it doesn't sell through car dealerships. Perhaps bypassing the lemon laws contributed to Tesla deciding to bypass the use of dealerships. Perhaps Tesla was aiming only a forcing binding arbitration so as to reduce its litigation costs (unfortunately making it a bit hard on its national customers having to arbitrate in California). But put aside such speculation as to Tesla's business decisions as Tesla clearly has a right to conduct business the way it wants to.

But society also has a right to examine the potential use of contract law in an abusive fashion. Perhaps we should have a national law that cannot be waived by any party -- a law applicable to all contacts not personally negotiated face-to-face and not likely to be read in full or turned over to a lawyer to do so. That law could forbid all extraneous contractual provisions not inherent in making a sale or

---

[1] Vielmetti, Bruce, "Wisconsin man claims $95,000 electric Tesla is a lemon," Milwaukee Journal Sentinel, April 8, 2014.

rendering a service, defined to include forced binding arbitration, confidentiality provisions and the like.

It should be obvious that contractual abuse of customers has already gone too far and promises to get worse. It does not help our economy nor speak well for America.

If such a law increases the cost of doing business, and it might, the cost could be passed on to customers to the extent that products and services are not already priced at what the market will bear. If the cost must be absorbed, it would only hurt the profits of the abusers, and they can walk away from the business just as they only give their customer the right to walk away from their services or products. Those who do not abuse would have no increase in cost.

Contract law can be and is being abused, with every indication that it will accelerate. And success in contractual abuse will encourage other types of legal abuse. We have to put a stop to all abuses of law.

THE UNEVEN LITIGATION PLAYING FIELD

Even good litigation practices can be carried too far.

The plaintiff who loses a law suit does not normally pay the legal costs of the defendant it sued. Having losing plaintiffs bear the legal costs of winning defendants would discourage plaintiffs from suing, and no public policy suggests that. However, where the litigation is abusive or there is an uneven litigation playing-field, it might be a good idea to have a losing plaintiff pay the legal costs of the successful defendant.

The uneven litigation playing-field is found where a large corporation sues a small company (or wealthy person sues a poor person) who cannot afford to defend. If the defendant doesn't have the wherewithal to hire a lawyer, to say nothing hiring a competent or specialized lawyer, the lawsuit would effectively amount to unfair competition or downright extortion.

Changing the law to have the losing plaintiff pay the defendants legal costs would allow the small or poor defendant to hire a competent lawyer on a contingent basis. The lawyer would undertake the defense if the lawyer thought he or she would win and collect the fee. If lawyer loses, the lawyer doesn't collect, but that is the risk in all contingent fee arrangements. Lawyers tend to do well with contingent fees (as they can be selective in accepting them) and the small and poor defendants are defended, win or lose.

To have losing plaintiffs always bear the legal costs of a successful defendant can be justified since it is the plaintiff who determines whether filing the lawsuit would be worthwhile. A loser-pays rule would only deter plaintiffs from filing questionable, weak or abusive lawsuits. A loser-pays rule should reduce the judicial workload, reduce the cost to society of maintaining the judicial system, and conserve the time and energy of all the players and allow them to move on to more fruitful things.

The other side of that coin is that shifting the legal costs of the defendant to losing plaintiffs could deter lawsuits against wealthy. The wealthy defendant can afford to run-up extraordinarily high legal bills and pay them as the loser. But if the wealthy wins, the plaintiff would be saddled with the huge legal bills, which would serve to deter plaintiffs from suing the well healed.

Instead of a hard and fixed rule, the presiding judge or a standing committee of judges could be authorized to determine which party should bear the legal costs and the amount thereof, and directed to take into account the economic position of the parties. Of course, the wealthy and powerful would call this un-American, but perpetuating an uneven litigation playing-field is also un-American.

The law and the courts do have an interest in leveling the litigation playing-field. This is shown by existing law allowing consumers (and others groups) to band together in class-action suits against large companies that would not otherwise be sued because the damage to each consumer is too small to justifying bringing suit. Thus, it is American, not un-American, to have laws that serve to level the litigation playing-field.

Of course, companies potentially facing such class-action lawsuits attempt to get the Supreme Court to curtail those suits, with the argumentation before the court and the questioning by the Justices making it difficult guess the outcome[1] Corporations have been successful in this, ostensibly dependent on the political make-up of the court.

---

[1] Liptak, Adam, "Justices May Limit Securities Fraud Suits," The New York Times, March 5, 2014.
Savage, David G., "Supreme Court is unlikely to halt class-action stock fraud lawsuits," Los Angeles Times, March 5, 2014.

The complaint leveled against these class-action suits is that only the lawyers bringing the lawsuits are enriched through the large fees they get while each claimant in the class gets very little. That is true, but the remedy is limiting the fees, not curtailing class-action suits. In class-action lawsuits, courts should limit the lawyer's share to a reasonable fee based on time spent, not based on a percentage of the total recovery because there are so many claimants involved and the total amount involved is large without adding that much to the lawyer's workload.

While the corporate defendant might be called upon to pay a large amount of damages even though each claimant in the class gets very little, it is clear that the playing-field is leveled by class-action lawsuits and that alone justifies class-action lawsuits.

A case in point is the class-action lawsuit by almost 65,000 software engineers against four of the biggest software and i-product companies.[1] Individually, the engineers would have gotten nowhere. Acting as a class, and probably helped because criminal activity may have been involved, they were successful in forcing a settlement and actually recovering significant damages.

In somewhat allied situations where workers are illegally short-changed in their wages, law enforcement officials effectively substitute for class-action lawsuits and obtain recoveries for the workers.[2]

---

[1] Editorial, "Wage Theft Across the Board," The New York Times, April 21, 2014.
[2] *Ibid.*

America should strive to protect ordinary citizens in lawsuits whenever it can since the litigation playing-field is so stacked against them, particularly when powerful interests are involved.

Just like America should not condone government of, by, and for the large and powerful, America shouldn't condone a legal system that is of, by and for the large and powerful.

EQUITY versus THE LETTER OF THE LAW

Abuses of the rule of law are to be found in how the courts seem to accept deception, subterfuge and lack of substance by sticking to the very letter of the law.

Shams, subterfuges and deceptions work since they are invariably designed to meet the letter of the law while they abuse, cheat and steal. And some judges seem to accept the rubric that anything not specifically forbidden is allowed under the rule of law. Since the shams, subterfuges and deceptions are not specifically forbidden in so many words in the law, the some judges feel obliged to allow them.

This is found in all areas of the law and in particular the complex ones like taxation and trade. In taxation, deception might rest in the lack of substance in the business structures used and in the intercompany arrangements. In trade, the difficulty might rest on where a product is made, which can be deceptively complex.

Say a product made in Country X is subject to a higher customs rate when it enters into the United States because the foreign government subsidized its manufacture. But, instead of finishing the product in Country X, the components were shipped to County Y for simple assembly and the claim is made that it is a product of Country Y and thus the higher duty rate is avoided.[1]

This is deception if there is no economic or other rational reason not to assemble in Country X. It lacks substance if very little is done in Country X. It's a sham if the whole thing was arranged to just to reduce customs duties. To give credence to such an arrangement because the law doesn't forbid assembly in a third country is an abuse of the rule of law and is the fault of judges rigidly honoring the letter of the law even when the law is being abused.

Other types of abuses are found in other areas of the law. Normally the rule of law works as a shield to protect those who follow and abide by it. Yet it is possible to abuse the rule of law by using it as a sword to deliberately hurt another or for extortion.

For example, a lien can be filed against property (a home, car, farm land etc.) by anyone. Even if there is no basis for the filing, the person filing the lien would face no deterrent, expense or penalty when the lien is removed because the underlying claim cannot be proven. The operation of this law sets the stage for using bogus lien-filings as a sword.

Bogus lien-filings are now being used for political purposes or just to get even with someone because, in

---

[1] Cardwell, Diane, "U.S. Solar Panel Maker Seeks to Close Loophole in Duties on Chinese Products," The New York Times, December 31, 2013.

removing the bogus lien, the property owner incurs expenses and must devote time and effort to it.[1]

When the law can be taken so far that it becomes a sword used to punish and harm, we should feel obliged to redress the law. That is, we should change the law but not in ways that burdens society with additional costs.

Criminalizing bogus filings is a way to go, as some states have done, but that adds another layer of expense to society in terms of increasing enforcement and judiciary costs in pursing the bogus filers.

The era of saddling society with more and more expense and diverting funds away from more fruitful endeavors is gone; we can no longer afford it. We have to find more creative ways to deal with our problems, getting rid of confrontational situations instead of relying on confrontation for justice.

For example, the purpose of liens is to help contractors collect their bills without resorting to the courts. Thus, the law assumes the contractor is the good person seeking what is owed, while the property owner is the bad person shirking payment. Yet, the contractor might be abusing the situation by trying to extort an excessive payment from the property owner. Society should try to be fair to both the contractor and the property owner. Society should aim to both stop the filing of bogus liens, and also to stop extortion.

For instance, the state could require the contractor to deposit a contingent fee upon the filing a lien, the fee to be

---

[1] Goode, Erica, "In Paper War, Flood of Liens Is the Weapon," The New York Times, August 23, 2013.

recovered when the contractors claim is paid in full or partially forfeited to the state if the lien claim proved to be excessive by not collecting it in full.

In still another area concerning the bankruptcy laws, sticking to the letter of the law can result in injustice. This is illustrated by how General Motors is attempting to limit its liability under the bankruptcy laws for defective ignitions switches (that led to many accidents and deaths) because the cars were manufactured by GM before 2009 and GM exited bankruptcy in 2009.[1]

Our bankruptcy law is a good law, as witness it keeping GM from being liquidated. Upon exiting bankruptcy, the bankrupt is protected from all prior claims. Yet the car owners did not then know they would have a damage or repair claim that should have been filed while the bankruptcy was pending in court.

Obviously, this is an injustice which gets a person to wonder whether the courts and the legislatures writing the laws ever consider equity and their power to make exceptions when equity calls for it.

Aside from GM when knew of the dangerous defect, which could be relevant, there is no reason to run a statute that time-limits the filing of a claim in bankruptcy (or the filing of any lawsuit) where the harmed person does not know nor could have known of the wrongdoing.

Or another more tailored approach could be used for bankruptcy proceedings. It is known that cars or other

---

[1] Stout, Hilary, and Vlasic, Bill, "G.M. Seeks to Fend Off Lawsuits Over Switch," The New York Times, April 22, 2014.

products can and do have defects that will become known on their own timetables. Estimates could have been made and reserved for before the bankrupt exited bankruptcy, with some residual creditor getting the leftovers a reasonable time after the bankruptcy closed.

To be sure, a statute of limitations is another good thing because it isn't fair to have potential liability hanging over a business indefinitely. On the same token, the corollary that necessarily flows from protecting the business from loss is that the loss is saddled on someone else, in this case the purchaser of the car. We tend to focus on the protection side while ignoring the shifting of loss to some innocent party.

Society chose to impose a statutory term-limitation of an appropriate length for pursuing a legal claim as being the greater good to the society, but the statute of limitations need not have been absolute. Although any limitation would favor one party over another, the limitation need not have applied in egregious situations which should include all instances where the harmed party did not know, nor could have known, that she or he had been harmed.

The point here is not to advocate any particular solutions, but to suggest that thought be given new ways to handle both abuse and egregious situations without increasing costs to society. It is about time that we got our legislators to clean-up our house instead of just trying to score points over the other political party.

And it about time that judges stop accepting shams, subterfuges, and deceptions in a rigid application of the rule of law and start looking to substance.

PURSUING FAVORITES & LACKING BALANCE

We all have favorites that lead us to go overboard in one direction or another. While it is said that some of us believe in "spending, spending and more spending" and other are anti-spending, it seems that we all favor spending on what interest us.

Some of us would spend boundlessly on the military and little on education, while others would do it the reverse way. We all see life though our particular glasses and some of us are myopic, seeing only what we want to see.

We all have our own roster of favorites with something to be said for every selection. Many Americans feel we need a strong military, and rightfully so, but where is the line to be drawn? Many Americans favor education, again rightfully so, and again it is a question of where the line is to be drawn?

It is the same all the way down the list of favorites, each of which has something to be said for it, and each needing a line drawn as to how much money should be devoted to it because we do not have the money to do everything.

Once again we encounter the American tendency to go too far in what we do, especially with an admittedly worthwhile effort (which, by definition, are the ones we favor). It is something we must learn to curb.[1]

Political parties might tend to favor one area or another, but there are many members in each party that have different

---

[1] Editorial, "Reality Sets In," The New York Times, November 9, 2013.

Editorial, "Putting Military Pay on the Table," The New York Times, November 30, 2013.

views. When a <u>bipartisan</u> Secretary of Defense, whose job is to manage and represent the interests of the military, advocated cuts in military pay, housing and health care benefits,[1] an uproar from the single-focus military crowd ensued.

Many of us tend to be singe-focus, going too far in endlessly advocating bigger and better in what we favor and brooking no cut-backs. Yet, the same people see nothing wrong about endlessly advocating cut backs in what the other guy or gal favors.

This is not a formula for national well-being. It is divisive and can only lead to dysfunction and decay. As a nation, America will get nowhere if there is not some give politically.

We must learn to accept the "other" and their views, and compromise. We can't fight about everything as that can only lead to disaster.

We are stuck with the "other." We can't get rid of them. So we must learn to compromise for our own good.

AFFIRMATIVE ACTION IN EDUCATION

Not only have the desirable affirmative action programs in our colleges gone too far, it now appears that instead of rolling them back they should be jettisoned.

I make this personal because I had been a strong advocate of affirmative action in our universities and colleges

---

[1] Miller, Jake, "Defense Secretary Chuck Hagel to recommend deep budget cuts targeting pay, benefits," CBS News, February 23, 2014.

and had recently changed my views, perhaps because the surrounding conditions have changes. The matter has eaten away at me for almost a decade.

I did strongly believe that America needed to aid blacks who had been so discriminated against, but I was surprised to learn that the affirmative action programs served more to aid blacks from abroad rather than descendants of America's slaves.

Moreover, I was truly shocked by the size of the SAT advantage given by one of the finest of universities, which to me would have made their minority students almost un-hirable because potential employers could not know how good they really were.

I had learned at a lecture that Princeton University gave preferences to black applicants that the lecturer quantified as being the equivalent of about 300 extra points on the SATS. Latinos were given about 150 extra points and Asians had about 100 SATS points subtracted, if my memory serves me correctly.

Asians now appeared to be the Jews of yesteryear who were discriminated against for crowding out others.

Not a word was mentioned at the lecture about academic excellence. The lecture was all about diversity; racial, national and even international diversity.

In my mind I started to relate the granting of seats in our top schools based on diversity rather than academic excellence with the beginning of America's decline in this world, although the connection may be tenuous.

Identifying, recruiting, and inducing the poor blacks to enroll in college and then giving them financial aid is expensive to the colleges that undertake such programs.[1] Voters in California abolished affirmative action by approving Proposition 209 in 1996.[2]

Thereupon affirmative action in California shifted to emphasizing programs aimed at overcoming the disadvantages all poor students face because of economic, social and family barriers. Academic standards for admission were not reduced for the poor, but programs were aimed at raising the poor's interest in education and improving their academic skills.

Colleges struggling for national diversity also add expense by departing from merely choosing between the equally qualified applicants from other states to adopting reach-out programs to bolster geographic diversity. While the advantage to students of encountering the "other" in college is not being questioned, the advantage in seeking students from every state and from countries as far flung as Madagascar does appear questionable.

A person might also wonder why it is in America's national interest to devote so many seats in our finest universities to accommodating foreign students, and, additionally, wonder why these universities should take it upon themselves to do so.

---

[1] Perez-Pena, Richard, "Universities Show Uneven Efforts in Enrolling Poor," The New York Times, May 30, 2013.

[2] Perez-Pena, Richard, "In California, Push for College Diversity Starts Earlier," The New York Times, May 7, 2013.

Adjusting for population sizes, 20% or so fewer seats in the top schools are available to American teenagers than was available to their parents or grandparents.[1] Many of the lost seats were devoted foreign students and international diversification.

And then we make it even harder for American teenage applicants. Most of them are being rejected by our prestigious school, up to 95% being rejected even though they are indistinguishable from those who get accepted.[2] The wisdom of affirmative action programs that reduce admission standards for others has to be questioned.

The question naturally arises as to why take any less-qualified student when the universities turn away so many qualified students? Imagine, 95% of applicants, all being of the best and brightest, are turned away. And the difficulty faced by the best and brightest American teenagers getting into the better universities is compounded by the large number of seats given to foreign students.

Where is the justice in this? And while this is on the table, let's also explore the justice of giving away seats to athletes, band players, or others on any basis other than academic excellence?

A number of affirmative action cases are pending in the

---

[1] Leonhardt, David, "Getting Into the Ivies," The New York Times, April 26, 2014.

[2] Perez-Pena, Richard, "Best, Brightest and Rejected: Elite Colleges Turn Away Up to 95%," The New York Times, April 8, 2014.

courts.[1] Opinion is divided as to what the Supreme Court should do.[2] It is up to the Supreme Court to set the pattern for affirmative action in our colleges.

However, in 2013, Miss Fisher challenged the constitutionality of a university's affirmative action program based on race and the Supreme Court avoided a direct answer, reprimanding the case for reconsideration.[3]

In 2014, the Supreme Court upheld a constitutional amendment approved by Michigan voters that banned affirmative action by the state's public universities, placing emphasis on the public vote.[4] It's not clear whether the Supreme Court is holding back, waiting for society to address the matter.

In my view, the universities are educational institutions, not social policy institutions, nor vehicles of their administrators. The university function is to graduate the best

---

[1] Editorial, "False Equality in Michigan," The New York Times, October 13, 2013.
Liptak, Adam, "Justices Weigh Michigan Law and Race in College Admissions," The New York Times, October 15, 2013.
Fernandez, Manny, "Texas University's Race Admissions Policy Is Debated Before a Federal Court," The New York Times, November 13, 2013.

[2] Espenshade, Thomas J., "Moving Beyond Affirmative Action," The New York Times, October 4, 2012.
Keller, Bill, "Affirmative Reaction," The New York Times, June 9, 2013.
Ifill, Sherrilyn A., "Race vs. Class: The False Dichotomy," The New York Times, June 13, 2013.

[3] Liptak, Adam, "Justices Step Up Scrutiny of Race in College Entry," The New York Times, June 24, 2013.

[4] Liptak, Adam, "Court Backs Michigan on Affirmative Action," The New York Times, April 22, 2014.

educated in the fields the students choose, and not try to impose any other standard or goal as to making students well-rounded or advocating the "good life" or anything else. These are the functions of other organizations and institutions and, of course, parents.

With our colleges being perennially short of funds and raising tuitions much faster than the pace of inflation, a person might well wonder why a college should allocate any funds for any purpose other than the pursuit of academic excellence. Not only is the purpose of our institutions of higher learning to educate and conduct research, it would appear they have no right to devote their funds to any other purpose.

Diversity efforts are expensive in terms of employing staffs to handle them, diverting the time and attention of the top administrators to these efforts, and incurring the out-of-pocket costs involved in these efforts, including the financial aid distributed to those accepted only for diversity purposes.

Not only are there now indications that the better colleges have largely failed in their efforts to recruit economically disadvantaged students,[1] there are indications that the disadvantaged students they were able to attract were "mismatched" and many did poorly at those colleges because

---

[1] Leonhardt, David, "Better Colleges Failing to Lure Talented Poor," The New York Times, March 16, 2013

Bellafante, Ginia, "A Chance at Learning," The New York Times, August 23, 2013.

they couldn't keep up.[1] They would have been better off elsewhere.

It might be provincial to suggest that the sole purpose of our higher-education institutions should be to educate (and further education by conducting research) and leave to others the efforts to make-up for past sins, to elevate the poor, and the like. Government on all levels already have programs to do this, and public-spirited citizens also contribute.

It seems that America should focus more on improving programs it does have, like the Pell Grants,[2] and keep the colleges from doing it. Also, America is beginning to focus on the elementary schools, even pre-school, and other programs[3] as having more potential to elevate and diversity.

We will get excellence in education only when the colleges stick to recruiting the best academically qualified students and only those, leaving diversity to others.

America sorely needs to seek excellence in education in order to stem its decline in education ranking compared to other nations and to help reverse its economic decline.

While our universities and colleges must necessarily discriminate amongst applicants on the basis of academic excellence, which is inherent in their function, it is unclear

---

[1] Slater, Dan, "Does Affirmative Action Do What It Should?" The New York Times, March 16, 2013.
[2] Baum, Sandy, and Conklin, Kristin, and Johnson, Nate, "Stop Penalizing Poor College Students," The New York Times, November 12, 2013.
[3] Rich, Motoko, "Pulling a More Diverse Group of Achievers Into the Advanced Placement Pool," The New York Times, November 26, 2013.

where they got the right to discriminate amongst applicants on any other basis.

It is time for the Supreme Court to strike down all affirmative action programs, and hopefully advocate an academic excellence standard. This would contribute much to stemming the decline of America.

EXPORTING DEMOCRACY

As individuals, we tend to promote what we personally have. We promote democracy because we believe in it or want to believe in it and yet give our legislators the lowest rankings ever.

We know our democracy is dysfunctional, but we blindly stick with it instead of re-structuring it. And we try to export our faulty product. Briefly put, if we can't get it right, we should stop telling others what to do.

And we shouldn't look to foreign practices to guide us domestically as the surrounding circumstance differ so much.

We were the first modern nation to be formed of, by, and for immigrants coming from diverse nations. Perhaps our founders invented a system of government based on the separation of powers because we were such a diverse nation -- since we were so diverse, we didn't trust each other and needed checks and balances. And, we proceeded to perpetuate that diversity by having a federal system with the states retaining powers that support diversity on a geographic basis.

The separation of powers suited us well, giving us the give and take in government between the diverse groups that allowed them to pull together and reach a consensus that satisfied everybody (until recent decades).

Even with the structure for consensus, some splits will always remain: poor and rich, young and old, secular and spiritual, and so forth. These differences can lead to war in the streets as we've recently seen around the world; wars that might be viewed as poor vs rich in Greece and secular vs spiritual in Egypt.[1]

We say we love our democracy, but have the lowest regard for how it works. Yet, democracy is engrained in us and we would naturally promote it abroad even though different considerations might influence our foreign policy. Trying to make the world look like us is not necessarily a valid foreign policy although it is natural to promote what we believe in.

Some would say our foreign policy should reflect our domestic laws and others say it should accord with international law, which is harder to identify. Even if the United Nations charter and practices is to be the international law standard, the ability of one nation to block United Nations action destroys the United Nations as any model.

Following domestic law and practices in our foreign policy might be viewed as the moral position for us, but some

---

[1] Kupchan, Charles A., "Democracy in Egypt Can Wait," The New York Times, August 16, 2013.

believe morality should not be the standard in our foreign affairs.[1]

In our endeavors to export democracy, we once again as a nation go too far in trying to extend what we consider to be a good thing. Despite its dysfunction, we love and honor our democracy but that does not necessarily mean we should try to export it or even try to advocate it abroad. The world is too diverse for that and our national interest might be otherwise.

RECIPROCITY WITH TAX-HAVEN COUNTRIES?

Respecting the sovereignty of other nations is the international law norm. But where there is no reciprocity of any sort and the foreign country supports itself at America's expense, there is no reason to recognize the sovereignty of that nation.

There is no law that addresses whether America should recognize a particular nation. If America wants, it can refuse to recognize the very existence of another nation or its government as a matter of foreign policy.

A noted advisor to President Kennedy advocated an amoral foreign policy,[2] one based on the national interest. Pursing the national interest is just fine when there is a moral side to it. With respect to tax-haven nations, it would be both against the national interest and outright immoral for America to extend normal treatment to tax-havens as it presently does.

---

[1] Schlesinger, Arthur, "The Necessary Amorality of Foreign Affairs," Harper's, August 1971.
[2] Ibid.

Tax havens harm us by extending their domestic bank-secrecy laws to foreigners, including Americans. What they do is right in America's face, designed to help Americans evade American laws, particularly the American tax laws. More has been said about this in the chapter on "*Economic Inequality.*"

Aside from depositing cash in tax-haven bank accounts, Americans also hide other assets in these banks or tax-haven trust companies. The banks and trust companies cannot disclose they have the deposits or assets because of the tax-haven secrecy laws. The US tax authorities cannot obtain any information from the tax-haven bank and the depositors escape US taxes. The other assets are hidden from other American who have claims against them and from American court orders.[1] Thus, the tax haven secrecy laws aid Americans in avoiding all sorts of American laws in addition to the American tax laws.

This can be stopped by Congress enacting a law forbidding American banks and other American financial institutions from sending or receiving money from those countries. The transfer of other assets to tax-havens could also be forbidden.

When America does this, those countries would become dreadful places for Americans to keep their money or other assets or set up trusts. Just the treat of enactment would be sufficient for the money and other assets to flee the tax-haven country, but America should actually enact such laws.

---

[1] Wayne, Leslie, "Cook Islands, a Paradise of Untouchable Assets," The New York Times, December 14, 2013.

Money and assets fleeing from the tax-haven counties to other countries where we have true reciprocity wouldn't present much a problem because those countries don't have such secrecy laws. Flowing the money and assets to another tax-haven country would accomplish nothing as our new law would cover or could be extended to cover all the tax-haven countries.

Thus, what is being suggested here is a program aimed at stopping America from being a patsy. Why America hadn't done something like this decades ago is not understandable. Perhaps it was the effectiveness of the lobbyists representing both foreign and domestic businesses and professional interests that benefit from the status quo. But supporting crime should not be part of the business of America.

TEACHERS' AND PROFESSORS' TENURE

The question presented is whether tenure, conceded to be a good thing, is being carried too far when it protects the incumbents who are no longer doing the jobs expected of them. But the rub is that the very purpose of tenure is to keep incumbents from being fired.

Perhaps tenure arose as a trade-off for accepting a job perceived to present limited advancement opportunity or lower compensation, but that does not appear to be the case. Teachers and professors earn decent, professional pay. Whatever the reason for tenure's existence in the schools and colleges, it exists.

By offering tenure, an implicit bargain was to be reached; do an adequate job for so many years and tenure would be granted on the assumption that the level of performance would continue in the future.

While an onlooker could reasonably accept that obvious misfits should not and would not have been conferred tenure, it also has to be accepted that performance can change over time and some teachers or professors can become below-par, lazy or incapable with age. But an implicit bargain was struck and society should live up to it (perhaps undertaking to review and tighten-up when tenure is to be granted).

The concept of tenure itself has recently been challenged as conflicting with the students' right to an education, the argument being that the poor performance of those with tenure deprive students of the education they should get and thus reduces future earnings.[1] Without getting into the legal arguments, the lawsuit is essentially an attack on the entire system of tenure.

The states and cities have rules and procedures as to both conferring teacher tenure (although one might raise an eyebrow about granting lifetime tenure after 18 months on the job) and as to removal for poor performance. As in the case of any endeavor, things do not always work out satisfactorily and the removal rules are not infallible, but that is no basis to dump the tenure system.

Going deeper, the purpose of tenure is to protect jobs. Most American workers have no such protection in their jobs

---

[1] Medina, Jennifer, "Competing Views of Teacher Tenure Are on Display in California Case," The New York Times, April 16, 2014.

whether they are janitors, salespeople, professionals or executives. They can be fired at any time and yet the pension roles show that many or most do keep their jobs until retirement age.

Just as with the administration of tenure, in commercial enterprise there are bad-case exceptions of terrible performers remaining employed and competent performers being unjustifiably fired, but that is no reason to dump our economic system. There are protections against unjust firings built into our economic system and into the tenure systems, which surely can be strengthened, showing that there is some recourse to be had by those unjustly fired.

So what is so special about teachers and professors that they alone as distinctive groups should have tenure? We would all like to get protection against unjust firing, but we all have to rely on what the law provides. Except, that is, for those in a position to impose their will on their employers.

If tenure is merely the result of having sufficient power to impose it on an employer, perhaps it is time to dump the entire system. The question is whether tenure exists just because one party was able to impose it on another, the stronger or more astute taking advantage of the weaker or less savvy, or whether the system of tenor for teachers and professors has reason and merit behind it.

Whether tenure has been taken too far is up to the courts. The issue now being litigated goes further; questing the entire tenure system because of the effect on the most important players, the students.

EFFORTS TO REHABILITATE PRISON INMATES

The day of the chain gang is rightfully gone and America has generally done a good job in humanizing its jails. We have adopted many worthwhile programs aimed at rehabilitation. We have gone very far in improving conditions and comforts in our jails, perhaps gone too far.

Yet, our system does not seem to deter criminality which could be ranked foremost amongst reasons for incarceration. We have the largest jail population in the world; we are the king of wardens.

It is about time we recognize that our programs and prison systems are failures. We have gone too far along a given path and it hasn't worked. Every year we incarcerate more and more. We can no longer handle the volume, so we outsource our prisons to profit-making businesses and it potentially costs us even more.

Now there is a new proposal to underwrite college classes for jail inmates in the belief it would improve their chances of finding jobs after release. It is also hoped that taking college class would moderate the personal behaviors traits of the selected inmates.

The proposal is every controversial because most citizens have to pay for sending their kids to college.[1]

Nevertheless, proposals like this deserve study based on the merits, starting with a review of how much it is likely to cost, including the cost of administration, how the student prisoners are to be selected from the inmate population,

---

[1] Keller, Bill, "College for Criminals," The New York Times, April 9, 2014.

whether there could be dangerous adverse reactions by inmates not offered college classes, and a host of other matters.

There must be solid ground for criticizing the program instead a pocketbook reaction that you personally had to pay for college or pay for sending your children to college.

And there must also be some proof that the program would produce the desired results as contrasted to speculation or self-serving professional opinions. That's enough of a job for the proponents and opponents.

But before the pros and cons are stacked up against the cost, there is another aspect that must be considered by our policy makers.

What kind of a message would society be sending if we educated jail inmates? Would we be making jail too comfortable, considering all the amenities already provided, for jail to be the deterrent to criminal behavior we want it to be? Could offering college classes actually turn out to be an incentive for criminal behavior? Would society be better off providing a less comfortable experience in jail, even some hard labor?

We hear so much about punishment and rehabilitation but not enough about how to reduce our jail population. Should we instead devote more time and attention in developing approaches that would reduce our jail populations? Should we stop being so pristine in putting people in jail for minor offenses? Should we devote more funds to pre-school and to broaching the esoteric topics of ethics and right and wrong in early education?

Let us try to estimate or guestimate how much it would cost to pull-out all stops on education and other programs aimed at deterring criminal behavior and compare that cost to the number of jail slots it would save. It seems to cost about $60,000 a year to incarcerate each inmate, before adding college classes.

Simply put, should society now put new money behind deterring criminal behavior instead of rehabilitation though incarceration? It seems that America has failed at both deterring criminal behavior (as witness the ever increasing jail population) and failed at rehabilitation (as shown by now needing to provide college classes to make rehabilitation work).

While it might not be clear whether America has already gone too far in improving its prison system, we can rightly say that we have gone too far in emphasizing rehabilitation and allowed it to overshadow efforts to deter crime. What we are doing is not working. That was implicitly recognized in coming forth with new rehabilitation proposals, like college classes.

Perhaps we should reverse course by making incarceration more of a deterrent to crime, and use the available funds on pre-school and youth programs aimed at curtailing criminal behavior.

How can we ourselves and others abroad have high esteem for America when it has more people in its jails than any other nation? Our ever increasing jail population, by itself, shows America to be on a downward path and fixing that should be part of preventing the fall of America.

PROTECTING INTELLECTUAL PROPERTY RIGHTS

Intellectual property rights deserve the highest degree of protection, but that also go can go too far.

The first requirement when it comes to property rights is that the property actually be owned. Ideas cannot be owned and thus cannot be protected. The product developed from the idea is what gets protected in the form of patents and copyrights. The underlying idea is still be available to all for additional research and development as long as those development patents and copyrights are not violated.

Substances that a person might find in nature or in the human body are not protectable, although many scientists have tried to protect what they had uncovered (e.g., specific genes) but not invented. The Supreme Court, in a rare unanimous opinion, rejected such a claim by deciding that the uncovering of what already existed is not an act of patentable invention.[1] Even though brilliance and creativity may be involved in uncovering what already exists, the found item was not invented, but an invented synthesized version would be patentable.

Society wants research and development to take place and thus it should rightfully protect the results. On the other hand, we want as much innovation as possible and broadly issuing patents keeps others from innovating in those areas.

Tightening the patent laws, as this Supreme Court case did, should foster innovation. The patent office should stop

---

[1] Liptak, Adam, "Justices, 9-0, Bar Patenting Human Genes," The New York Times, June 13, 2013.

issuing overly broad patents that have more potential to stifle innovation by others than protect the patent owner.

The practice of the patent office issuing overly broad patents has created an incentive for a large company to file for as many sweeping patents as possible as defensive tools even if the patents are unlikely to issue.[1] Gaming the patent laws, like gaming other laws, may be entering the scene. The matter is getting legislative attention in some states but not yet in Congress.[2]

It would make sense if patents should expire if not put to actual use in making and marketing real products in a reasonable period of time considering the nature of the patent. If the inventor can't make use of the invention in a reasonable period of time, it makes sense to let someone else try. We are unlikely to see this because definitions would be exceedingly difficult. Reducing patent life is also unlikely.

A fine line must be drawn between promoting innovation and protecting intellectual property rights. Those closest to patent work should propose solutions to outstanding problems and work with others on developing a patent policy for America because they are in the best position to do so.

The matter is too important to leave unattended because the future of America depends on innovation bolstered by effective intellectual property protection.

---

[1] Duhigg, Charles, and Lohr, Steve, "The Patent, Used as a Sword," The New York Times, October 7, 2012.

Feldman, Robin, "Slowing the Patent Trolls," The New York Times, March 28, 2014.

[2] Walters, Edgar, "Tech Companies Fight Back Against Patent Lawsuits," The Texas Tribune, January 23, 2014.

ABUSES BY OWNERS OF PATENTS

A new industry has sprung up: the patent-buying businesses. The new business entails buying patents and then bringing a host of lawsuits based on those patents.

Those businesses claim that they help inventors get what is due them since inventors do not have the inclination, time or money to pursue infringers. Other have shown that these firms pursue flimsy patent claims as a means of extortion, and are frequently called patent trolls.[1]

Flimsy claims are normally lost if litigated, but litigation is an expensive proposition for the defendants. Some defendants having no option but to pay-up, because the cost of litigation would be prohibitive.

Bringing the flimsy lawsuit using a contingent-fee lawyer would cost the patent troll nothing if it loses the lawsuit, but would cost the successful defendant plenty in legal costs to defend against the suit. It's a set-up for extortion. Legislatively shifting the burden of legal expenses, as previously suggested, would help but that is a long way off.

Legislative action to stop the patent trolls has been meager and the troll lawsuits crowd the courts, waste time and effort, and cost defendants tens of billions of dollars.[2] Federal judges have the power to shift the cost burden of litigation but don't do it very often.

---

[1] Wyatt, Edward, "Inventive, at Least in Court," The New York Times, July 16, 2013.

[2] Rader, Randall R., and Chien, Colleen V., and Hricik, David, "Make Patent Trolls Pay in Court," The New York Times, June 4, 2013.

Foreign government sponsored and owned companies are now being formed to acquire American patents. These patent troll-like companies have been launched by South Korea and France, with China and Japan also making moves into the business.[1] It is not known whether the purpose is to file lawsuits for profit as the American patent trolls do, or whether it is protective of their competing industries, or whether it is to obtain American innovations through the back door.

The matter is clearly getting out of hand. It is imperative for knowledgeable patent professionals to get together to devise ways to stop the trolls and protect American innovation.

---

[1] Levine, Dan, and Kim, Miyoung, "Nation-states enter contentious patent-buying business," Reuters, March 10, 2013.

Chapter 5

Personal Freedoms

Above most things, Americans cherish their personal freedoms, their rights, and their privileges. Many are granted by the U.S. Constitution, some are launched by the courts as being implied by the constitution, and all are limited in some fashion. The limitations show that our personal freedoms, rights and privileges are not absolute.

Most American insist on standing on their rights, not quite understanding that there can be limitations and the limitations can apply to them. Usually, it is one right confronting another as where one person's free speech endangers the right to security of another person. Or it could be claiming a religious freedom exemption from following a law that other Americans follow.

Just like Americans generally take good things too far, so too our personal freedom claims have gone too far and it is time to examine and roll-back the excesses. It is a most controversial matter as it seems that our personal freedoms are being attacked.

However, our personal freedoms are neither being attacked nor questioned. The discussion revolves around only those situations where we have taken our personal rights too far and roll-backs should be considered.

Cast in no particular order, the right to privacy is first addressed, followed by the right to bear arms, the freedom of religion, free speech, free press, free assembly, equality, protecting minorities and freedom of choice. Following that is a discussion of corporate "rights" taken too far.

Going Too Far With the Right to Privacy

Our Constitution does not mention any right to privacy. Without going into details, which would yield little, the courts created a right to privacy by interpreting the constitution to provide that right.

Amendments to the constitution, primarily the Bill of Rights, are cited as the constitutional basis for the right to privacy. A reading of the Bill of Right would show that the word "privacy" is not mentioned. However, there is much in the Bill of Rights that could be viewed as alluding to a right to privacy.

Thus the right privacy, which has taken a foremost position amongst the rights and freedoms of Americans, was created by a long line of cases, primarily Supreme Court cases. Or more accurately, it was based on the many allusions to the right of privacy found in the Amendments contained in the Bill of Rights.[1]

Thus, we have nothing concrete in the constitution about the right to privacy. At best, we have court cases, essentially Supreme Court cases that declare the right to privacy exists in the particular circumstances addressed by those cases. And those rights are not absolute, as they were limited by other case law.

For instance, citizens cannot be deprived of "life, liberty, or property, without due process of law," (Amendment XIV). Due process of law broadly laws refers to laws duly adopted under fair procedures.

Yet, society can deprive you of your "life" (for committing a crime), deprive you of your "liberty" (by jailing you) and deprive you of our property (by fining you). "Liberty" was also found to allude to the right to privacy, and that too can be limited or restricted by law. The Supreme Court, having found a right to privacy to exist, can apply that right as broadly or as narrowly as it desires.

In its decision in *Roe v. Wade*, the Supreme Court determined that the right to have abortions was founded on

---

[1] Forbidding enactment of any "law respecting an establishment of religion" (Amendment I) is said to create a right to belief, which in turn creates or suggests a right to privacy. Not permitting, in peace time, the quartering of soldiers in a house (Amendment III) is said to create a right of privacy of the house, which in turn creates or suggests the right to privacy in one's home. "The right of the people to be secure in their persons, houses, papers, and effects, against unreasonable searches and seizures..." (Amendment IV) is said to create a privacy of the person, without any limitations as to security or reasonableness. "The enumeration in the Constitution, of certain rights, shall not be construed to deny or disparage others retained by the people." (Amendment IX) could be said to create some generalized right to privacy.

the person's right of privacy. But, like all other rights, the right to have an abortion can be limited.

LIMITATIONS ON THE RIGHT TO PRIVACY

Whichever constitutional amendments the Supreme Court used to justify the existence of the right to privacy, limitations on the right can be found.

For example, we might be forced to testify in a court of law, which some people would say interferes both with their right to privacy and the right to liberty. Various laws allow you to be searched under certain circumstances, which is a limitation of the right to privacy emanating from the right to be secure in your person. The right to privacy arising from the right to be secure in your house can be breached by court orders and reasonable searches.

It would seem that the moment we leave our homes, we yield our right to privacy. Anybody can take our picture, including a police surveillance camera.[1] Anybody on the street has a right listen to listen to you conversing on your cell phone if they are close enough to do so, even though the circumstances indicate that the conversation was meant to be private. But the picture changes when electronic means of listening to the phone conversation are used, and the courts will grapple with that.

DATA-MINING AND THE RIGHT TO PRIVACY

Data-mining, by both businesses and law enforcement, has become an area of concern. It would seem difficult indeed to restrict businesses from collating information

---

[1] Sengupta, Somini, "Privacy Fears Grow as Cities Increase Surveillance," The New York Times, October 13, 2013.

legally obtained or voluntarily given. Usually the mined data is used in marketing to that person, or sold to others for that purpose.

The internet has been a significant source of data-mining, triggering a proposal for a Consumer Privacy Bill of Rights to protect against prying by internet companies.[1] That proposal went nowhere, but led to a write up of other proposals by privacy experts.[2] Databases have become secret blacklists where sensitive personal information has been accumulated under questionable circumstances or in violation of consumer protection laws.[3]

Mining bank data by the Central Intelligence Agency is allowed by the Patriot Act (overseen by the Foreign Intelligence Surveillance Court), other laws allow the National Security Agency to mine phone calls, and still other laws allow other privacy invasions by law enforcement.[4]

These laws limit the right to privacy in deference to the basic government function of protecting its citizens from harm by other citizens or foreigners. America has entered in no suicide pacts, which is what it would seem like if our courts allowed the right to privacy to keep the government from protecting us. Thus, there is justification for having different right-to-privacy limitations in the private and law enforcement spheres, with court the drawing the lines.

---

[1] Editorial, "A Second Front in the Privacy Wars," The New York Times, February 23, 2014.

[2] Nocera, Joe, "The Wild West of Privacy," The New York Times, February 24, 2014.

[3] Clifford, Stephanie, and Silver-Greenberg, Jessica, "Retailers Track Employee Thefts in Vast Databases," The New York Times, April 2, 2013.

[4] Savage, Charlie, and Mazzetti, Mark, "C.I.A. Collects Global Data on Transfers of Money," The New York Times, November 14, 2013.

Life and death considerations lead to special rules that have no bearing on commercial data-mining. The courts have to draw the between permissible data-mining by businesses and the public's right to privacy, which should also keep the courts busy.

Perhaps we can free the courts and society of this litigation burden by motivating Congress to pass a law making data-mining a contractual matter, allowing businesses to conduct data-mining if the customer explicitly opts-in, while forbidding the opt-out approach.

UNDERCUTTING THE RIGHT TO PRIVACY

As the right to privacy was created by litigation in the courts, an incentive to litigate is created for parties who want to limit or expand the right. And there is no end to legal creativity, pro or con.

Not all attacks on the right to privacy are direct and open. Subterfuges are being used to undercut the right to privacy.

For instance, the right to have an abortion as established in the *Roe v. Wade* Supreme Court case is founded on the right to privacy. There is still much opposition to abortions, with the Governor of Texas being quoted as wanting to "make abortion, at any stage, a thing of the past,"[1] and Texas passes a law in the name of health and safety that effectively closes most abortion clinics in the state.

There might have been justification in the health and safety claims, but perhaps not sufficient to justify particular remedy Texas enacted. Thus, it becomes difficult to determine whether the Texas law was just a subterfuge to

---

[1] Fernandez, Manny, "Abortion Law Pushes Texas Clinics to Close Doors," The New York Times, March 6, 2014.

curtail the right to abortion or there were sufficient, real medical concerns.

This is certain to get back to the Supreme Court, which should be able to deal with both subterfuges and real concerns. Hopefully, the court would also deal with the apparent right to endless litigation that so burdens America.

Also being pitted against the right to privacy is the freedom of the press to engage in what is said to be unwarranted snooping on the one hand or good journalism on the other hand.

Government as well as corporations can claim a similar right to privacy so as to protect their secrets from being leaked. Britain has an Official Secrets Act and other laws that protect government secrets even though those secrets were previously disclosed.[1] This allows the British government to limit dissemination of the disclosed secret.

Being stopped on the street and frisked by law enforcement pits the obligation of government to protect society (creating a citizen's right to protection?) against a citizen's right to be secure in her or his person. The showing that 90% of those stopped had broken no law[2] would be appalling condemnation of law enforcement to some people. Others might focus on the 10% that had broken laws, not an inconsequential number, and applauded law enforcement.

Undoubtedly the right to privacy is good. The courts will continue to define and redefine the right to privacy, limiting or expanding it as the surrounding circumstances require. But we shouldn't go too far in extending the right.

---

[1] Editorial, "British Press Freedom Under Threat," The New York Times, November 14, 2013.
[2] Editorial, "The Stop-and-Frisk Case Takes Another Turn," The New York Times, November 14, 2013.

For instance, we should not in the name of privacy allow corporations to hide the identities of their beneficial owners,[1] whether their shares are held in individual names or hidden in fiduciary accounts. We should not in the name of privacy allow contributors to any type of political organization or funneling vehicle to hide their names or the amounts contributed.

Perhaps it is time for America to legislatively define America's privacy policy. But considering our inability to come up with energy, industrial, tax or trade policies, writing a privacy policy would appear to be hopeless at the present time.

Defining and redefining our right to privacy should keep the courts busy.

Going Too Far With the Right to Bear Arms

The right of the citizenry to bear arms is well established in the constitution,[2] although the wording connects it to the need for a militia. That wording was disregarded in the passage of time, while the right of the people to keep and bear arms <u>without infringement</u> remained clear-cut.

---

[1] Somaiya, Ravi, "Obama Urged to Back Plan to List Owners of Shell Firms," The New York Times, June 9, 2013.
Editorial, "Change the Rules on Secret Money," The New York Times, February 18, 2014.

[2] "A well regulated militia, being necessary to the security of a free state, the right of the people to keep and bear arms, shall not be infringed." Amendment II (Bill of Rights) to the United States Constitution.

"Without infringement" also fell by the wayside over the years as enacted laws and court decisions placed various limitations the right to bear arms as was done with other rights found in the constitution.

Today there are limitations on carrying concealed arms, on the type of arms, on who cannot own arms, on how arms are sold and so forth. Thus, the question presented is always whether a proposed limitation is reasonable as a matter of public policy. If not, the constitution protects against it being implemented.

The National Rifle Association (NRA), a privately supported non-profit organization, is noted for its efforts to protect the right to bear arms. That endeavor has to be unobjectionable, and the NRA does a good job at it.

Yet, some would say that the NRA goes too far in its absolutist approach, which appears based on the camel's-nose-under-the-tent theory. Under this theory, once the camel gets its nose under the tent, there is nothing to stop the camel from going all the way into the tent -- that is, once a gun limitation is accepted, the right to bear arms will eventually be lost.

Yet, limitations do exist, duly passed by the legislature and approved by the courts. This shows that our society is perfectly capable of drawing lines. Considering all the limitations that are already in place, including some recent ones that the NRA found acceptable, it appears that society and the NRA can control the camel when they want to and they have done so.

Thus, once again it is incumbent on us to look at each limitation proposal on the merits. For instance, it wouldn't be outlandish if military caliber weapons like machine guns were bared or if proven crazies were barred from owning arms. Big cities might want to limit the carrying of concealed weapons in their streets lest road rage or petty squabbles result in shoot-outs.

We all have our own opinions as to what limitations are okay. We shouldn't take absolutist positions and we should listen to the other guy and debate the matter.

But, as usual things, can be taken too far. When there is a shooting at a school, at a shopping mall, or at an airport,[1] the suggestion is to arm the teachers, or to arm the inspectors or ticket takers, or to insert armed guards into the scene, all of which would put us on the path to a police state.

A person has to wonder why the protection of the right to bear arms had blossomed into proposals to expand gun use, perhaps with commercial prodding.

Putting that aside, it would seem better to deter such publically displayed shooting by taking other security measures, like using gun detectors, or ridding ourselves of assault weapons that lead to multiple killings,[2] or using background checks for mental illness (with due modifications of the privacy laws) so as to keep guns out of unreliable hands.[3]

Some people go too far in pushing their personal positions on the right to bear arms. While there can be no objection to anyone being a staunch supporter of the right to bear arms, trying to pass state legislation making it a state

---

[1] Editorial, "Arming the T.S.A. Is Not a Solution," The New York Times, November 4, 2013.

[2] Kaplan, Thomas, "U.S. Judge Upholds Most New York Gun Limits," The New York Times, December 31, 2013.

[3] Parker, Ashley, "Obama Announces Gun Control Actions," The New York Times, January 3, 2014.

crime for federal agents to enforce federal gun laws in the state[1] would seem to go too far. While states cannot repeal duly enacted federal laws, state are free to spearhead efforts to get Congress to change the federal law. While a law exists, we should all abide by it and welcome enforcement.

Exacting retribution for opposing or seeming to oppose gun rights takes us to the seamy side of absolutist positions. A gun stalwart who had done much to expand the right to bear arms came around to thinking that there should be mandatory training for gun owners and wrote an opinion piece on it for a magazine.[2] The retribution from other gun stalwarts, backed up by gun manufacturers, was brutal and smacked of tyranny and a police state.

The newly proposed, and expanded, stand-your-ground law in Ohio[3] is fraught with the danger of neighborhood mayhem. Even the police in Sanford, Florida, (where Mr. Zimmerman killed Mr. Martin) are having second thoughts about the desirability of armed neighborhood-watch programs.[4] Also professional police organizations in Ohio itself oppose the new law which promises to expand gun use.

The effectiveness of gun control laws in reducing gun use is being question based on evidence that the onerous

---

[1] Schwartz, John, "Gun Bill in Missouri Would Test Limits in Nullifying U.S. Law," The New York Times, August 28, 2013.
[2] Nocera, Joe, "When a Gun Advocate Dissents," The New York Times, November 8, 2013.
[3] Editorial, "More 'Stand Your Ground' Fantasizing," The New York Times, November 23, 2013.
[4] Editorial, "Second Thoughts on Neighborhood Watches," The New York Times, November 6, 2013.

sentencing laws for illegal possession of a gun have not reduced gun violence and violent crime rates.[1]

Reducing the draconian jail sentences for nonviolent offenders has led to a call for repeal of the mandatory sentencing laws, which are now considered to be counterproductive due to the adverse effects on lives, families and communities and the huge incarceration costs borne by taxpayers.

Apparently, the gun control laws are not effective in depriving the criminal element of guns, but the gun control laws might be very effective in keeping guns out of the hands of the mentally disturbed (based on approved investigative procedures) and of careless youths (due to home gun lock-up requirements).

For those who favor gun control the NRA has become the enemy that must be countered. A billionaire, Michael Bloomberg, took on the job by establishing and funding an effort to counter the NRA.[2] Both sides are aggressive. With both sides now being more adequately funded, perhaps a happy middle ground will be found.

Criticism has been levied at the courts for both expanding the right to bear arms and also limiting the right. Some would say that they did too much of one or the other. Yet the court also seems to avoid certain issues.

The right to carry guns in public for self-defense is such a situation, where the Supreme Court turned away a case giving no reason. That's easily understandable with all the shootings

---

[1] Schenwar, Maya, "Reduce Gun Penalties," The New York Times, March 14, 2014.

[2] Peters, Jeremy W., "Bloomberg Plans a $50 Million Challenge to the N.R.A.," The New York Times, April 15, 2014.

taking place in the schools and elsewhere. Perhaps the court is backing away from this issue in fear of their being criticized for cowboy or rage type shoot-outs in the streets, and rightfully so. Hopefully, America will find some modicum of balance along the way.

Going Too Far With the Freedom of Religion

Our freedom of religion is grounded in the United States Constitution, in relatively direct words. Amendment I (Bill of Rights) states that "Congress shall make no law respecting an establishment of religion, or prohibiting the free exercise thereof…."

Thus, America can take no steps to establish a religion, which was quite a concession to religious freedom because America was basically a Christian nation, then and now. With our founding fathers being Christian and with currently about 75% of Americans being Christian, it is understandable why America can be viewed as a Christian country. The founders could have but did not establish any religion. Rather, they did what they could to keep the new government from establishing any religion.

ESTABLISHMENT OF RELIGION

Notwithstanding that, America officially recognizes the Christian Christmas as a national holiday, but does not recognize any holiday of any other religion as an official holiday. Christmas trees abound in official settings and our coinage refers to religion. This appears to be okay with most people, since non-Christians also seem to celebrate the joy and trimmings of Christmas if not the religious message.

States exempt religious institutions from real estate and other taxes and laws, which smacks of establishment of religion as such but not the establishment of any particular religion. And America gives tax deductions for contributing to religious institutions.

Yet, issues continue to arise, like a New York Town Board opening their meetings with mostly Christian prayers. Some people objected by litigating the matter[1] and the Supreme Court allowed the prayers.[2] The town neither edited nor approved the prayers, and others were free to offer payers even though only Christians did so.

Both religious and anti-religion zealots go at each other about this and other religious matters, but with no meaningful impact.[3]

This is more or less acceptable to most people. It cannot be denied that America is basically a Christian nation that accommodates all religions and also accommodates the absence of religion. A balance seems to have arisen, with the Christians not going too far in attempting to impose Christianity on others and non-Christians not going too far in objecting to the existence of Christian holidays and the like.

---

[1] Liptak, Adam, "Justices Weigh Constitutionality of New York Town's Prayers," The New York Times, November 6, 2013.
[2] Liptak, Adam, "Town Meetings Can Have Prayer, Justices Decide," The New York Times, May 5, 2014.
[3] Collins, Gail, "Cultural War Games," The New York Times, December 4, 2013.

Yet, others do not see it this way and there is much to be said for their position. Muslims in New York City are beginning to agitate for making the most sacred Muslims holidays into school holidays just like Christmas and Easter are.[1]

The Muslims are correct in that having a holiday of one religion (Christianity) officially recognized obviously offends the constitutional mandate of not establishing a religion. That the Jewish population of New York City hadn't been as vocal about the Jewish holidays does not detract from the argument made by the Muslims.

Many people do not object to the Christian holidays because the nation was in fact established by Christians and remains largely a Christian nation, but one that basically does honor the separation of church (Mosque or Temple) and state. But, still, honoring only Christian holidays does seem to fly in the face of the constitution.

Nevertheless, also recognizing Muslim, Jewish or other holidays in the school calendar, or any other calendar maintained by the state, is not the way the go. While many if not most people might prefer to leave things as they are, if push comes to shove the elimination of all religious holidays from official calendars would be the way to go.

And, at the same time, all the symbols of religion should be eliminated, like "in God we trust" on our coins and the like.

America can no longer continue to maintain the old ways, no matter how comfortable and acceptable that had

---

[1] Otterman, Sharon, "Muslims in New York City Unite on Push to Add Holidays to School Calendar," The New York Times, April 17, 2014.

been, because the old ways now fester more and will divide us much more than we have ever been divided.

Had America actually become one nation out of many (E PLURIBUS UNUM) and a true melting pot (discussed in the chapter "*Dysfunctional Democracy*"), it would have mitigated controversies of this kind. But with diversity wrecking the melting pot, conflicts can be expected.

However, there might be a silver lining in adopting total blindness to religion. It would undermine fanatics of all religions who continue to attempt to impose their views on everyone else and also undermine religious believers who claim that they are exempt from laws that every else must obey.

RELIGIOUS FREEDOM OVERRIDING CIVIL LAW

America has many civil laws which can be viewed as conflicting with the constitutional right to freely exercise one's religion. That is, compliance with the civil law requires a person to act in contradiction to religious belief or practice.

Much litigation is pending based on claims that ordinary civil laws law need not be followed where compliance would be in conflict with one's religious beliefs or practices. The constitution bars Congress from passing laws prohibiting the free exercise of religion. A law specifically targeting free exercise of religion would be barred, but not necessarily one of general application that only incidentally falls that way.

These claims can relate to using poisonous snakes in religious practices in violation of wildlife laws.[1] It can also

---

[1] Blinder, Alan, "Tennessee Pastor Disputes Wildlife Possession Charge by State," The New York Times, November 15, 2013.

apply to corporations[1] and the Boy Scouts of America[2] disregarding anti-discrimination laws based on their religious dictates, to corporations refusing to offer employees required contraception services,[3] to nuns objecting to filing legally required paperwork,[4] and more all based on religious beliefs.

The constitutional right to freely exercise a person's religious beliefs, practices or demands is constantly being pitted against an existing law that would impinge on that free exercise of religion. Simply put, religion is being claimed as a justification for not following the law.

There are three major problems with this position. First, honoring the religious claim to defeat the civil law effectively operates to establish religion which is forbidden by the

---

[1] Wayne, Alex, "Religious Exemption for Birth Control Won't Be Expanded by U.S.," Bloomberg, June 29, 2013.
Editorial, "Religion, Contraception and Bosses' Rights," The New York Times, November 7, 2013.
Liptak, Adam, "Court Confronts Religious Rights of Corporations," The New York Times, November 24, 2013.
Editorial, "Another Challenge to the Health Care Law," The New York Times, November 26, 2013.
Greenhouse, Linda, "Doesn't Eat, Doesn't Pray and Doesn't Love," The New York Times, November 27, 2013.
[2] Bruni, Frank, "Religion Beyond the Right," The New York Times, May 6, 2013.
[3] Editorial, "A Missing Argument on Contraceptives," The New York Times, February 5, 2014.
[4] Kenny, Steve and Pear, Robert, "Justice Blocks Contraception Mandate on Insurance in Suit by Nuns," The New York Times, December 31, 2013.
Liptak, Adam, "Health Law Challenge Opens Up New Front," The New York Times, January 1, 2014.
Editorial, "No Burden on Religion," The New York Times, January 2, 2014.

constitution. Honoring religious law or dogma over secular law is the establishment of religion.

Second, in many instances the religious law or dogma is not all that clear in the religion or its scripture, making the claim of religious freedom optional to believers. Not all religious dogma is cast in stone.[1]

This is seen in believers in a religion not following the claimed religious beliefs that others of the religion claim. Thus, the religion itself not requiring believers to comply contradicts the claim that they must comply with religious dictates.

And there is no telling how many specious religions or religious claims can be dredged up by the unscrupulous so as to avoid adhering to a civil law. Thus, the civil law could be disregarded merely on the say-so of an individual because the courts cannot and will not sit in judgment as to which religions are "legitimate" religions or what religious claims are "legitimate."

And, third, civil law should apply equally to all citizens. The equal protection clause of the constitution demands that citizens be dealt with equally, with the court applying it to the federal government as well as the states. If some people can claim exemption from a duly passed law that provides no special treatment for anyone, it would seem that the law would be applied unequally.

A fourth problem forcefully surfaced in 2014. A denomination of a major region challenged a state law that effectively barred clergy members from blessing gay and

---

[1] Goodstein, Laurie, and Povoledo, Elisabetta, "Pope Sets Down Goals for an Inclusive Church, Reaching Out 'on the Streets,'" The New York Times, November 26, 2013.

lesbian couples, which that denomination felt they had a religious right to do.[1] The state banned gay and lesbian marriages.

Before this case, religious freedom suits were primarily aimed at claiming a religious right to disregard state law that allowed such marriages, or by refusing to sell to gays and lesbians. In this case, the claim goes the other way, claiming a religious freedom right to effectively disregard a state law that didn't allow such marriages, claiming a religious right deal with married gays and lesbians.

Moreover, the case wasn't brought by an individual believer, by a member of a church, or by church clergy, but rather was brought by a domination of the church, which is an integral part of the religion itself.

This emphasizes the absence of a uniformly followed doctrine in the church itself, and that the religious freedom claim is essentially based on personal inclination rather than religious doctrine. Claims based on personal inclination might not appear to a court to be claims of religious freedom.

In a 1990 case, the US Supreme Court condoned a state denying certain benefits to a person using the illegal drug peyote as part of a religious ceremony, thus denying a freedom of religion claim to override ordinary civil law. That would have settled the matter, but the public thought the decision unfair to the Native Americans involved.

A law (Religious Freedom Restoration Act of 1993) designed to upset that decision was pursued, passed and later found illegal although there are still some areas where the law applies. Basically the law required that the burden on

---

[1] Paulson, Michael, "North Carolina's Gay-Marriage Ban Is Challenged by Church," The New York Times, April 28, 2014.

religious believers to follow the civil law must serve a compelling government interest and the legal mandate is the least restrictive means of doing that.

These so-called tests might resolve down to mere matters of semantics. It could be argued that government does have a compelling government interest in stemming the use of illegal drugs like peyote and forbidding its use is the least restrictive means of doing so, which runs contrary to what the new law was aimed at doing.

Needless to say, a civil law that is directly targeted against a religion (as contrasted to being aimed at the general public only incidentally affecting religion) should run afoul of the right to freely exercise one's religion.

Where the civil law is applicable to all and has an ordinary subject matter, that law should apply equally to religious persons or we'll have a system of duel laws and we will be establishing religion.

Adherence to the law should be our standard in all cases. If an individual or group does not like the law, they are free to pursue a legislative change applicable to everybody, not just for themselves. Until that happens, they should follow the law.

TAKING ADVANTAGE OF RELIGIOUS FREEDOM

Religious freedom claims can permeate many aspects of our society. Religions abound and religious beliefs range wide. There are no clear ways to determine whether religious freedom claims are sincere or just made-up for the occasion for self-serving reasons.

The courts would be reluctant to decide whether a religion is legitimate, whether the claim is supported in that religion's dogma, and whether the claimant is of that religion and believes in it. Administrative bodies that have to deal with such claims would also be reluctant to do so.

Rather than disregard the civil law entirely, responsible officials could look to finding an accommodation so as to be fair to all, not allowing the claimant to entirely escape compliance. Thus, they could substitute an appropriately related burden that would not violate religious dictates.

It was on this basis that religious conscientious objectors could claim exemption from military service by undertaking alternate service. Perhaps it wasn't an equal burden since the conscientious objector was not placed in harm's way, but some compulsory service was required. The issue is not just an American one.[1]

In other contexts, accommodating a religious requirement can be expensive. For example, statistics showed that less than 1.5% of the jail inmates were Jewish, but the jail was swamped with claims for kosher meals that were considered better than the ordinary meals and cost the state 4 times as much.[2]

Passing back the costs involved to the inmate claiming the more expensive meal could be a way to deal with the matter, but not likely an effective one.

The courts should be able to deal with a religious claim, perhaps of a religion not before heard of, that requires eating

---

[1] Strother, Jason, "In South Korea, a Student Battles Against Compulsory Military Service," The Wall Street Journal, January 21, 2014.
[2] Alvarez, Lizette, "You Don't Have to Be Jewish to Love a Kosher Prison Meal," The New York Times, January 20, 2014.

of beef or lobster every other day, but even that might prove difficult. Who is to say that the new religion was established with that in view?

In this case, there is no doubt that the religion existed from the most ancient days and that it required the eating of kosher foods even though that was not strictly adhered to by believers.

But who is to say that the inmate claiming kosher food were not Jewish? Would the particular clergy (in this case, the Rabbinate) willingly take on such responsibility by quizzing religious knowledge or otherwise? What degree of religious knowledge on the part of the claimant is required, or even relevant?

Would or could the jail warden undertake to determine legitimacy? Everyone would probably shy away from this. But the courts might be forced into this quagmire if they allow religious exceptions to the enforcement of ordinary laws. And wouldn't providing kosher food to just a few inmates deny the right to equal treatment to other inmates?

In a very different and heart rendering context, but also involving issues of religious belief and burdensome cost to society, a state law mandated continued life support to a brain-dead pregnant woman against the wishes of the family and her declared desire to be taken off life support when the time came.[1]

Here it was the state and not the individuals involved which pursued keeping an unborn child alive. Also, it wasn't clear who would bear the cost of rendering the required life support, but it would seem that the state should pay the bill

---

[1] Fernandez, Manny, and Eckholm, Erik, "Pregnant, and Forced to Stay on Life Support," The New York Times, January 7, 2014.

although the cost of complying with legal requirements isn't normally borne by the state.

Obviously, an approach must be found to say "no" to a claim of religious freedom, as distasteful as that might be. Saying "yes" would be still another instance of America taking a good thing (this time, religious freedom) too far.

Finding ways to accommodate the claim for a religious freedom exception might be fair to the religious but unfair to the non-religious. The best thing America can do is to provide no accommodations at all. That is, religious freedom should not force exceptions.

Following the no-exception approach would be of benefit to America in a number of ways.

It would stop bogging America down with still another area where the equities are not clear.

It would stop the constant flow of adversarial litigation that tears America apart.

It would allow America to devote its time and attention to other matters that need attention.

It would free America from perpetuating still another controversy that contributes to dysfunctional government.

Going Too Far with Free Speech, Free Press & Free Assembly

The Bill of Rights turns to the freedoms of speech and of the press and the rights to assemble and petition government (the subjects covered here) after starting off with religious freedom.[1]

While the text is cast in absolute terms of Congress making <u>no law</u> abridging these freedoms and rights, many laws have been enacted by Congress that do so and the courts have approved those laws. It is best that we all realize at the outset that all of our constitutionally granted rights are abridged or limited in some fashion.

A popular example of a speech limitation is that you cannot yell "fire" in a crowded theatre where there is no fire. There are speech limitations directed at stemming defamation, obscenities, hate speech and even provisions for outright censorship during wartime.

The right to peaceably assemble, parade, march, picket, pamphlet, petition and the like is akin to freedom of speech in that they modes to express protected speech. But, there too, the courts have approved all sorts of limitations, like having to get a permit to parade.

Freedom of the press faced less legislative tinkering, but provoked a host legal challenges when government secrets are published and the press refuses to disclose sources of information.

---

[1] Amendment I, United States Constitution: "Congress shall make no law respecting an establishment of religion, or prohibiting the free exercise thereof; or abridging the freedom of speech, or of the press; or the right of the people peaceably to assemble, and to petition the Government for a redress of grievances."

RIGHT TO FREE SPEECH

Predicated on the basis that we are all free to hold any opinions or maintain any views we want, our constitutional right of free speech protects our right to communicate those opinions or views.

Restrictions or limitations on free speech arise when the rights or reputations of others are harmed by speech and when national security or public order, health or morality are endangered by speech.

The context or surrounding circumstances sometimes have a significant bearing on whether a person's freedom of speech is being violated. The academic context is a difficult one.

Academic freedom can lead to exploring unpopular topics that can hurt others, so "academic justice" is advanced as an alternate guiding principle in order to bar exploration that would be unjust to others.[1] Core values get involved in such controversies with there being no correct path. Once again it is the eyes of the beholder.

The restrictions and limitations on speech that have developed over time seem reasonable and unobjectionable. The issues that arise today seem to relate less to censorship, content, context or purpose and relate more to what actions are to be treated as speech.

For instance, there are limitations as to how much money a person can contribute to the election of a particular candidate, that limitation being challenged on the basis that

---

[1] Douthat, Ross, "Diversity and Dishonesty," The New York Times, April 12, 2014.

the limitation itself violates the contributor's right to free speech.[1] That is, the spending of money is being promoted as being symbolic speech.

Does the spending of money constitute speech? In the modern era, speech can take many forms in addition the oral speech and the writings of our founders. Modern speech might be through radio, TV, cellphones, social media, the internet or even blimps in the sky. But as speech went beyond the soap-box in the park and became more sophisticated, other public concerns arise.

For example, some people might object to the blasting of the sound truck, not to the message blasted. People might just object to the noise or to being constantly bombarded with messages, basically matters involving respecting privacy. One person's speech might invade another person's privacy. Conversely, one person's insistence on privacy might keep another person from speaking out.

Such issues, which basically pit the freedom of speech against other person's rights, will be resolved in the courts on a case by case basis as there aren't any generally applicable standards or principles to be applied.

FREEDOM OF THE PRESS

Technically, the constitution refers to freedom of the press, not specifically to the press's right of free speech. Obviously, the purpose of the press is to speak out.

---

[1] Editorial, "Politicians for Sale," The New York Times, October 7, 2013.

Freedom of the press might contemplate more than free speech, but certainly not going as far as permitting actions like breaking and entry in order to obtain information.

Freedom of the press is not carte blanch freedom for reporters to do whatever they want to do or say whatever they chose to say. As with all the other seemingly absolute constitutionally granted freedoms, limitations have arisen and have been approved by the courts.

A major issue facing the press is whether publication of secret government information is against the public or national interest and can be prohibited. Sometimes the issue is framed in terms of the right to privacy.[1]

The existence of a free press, like we have, is extremely important in a democracy. We can make a case for a free press over censorship in a restricted country like China. We also have to also acknowledge that the press in a free country like Great Britain is not all that free.[2]

The British have an Official Secrets Act that make it a crime for a government employee to disclose confidential government information, and a crime for journalists to print it. Interestingly, disclosure is still a crime if the information is already in the public domain, with journalists repeating the information also subject to prosecution. This is apparently aimed at stemming further dissemination of the tainted disclosures.

---

[1] Hardy, Quentin, "Privacy in the War Without End," The New York Times, March 17, 2014.
[2] Carr, David, "Where Freedom of the Press Is Muffled," The New York Times, December 8, 2013.

This mindset, of going far in protecting government secrets, might account for the British press being given a hard time for covering the Edward Snowden disclosures. America does not have such an Official Secrets Act, which wouldn't be a bad idea if counterbalanced with strong internal ombudsman practices.

America has not entered into any suicide pact that would justify protecting the press when it harms America by disclosing government secrets under the seeming protection of freedom of the press and the claimed need of the public to know. Many citizens would prefer on relying on the government to determine whether there is truly a need for the public to know or when the national interest requires silence. Others citizens feel otherwise; that protecting the freedom of the press is more important.

Again, it is a question of how far we should go with a good thing. The freedom of the press is extremely important and it should be protected, but not when pitted against protecting the nation. The preamble to the constitution includes the common defense as a stated purpose for forming the union. Common sense also dictates it.

The other major issue facing the press is whether reporters can legally refuse to reveal their sources of information. Lawyers and clergy cannot be forced to reveal the content of communications, but that privilege is not important to the press as the press doesn't strive to keep content private as their very purpose is to disclose the information they unearth.

The press strives to keep the names of their sources secret in order to induce them to reveal information. Yet the attorney-client privilege does not normally extend to baring disclosure of the existence of a lawyer-client relationship, which would disclose the identity of the client. In that sense, the press is asking for greater privilege than lawyers have.

Again, in forming a union and in granting our freedoms and rights, our founders were not entering into a suicide pack. But wait! These freedoms and rights were not placed into the constitution by our founders. The freedoms and rights were added by others through a later amendment, the Bill of Rights. So perhaps the founders were concerned with the granting of constitutionally authorized freedoms and rights, preferring to leave it to the courts to rule on it. Even so, a case can be made for society being better served if the press could protect its sources in all but national security instances.

RIGHT OF ASSEMBLY

As with all other constitutionally granted rights, there are limitations to the right of assembly. In this instance, the limitations are usually based on the need to maintain public order (or to "insure domestic tranquility" as expressed in the preamble to the constitution).

While these concepts normally seem to arise where the public is interfacing with government, they have been give broader application as in a fray between college administrators and student protesters.[1]

The constitutional right to assemble and the allied right to petition government protects public dissent that is so vital in a democracy. That dissent can and frequently does encompass civil disobedience, and that too has many aspects to it.

A hacker breaking into corporate and government computers justified hacking as an act of civil disobedience in the proud US tradition of protest, but the court found that there is no right to be civically disobedient.[2]

Equality, Protecting Minorities & Freedom of Choice

The equal protection amendment[3] to the constitution grants citizenship to everybody born or naturalized in America and also protects them against discriminatory laws.

---

[1] Kaminer, Ariel, "2 New York City Colleges Draft Rules That Restrict Protests," The New York Times, December 10, 2013.

[2] Mazzetti, Mark, "Hacker Receives 10-Year Sentence for 'Causing Mayhem,'" The New York Times, November 15, 2013.

[3] 14th Amendment, Section 1: "All persons born or naturalized in the United States, and subject to the jurisdiction thereof, are citizens of the United States and of the State wherein they reside. No State shall make or enforce any law which shall abridge the privileges or immunities of citizens of the United States; nor shall any State deprive any person of life, liberty, or property, without due process of law; nor deny to any person within its jurisdiction the equal protection of the laws."

It applies equally to the federal government and to the states, with Congress being the enforcer.[1] Although ratified back in 1868 to protect the recently freed slaves, it applies broadly in many contexts, like women having the same right to vote as men have.

The equal protection amendment refers the privileges and immunities of citizens but does not directly indicate what the privileges and immunities are. They are as stated or implied in the constitution as interpreted by judges and massaged over time.

The constitution makes persons born or naturalized in the United States citizens, entitled to the privileges and immunities of citizens which would include being protected by the government. Yet, the security needs of the nation could conflict with the nation's duty to protect its citizens.

It comes into focus when a US citizen effectively declares war on America and an uproar is heard when a US drone is dispatched to kill the citizen. The British seem to limit the backlash by stripping citizenship from those considered terrorists, making them fair targets for reprisal.[2]

The equal protection amendment also states that we are not to be deprived of life, liberty and property, but that is not absolute. Our laws can take life, liberty and property as long as the exceptions and limitations are based on reasonable classifications legally adopted through the application of fair procedures (it's called "due process"). This largely takes us

---

[1] 14th Amendment, Section 5. "The Congress shall have power to enforce, by appropriate legislation, the provisions of this article."

[2] Bennhold, Katrin, "Britain Increasingly Invokes Power to Disown Its Citizens," The New York Times, April 9, 2014.

back to matters of fairness which ultimately resides in the eyes of the beholders, the judges.

EQUALITY

We are not equal. Some of us are bigger or smaller, faster or slower, richer or poorer, or smarter or duller than others. The concept of equality relates to the law; that we are all equal in the eyes of the law.

The battle for equality in law contends with racial discrimination and now also faces matters like same-sex marriage, voting oversight, job discrimination, affirmative action, and other uses of discriminatory classifications.[1] Yet, there are exceptions to equality under the law, just like there are exceptions and limitations to all our constitutionally granted freedoms and rights.

On the one hand equal protection expanded from its original purpose of combating racial discrimination.

On the other hand, equal protection was diminished by exceptions and limitations that encroach on life, liberty and pursuit of happiness and ever more encroach on property rights.

It seems that equal protection depends on the glasses worn by generation after generation of Supreme Court judges, although the trend seems to be toward ridding American society of legally created inequality and curtailing exceptions and limitations to equal treatment. Economically created inequality is a separate matter and is dealt with separately.

---

[1] Liptak, Adam, "Supreme Court Weighs Cases Redefining Legal Equality," The New York Times, June 23, 2013.

However, it would appear that the Supreme Court will face more complex cases as those persons who would discriminate have become more sophisticated in their ways.

For instance, discriminatory classifications in the laws could diminish or disappear while being replaced with how a non-discriminatory law is designed to fall on various groups. Such subterfuges can be uncovered and dealt with,[1] but the cases will become more complex.

How a law falls could depend on where public funds are spent and that could involve courts in vetting how a legislature allocates funds. In a state court case, the court faced the duel issues as to whether the public school system was adequately funded in accordance with state legal requirements and whether there were disparities (discrimination) between school districts in how the allocated funds were actually spent.[2]

The first issue concerning adequate funding was reprimanded to a lower court. On the second issue, the court found that a discriminatory gap existed in the actual spending between the districts and ordered the legislature to allocate state funds to the short-funded districts so as to bridge the gap. The first issue depended strictly on state law, while the second issue also involves the equal protection clause of the federal constitution which specifically applies to the States.

Thus it would appear that the courts do have a basis to get involved in what was previously considered a legislative matter -- how state revenues are spent. But it is a limited

---

[1] Robles, Frances, "Florida Law on Drug Tests for Welfare Is Struck Down," The New York Times, December 31, 2013.

[2] Graff, Trevor, and Eligon, John, "Court Orders Kansas Legislature to Spend More on Schools," The New York Times, March 7, 2014.

involvement aimed only at assuring that all the citizens of the state get equal treatment.

More money could be spent in one district or another if there is a justification for it that would past judicial muster. But if the expenditures fall into a discriminatory pattern that violates equal protection, it would not past judicial muster and the court could order an appropriate remedy.

For instance, if more funds dedicated to a specific purpose is spent in richer districts than is spent poorer districts or more is spent in white districts than in black districts, then it would seem at first blush that the citizens living in the poorer or black districts were not getting equal protection of the laws.

The courts would have to get involved in complex matters, deal with details and statistics, affirm or deny the existence of discrepancies and hear endless justifications for the discrepancies, matters that the judiciary is perfectly capable of handling even though time consuming.

And, instead of just passing on the constitutionality of legislation, the judicial branch would be sending orders to the legislative branch to allocate or reallocate funds, matters the legislators would surely oppose. Yet, the constitution does seem to call for it.

All this is to the good because it seems that sophisticated modern day discrimination practices are based on how the law falls in actual practice. It might also apply to bar gerrymandering if the strange salamander patterns of laying out equal voting districts fall in a discriminatory pattern and the courts use that to stop gerrymandering.

PROTECTING THE MINORITY

Minority groups are clearly entitled to equal protection under the law. The constitution already protects minority groups from discrimination. Thus "protecting the minority," if it actually exists as a separate right to protection, must have nothing to do with discrimination but rather be something like protection against oppression by the majority.

Racial profiling, a form of oppression, is aimed at minorities. It is aimed at certain races, religions, national origins, gender, and sexual orientation and could be extended to include to mapping neighborhoods and other things.[1] The oppressor would be law enforcement, possibly by any level of government.

The Justice Department is busy revising its rules so as to balance the security needs of the nation with the rights of the groups usually profiled. The competing interests are very strong and neither side is likely to be satisfied when all is done. There is right on both sides, making balance difficult.

In addition to the discriminatory aspects surrounding minorities, there are political aspect brought about by elections of one sort or another which produces a winner (the majority) that has the ability to oppress and also produces a loser (the minority) that has the ability to obstruct.

The "right" of the minority not to be oppressed by the majority seems to have evolved out of ethical principles of fairness, not from any constitutional or legal mandate. The minority claims a right to be heard, the right to obtain information, the right to debate and to try to convince the majority.

---

[1] Apuzzo, Matt, "Profiling Rules Said to Give F.B.I. Tactical Leeway," The New York Times, April 9, 2014.

Our legislatures confer such minority "rights" or some semblance of it in the rules the legislatures establish to govern the way they operate. Those rules are perpetuated by the majority in power with an eye from benefiting from the rules when the other political party becomes the majority. However, the minority can also take advantage of these operational rules and procedures to obstruct and delay the majority.

Protecting the minority against an overbearing majority can be, as with many other good features of our society, taken too far. Thus, the minority has a right to enter the debate and be heard on a pending bill, but shouldn't be able to keep the majority from voting on the bill through what is known as a filibuster. The majority won the legislative mandate in the election and thus has the right and obligation to govern, and the minority should not be able to interfere with that.

Also, voluntarily giving a minority extra clout though creating the need a supermajority to pass a bill goes too far as it contributes to a dysfunctional government. There is no provision in the constitution that requires a supermajority vote, other than to ratify treaties with other nations. The reasons behind these extraordinary grant of powers to the minority through the operational rules of the legislature has been discussed in the chapter "*Dysfunctional Democracy*."

Legislation should be fully discussed on its merits; not in order to protect any rights the minority might have or claim, but rather to get a better end-product for the benefit of all. While the majority should not abuse the minority, on the same token the minority should not be able to take advantage of the majority. Since the majority won the legislative mandate and has the right and obligation to govern, the greater harm comes from a minority that can obstruct governance.

THE "RIGHT" TO CHOOSE

The so-called "right to choose" or "freedom of choice" is being claimed without there being any constitutional or legislative support for the existence of such right or freedom. The call for such a right or freedom is basically an argument against limitations, against restrictions, and against regulation.

If the philosophical purpose of government is to keep people from harming each other, there should be no bar to allowing people to harm themselves. We should have the right to smoke, eat junk foods, overstuff ourselves and engage in any behavior that does not harm others, or so the purveyors of such products and sponsors of such behaviors would advocate.[1]

Yet, smoking and obesity not only harms the smoker or glutton but also harms others in terms of the indirect effects (like second hand smoke) and medical treatment bills that others have to bear through the taxes they pay. Smokers and gluttons who rely on society to pay their medical costs do burden others. So too for alcoholics and drug addicts who directly and indirectly harm others and increase societal costs in a host of ways.

Yet, those who profit from supplying smokes, junk food, alcohol and drugs try to create a "right to partake" and any restriction on that is claimed to be un-American. Rather, it

---

[1] Bittman, Mark, "Rethinking Our 'Rights' to Dangerous Behaviors," The New York Times, February 25, 2014.

would seem that allowing any such right would be un-American because the nation has a right and obligation to protect its citizens from harming themselves because that invariably also harms others, harms our economy and harms our social fabric.

Somewhat allied to this is the claimed right to disobey the law. Obviously, nobody has the right to disobey a law. A person might protest a law, as to which they have a right, but there is no right to actually disobey the law. Yet, some people do claim such a right when they disagree with a law.[1] And sometimes they get away with it though the kind-heartedness of law enforcement officials.

Corporate "Rights" Taken Too Far

Corporations are not people. They are not endowed with any inalienable rights, but only with the rights the law chooses to give them. They are creatures of the law, existing only in legal contemplation. Their creator, normally state law, gives them whatever rights, attributes and legal status state law chooses to give them.

Corporations cannot do things. Only people can do things. People are hired in the name of corporation and they act in the name of the corporation. Corporations can own things, but people have to buy those things in the name of the corporation or transfer the property to the corporation.

---

[1] Krugman, Paul, "High Plains Moochers," The New York Times, April 27, 2014.

What the corporation can and cannot legally do, or more accurately what the employees of the corporation can and cannot legally do in the name of the corporation, is determined by the government entity that created the corporation. What the corporation actually does is determined by the people who founded the corporation and the board of directors and executives who run the assets held in the corporate name.

The legal fiction of the corporation is brilliant. The law recognizes the corporation as a separate entity, separate from that of the real persons who own it. The real person contributes property to the corporation in exchange for shares of corporate stock (pieces of paper that represent proportionate ownership in the corporation). The corporation is legally endowed by the law to own and hold the contributed property in its name and to have that property managed in its name. Thus, the real people own the shares of the corporation and the corporation owns and manages the property.

Corporations have two basic advantages over real people. They need not die; they can and do go on forever (perpetual life). And corporations can be owned by any number of real people, allowing them to achieve enormous size, dwarfing their individual investors. Many corporations own assets worth billions and billions of dollars while there aren't that many real people who are billionaires.

If wealth equates to power, overriding power would be concentrated in those who ran the corporations and the few billionaires around. The rest of the wealth, and thus power, would be spread over so many real people that they could only play a secondary role.

Yet, the real people get to vote for the governments that created the corporations and defined the corporate rights, attributes and legal status. Theoretically, the real people, the voters, ultimately determine what corporations can and cannot do, and what rights, powers, responsibilities and protections corporations have. Practically, corporations influence the legislative process with some persons maintaining that they control it.

As America tends to do, America has taken the legal fiction of the corporation too far. However, having given the corporation legal entity status, there is no obligation for the law to treat the newly created entity as a real person having the rights, attributes and legal status real persons have. Yet, we tend to do this.

That is, we tend to treat the corporation as a real person and unnecessarily endow it with a multitude of rights and attributes a real person has.

This has not served us well and it is about time that we reviewed what rights, attributes, capacities, and status a corporation should have in our society. That is, we should review what a corporation should be able to do or be barred from doing, what responsibilities it should have and what disclosures it should make.

BARRING CORPORATE VEILS FOR SUBSIDIARIES

Allowing a parent company to avoid the debts of its subsidiary corporations extends the corporate veil much too far. This has been covered in more detail in the previous chapter "*Government Programs and Laws.*"

It is understandable why society should want to induce risk taking by real people entering into businesses that serve society, even though protecting the investor serves to shift losses to others. As in everything else, there is no free lunch. The protection that investors get is paid for by the risk cast upon others. The losses that do not burden the investor become the burden of others. That is the public policy decision society reached in authorizing the corporate veil.

However, there is no policy justification for society extending the corporate veil to subsidiary corporations formed by a parent corporation (the corporation that is owned by real people).

Why should society pick-up the huge losses on the next deep-sea oil spill if it was caused by a subsidiary corporation with limited assets and the parent corporation claimed the protection of the subsidiary's corporate veil? There is no valid public policy that justifies this and the corporate veil for corporate subsidiaries should be entirely eliminated and parent corporations be made liable for losses of their subsidiaries.

LIMITING LAWSUITS AGAINST CORPORATIONS

There is a tremendous litigation inequality between the rich and powerful and the average person when it comes to litigation. As was pointed in the chapter "*Government Programs and Laws*," there are a number of things America can do to make the litigation playing-field less stilted in favor of the rich and powerful.

The injustice of the uneven litigation playing-field exists when wealthy people sue average or poor people but fortunately there isn't much of this kind of litigation. However, there is a lot of potential lawsuits by average or poor people against powerful corporations when these people are harmed by the products and services purchased from these corporations. As to this, the uneven litigation playing-field would effectively bar these people from suing but for the possibility of using a class-action lawsuit.

Keep in mind that the law gave corporations the ability to obtain and concentrate the wealth of many individual investors, thereby allowing the corporations to achieve the enormous size that created the uneven litigation playing-field. Turnabout being fair game, that itself justifies individuals banding together to sue these corporations in class-action suits. For the most part, the law allows such class-action suits against corporations but the courts have gone too far in limiting those lawsuits.

Some people claim that the courts have gone too far in protecting corporations against all sorts of law suits by individuals including class-action lawsuits.[1] When this happened, Congress has occasionally stepped in and passed laws effectively reversing the court holdings. Class-action lawsuits, the great equalizer, should not only be protected but should be expanded wherever possible.

On the same token, America should limit the incentive for lawyers to bring class-action suits that are unwarranted or suits deliberately aimed at punishing the corporate defendants. Since the suing class might consist of tens of thousands of plaintiffs, the winning lawyer can get huge fees. This creates an incentive for bringing as many cases as

---

[1] Chemerinsky, Erwin, "Justice for Big Business," The New York Times, July 1, 2013.

possible, some cases with dubious merits that serve extortive type purposes and other cases that are meritorious that deserve good fees, but not exorbitant fees that unfairly cut into the plaintiff's recovery.

A lawyer winning a case on behalf of 10,000 plaintiffs should not get 10,000 times the normal fee for her or his time and effort. One way to limit fees is that the winning lawyer should get a fee no larger than say 100 times the recovery by the average plaintiff, and perhaps reduce that by half if the case is settled without trial. Such a limitation might also serve to assuage the concern of "pro-business"[1] courts that protect corporations from class-action lawsuits.

FORCED ARBITRATION CLAUSES

The courts have held that class-action suits are barred where customers have entered into mandatory arbitration clauses when they contracted for corporate services.[2] This holding effectively allows corporations to avoid all class-action suits as these corporations insist on such clauses in their service contracts. Customers have no choice but to comply because all the corporations rendering particular kinds of service insist on mandatory arbitration.

Why not force arbitration? Individual customers who are harmed could hardly sue the corporation because it would be expensive and there wouldn't be that much money involved to justify an individual lawsuit. Yet, the same harm likely

---

[1] Liptak, Adam, "Corporations Find a Friend in the Supreme Court," The New York Times, May 4, 2013.
[2] Chemerinsky, Erwin, "Justice for Big Business," The New York Times, July 1, 2013.

befell all the customers of that corporation and the class-action suit would appropriately level the litigation playing-field.

There should be a public policy prohibition on all mandatory arbitration clauses in contracts with the general public. Arbitration clauses in standardized contracts should be distinguished from separately negotiated contracts between equals that contain negotiated arbitration clauses. Efforts to limit forced arbitration clauses have commenced with the Consumer Financial Protection Bureau[1] but the need to bar forced arbitration is at least as great in non-financial areas. Thus, there is need for congressional action when the Washington gridlock disperses.

THE CORPORATE CLOAK OF SECRECY

Secrecy facilitates both cheating and outright stealing. Some countries recognized the value of this by extending their bank secrecy laws to foreigners by forbidding the banks to disclose anything about their customers.

This is not bank secrecy like you would expect from your local bank in America. Of course, American banks cannot and will not voluntarily reveal your deposit and other information to your neighbors or anyone else. But American and most other developed-country banks would allow authorized law enforcement authorities to demand and uncover bank information.

The countries that wouldn't allow their banks to reveal information to anybody, including law enforcement, became

---

[1] Editorial, "A Tool Consumers Need," The New York Times, December 29, 2013.

tax-havens when they extended their bank secrecy protection to foreigners. Secrecy was the license to cheat and steal, which is what the tax evaders do. But there is much more than mere tax evasion fostered by a cloak of secrecy.

Governments and tax authorities around the world got wise and started to go after tax-haven countries that provided bank secrecy to foreigners, deliberately inducing Americans and others to open bank accounts in those countries so as to avoid taxes in their home countries. The international crackdown on tax-haven secrecy had begun years ago and continues, with little success since so many lawyers, financial planners and others benefit from it.

There is no crackdown on America's domestic equivalent which is primarily and overwhelmingly the State of Delaware (others are Nevada and Wyoming). These states allow the formation of privately held corporations that need not reveal who their beneficial owners are. As these states do not require this information, the states do not know who the owners are and thus cannot respond to law enforcement inquiry. The corporate law in these states not only created artificial persons called corporations, but these artificial persons can be a ghosts, something real people cannot be.

Thus, these American states facilitate underground activities, illegal political contributions and graft, tax evasion and other nefarious deeds as they solicit such covert business and induce other states to join them in a race to the bottom.[1]

---

[1] Cassara, John A., "Delaware, Den of Thieves?" The New York Times, November 1, 2013.
Wayne, Leslie, "How Delaware Thrives as a Corporate Tax Haven," The New York Times, June 30. 2012.

A proposal requiring corporations formed in the United States to disclose the names of their beneficial owners to the U.S. Treasury has gone nowhere.

A proposal that could work and has international backing is for governments to require corporate-registrars to collect and make publically available the ultimate beneficial ownership of corporations they register.[1] Failure to submit accurate beneficial ownership information would should invalidate the corporate charter right from the beginning (as if the charter were never issued), making property transfers to it invalid and creating deserved havoc (a tremendous deterrent). Criminal penalties on the incorporators might also work. However this is approached, real teeth are need to prevent cheating.

Not having uniform corporate-registration practices throughout America has allowed these states to parasitically bugger their neighboring states and rake in corporate-registration revenues. It is getting to the point that the neighbors feel pressure to join them and create a level playing-field for corporate secrecy throughout America. There is every reason to protect trade-secrets and the like but there is no public policy justification for providing privately-held corporations with cloaks of secrecy.

It is interesting that most states require businesses that operate in the state under fictitious names to obtain fictitious-name licenses or to register such names so as to publically disclose who is behind those names. The State of Delaware requires the registration of Trade, Business and Fictitious Names, the payment of a fee for such registration, and has a

---

[1] Somaiya, Ravi, "Obama Urged to Back Plan to List Owners of Shell Firms," The New York Times, June 9, 2013.

publically available database of such registrations. The registration form requires the names and addresses of all owners:

"In Delaware, no person, firm, association, or company can transact business without using their actual legal name within the State unless you file a Fictitious Name Certificate.

This includes, but is not limited to sole-proprietors.

The bottom line – you need to be accessible."[1] [Emphasis added]

It is interesting that only the small guy who uses a fictitious name on a store or garage has "to be accessible" in Delaware. Yet, where more money is involved and where Delaware can rake in registration fees, Delaware will allow the creation of corporations without making the owners accessible by requiring beneficial ownership information. It is noted that all corporate names are fictitious names, and the corporation itself is a legal fiction.

Once again America has gone too far with a good thing. There is no public policy that would justify America's aiding and abetting persons who would take advantage of others or who would commit illegal acts which is what the corporate cloak of secrecy invariably does.

As such secrecy harms law enforcement throughout America, one begins to wonder whether the courts have grounds to stop the carnage by using the interstate commerce and the equal protection clauses of the constitution and by brushing aside corporate claims to having a right to privacy in terms of keeping their ownership secret.

More than hiding assets from due legal process or covering up criminal activity is involved because such

---

[1] http://www.delawarebusinessblog.com/?p=91

secrecy allows the flaunting of our election laws[1] and so endangers our very democracy. At a minimum, all state corporate-registrars should be required to obtain beneficial ownership information (with criminal penalties for false information being filed) on the registration of privately-held corporations and disclose it.

Instead of prosecuting corporations for crimes, there is a tendency for the Justice Department to substitute penalties and require improvement in future compliance.[2] Indications are that corporations escape prosecution in cases where individuals would be prosecuted, creating a double standard.

We should know by now that nothing gets attention like a picture of a Wall Street insider or a corporate executive in handcuffs. Nothing would be a better deterrent for the corporate elite who wouldn't personally be as concerned with penalties as they would be with handcuffs. Penalties levied on multibillion dollar companies are hardly deter and there is rarely a public admission of guilt.

Avoiding burdening the courts with unnecessary litigation is a good thing but it has been taken too far when penalties (particularly when not accompanied with a public admission of guilt) are used as a substitute for open trials and public admissions of guilt. If we had more airing of corporate misfeasance, as we have with individual misfeasance, we might foster a more ethical society which we sorely need. Only in minor cases, unimportant cases, should the penalty

---

[1] Editorial, "Change the Rules on Secret Money," The New York Times, February 18, 2014.
Confessore, Nicholas, "Tax Filings Hint at Extent of Koch Brothers' Reach," The New York Times, September 12, 2013.

[2] Uhlmann, David M., "Prosecution Deferred, Justice Denied," The New York Times, December 13, 2013.

approach be acceptable. Double standards rarely make sense and they are usually unjust.

IS THERE A CONSTITUTIONALLY GRANTED CORPORATE FREEDOM OF SPEECH?

There is much to object to when corporations claim to have a right to free speech. As with other aspects, we have gone too far in treating corporations as persons, while they are artificial creatures having only such rights as society decides to extend to them.

As was said in the context of corporations claiming religious freedom, corporations don't eat, don't pray and don't love all of which make it difficult to accept they can engage in religious exercise.[1] The same might be said with respect to the absence a corporate constitutional right of freedom of speech.

What corporations try to elevate to the level of constitutional freedom of speech should be limited to the so-called commercial speech that addresses their products and the services they render. Corporations should be free to advertise their products within the constraints of the truth in advertising laws, required health warnings and notices and other restrictions which are matters of commerce. Corporations should be barred from issue advocacy or advertising and other forms of political advocacy.

---

[1] Greenhouse, Linda, "Doesn't Eat, Doesn't Pray and Doesn't Love," The New York Times, November 27, 2013.

A distinction should be made between a corporation trying to influence voting on political issues and a corporation making its views known to legislators when its direct interests (that is, its products or services) will be impacted. Normally, this would be done in presentations before legislators in committee hearings, or even in private talks to legislators.

America goes too far when it allows an artificial person, a fictional entity, to claim the constitutional freedom of speech that real people have. America should bar all corporate issue advertising as contrasted to product advertising and all advertising directed to voters as contrasted to consumer advertising.

As there is no corporate right to free speech, there will someday be a Supreme Court that will reverse its decision in the Citizens United case, which will go far to restore our democracy.

References

Books & Documents

Old Testament/Hebrew Bible, any version

Frankfurt, Harry G., *"On Bullshit,"* Princeton University Press, 2005.

The Constitution of the United States of America

The Joint Committee on Taxation, "Modeling the Distribution of Taxes on Business," (JCX-14-13), October 16, 2013.

Media

Newspapers:
Los Angeles Times
Milwaukee Journal Sentinel
The Christian Science Monitor
The New York Times
The San Diego Union-Tribune
The Texas Tribune
The Wall Street Journal

Other Media:
BBC News, Europe
Bloomberg
CBS News
Cruise Law News
Harper's
MarketWatch
National Affairs
Reuters
The Nation
www.delawarebusinessblog.com

Index

Academic excellence 246, 348, 350, 352-354,
Accounting 161, 174, 176, **188-199**, 254, 285, 294, 295,
Advice and consent 48, 49, 52, 55, 64, 110,
Advocacy groups 21, 22, 94, 115, 116,
Affirmative action 274, **347-354**,
Air waves 159, 162, 164,
Airline(s) 223, 224,
Amoral 356,
Anti-dumping law 213
Anti-trust law 212, 224,
Apple 207-209, 248,
Apprenticeship 245, 271,
Assembly 140, 209, 210,
Assistance (programs) 263, 268,
Attorney's General 291,

Auditing, auditors 190, 196, 200,
Austerity 141, 146-149,
Australia 122,
Austria 304,

Bangladesh 233, 235,
Bank(s) 227, 276, 304, 305, 357, 412,
Bankruptcy 191, 230, 242, 273, 344, 345,
Bayer 258,
Bloomberg, Michael, 232, 380,
Blue slip(s) 33, 48, 59, 62, 105, 127,
Board(s) of Directors 218, 219, 283, 285, 289, 293, 296, 297,
Board(s) of Elections 25,

Board(s) of Trustees 290,
Bonds 170, 183, 184, 191, 243,
Brandeis, Louis, 193, 199,
Bribery 25, 28, 49,
Britain, British 179, 237, 375, 395, 399,
British Petroleum 317,
Brussels 226,
Budget(s) 4, 113, 141, 146, 148-151, 157, 160, 210, 239, 266, 280, 308, 310,
Buffett, Warren 289, 298, 308, 309,
Building code 233,
Burdening the next generation 151-153,
Bureau of Land Management 130,
Bush, George W. 321,

California 83, 84, 94-101, 182, 185, 186, 197, 223, 322, 336, 349,
Canada 131, 204,
Cap-and-trade 228-230,
Capitalism 147, 279, 281, 311,

Carbon 92, 170-173, 232, 246,
Cash committee 31,
Celebrities 20, 100, 101, 281,
Cell phones 3, 112,
Census 71, 82, 83,
Central Intelligence Agency 373,
Certified Public Accountant(s) 174, 189,
Charitable donations 160, 201,
Cheerios 335,
Chicago 272,
Chief Executive Officers 136, 137, 292, 296,
China, Chinese 139, 205, 207, 208, 210, 220, 221, 229, 234, 238, 241-244, 253, 255, 256, 367, 395,
Christian conflicts 386, 387,
Christian holidays 382-384,
Christian nation 382,
Christian prayers 382
Citizens United 17, 19, 418,
Class-action lawsuits 330, 339, 340, 410,

INDEX

Class warfare 154-156, 264, 277, 279, 280, 282, 289, 303, 311,
Cloture 52, 53, 56, 108,
Coal 172, 230,
Coast Guard 179,
Commercial speech 417
Communications 3, 125, 213,
Compensation consultants 283-285, 291
Competition **203-219**,
Computer(s) 3, 140, 251,
Congress 27, 33, 35, 36, 43-46, 50, 74, 97, 104, 105, 126, 142-145, 199-201, 218, 247, 285, 295, 297, 302-305, 357, 374, 379,
Consumer Financial Protection Bureau 412,
Consumer Privacy Bill of Rights (proposed) 373,
Consumer Product Safety Commission 234, 323,
Contract law **329-337**,
Copyright(s) 165, 364,
Corporate veil **314-320**, 408, 409,
Corporation(s) 4,
Corrupt(ion) 23-26, 29, 30, 33, 34,

Counter-productive programs **324-325**,
Courts directing legislatures 401,
Crime(s), criminal 26, 28, 29, 188, 235, 323, 324, 361-363, 379, 380, 395, 414-416,

de Tocqueville, Alexis 2,
Debt 9, 67, 132, 135, 141-146, 148-154, 193-196, 242, 243,
Debt ceiling 67, 141-145,
Delaware 413-415,
Democracy 5, **7-137**, 167, 309, 310, 353-356, 418,
Democrat(s) 5, 6, 59, 99, 270, 321,
Depreciation deductions 173, 174,
Deterring crime 363,
Dick Tracy 3,
Disability program 326,
Disneyland 3,
Distrust 128, 129,
Diversity 75-78, 275, 348, 349, 352-354, 384,
Dollars (physical) 242, 243,

423

E Pluribus Unum 74, 75, 384,
Ecology 153, 204, 319, 320,
Economy 5, 39, 139, 147 149, 167, 169, 188, 190, 195, 218, 231, 239, 240, 245, 251,
Education 4, 5, 10, 122, 166, 188, 213, 245, 253, 267, 274, 275, 280, 291,
Elderly 168, 170,
Energy 166, 214, 223,
Engineer(ing) 247-250,
England 238,
Enron, 189,
Entertainment 3, 47, 214,
Entitlement(s) 10, 321,
Equity versus the Letter of the Law **341-345**,
Espionage 241, 244,
Ethics(al) 10, 12, 26, 43, 43, 207, 217, 229, 236, 263, 362, 403, 416,
European Union 222, 284, 304,
Exclusivity 164, 165,
Executive compensation (packages) 196, 263, 277, 280-286, 289, 290,
Executive salaries 287,
Exporting democracy **353-356**,
Expropriation 256, 257,
Extort(ion) 29, 30, 58, 109, 110, 144, 181-183, 215, 342,

Failing cities 273,
Fair(ness) 156-158, 298, 300, 399, 400,
Family instability 264, 267, 274,
Fast food 269,
Favoritism lacking balance **346-347**,
Federal Election Commission 31,
Federal Reserve Bank 168,
Fictitious names 415,
Filibuster 8, 11, 33, 55, 56, 90, 94, 95, 106, 108, 127,
Financial disclosure(s) 27,
Financial Services Committee 31
Fine(s) 94, 122, 123,
Fire code 233, 234, 236,
Fireflies 246,
Flood(s) 180,
Food stamp program 265,

Foreign Intelligence
 Surveillance Court 373,
Foreign subsidiary(ies)
 39, 140, 141, 205, 206,
 239, 257,
France, French 2, 155,
 200, 204, 253, 281, 288,
 310, 367,
Fraud-prone programs
 326-329,
Free-trade zones 212,
Freedom of Religion
 369, **381-391**,
 Establishing Religion
 382-384,
 Overriding Civil Law
 384-388,
 Taking Advantage
 389-391,
Freedom of Speech **392-394**,
Freedom of the Press
 393, **395-397**,

Gates, Bill, 280, 308, 309,
General Mills 335,
Genome 3,
Gerrymander(ing) 7, 73, 82-85, 94-97, 99, 100, 106, 402,

Gibbon, Edward 1,
Glass-Steagall Act 223,
Globalization 203, 204, 207,
Golden handshake 283, 288,
Golden parachute 283, 288,
Good life, the, 246, 247, 352,
Google 104,
Government programs **320-324**,
Great Seal 74,
Greater good 158,
Gridlock 4, 8, 412,
Gulf of Mexico oil spill 317,
Gun(s) 68, 70, 130, 188, 192,

Happiness index 150,
Health care 10, 41, 42, 65-67, 166, 321, 328,
Hidden names and identities 376,
Hold(s) 12, 33, 48, 62, 63, 105, 127,
Hollywood 3,
Holocaust 75,

House of Representatives 31, 49, 75, 82, 96, 144, 270,
Hurricane Sandy 180,

Identification card(s) 81, 82, 94, 111,
Immigration 247, 250, 252
Impeachment 48-51,
In God We Trust 74,
Inauguration day 94, 125, 126,
Incumbent(s) 57, 84, 95, 103, 107, 113, 117,
India 207,
Industrial Policy **203-219**,
Industry organizations. *See* Trade organizations
Inequality 5, **261-312**,
Influence 14, 23, 25, 29, 30, 32, 34, 35, 42, 45, 101, 113, 114, 116, 117, 164, 166, 186, 189, 274, 284, 309, 408, 418,
Information, 7, 10,
Infrastructure 10, 76, 92, 147, 149, 151, 152, 166, 212, 240, 272, 273, 309,
Inherited wealth 279, 309, 310,

Innovation 2, 214, **237-259**, 364, 365, 367,
Insurance 180, 181, 318 320, 333,
Intellectual Property Rights **237-259**, 277, Protection **364-365**,
Internal Revenue Service 133, **199-203**, 302,
International Monetary Fund 166,
Internet 3, 164, 210,
Investment(s) 28,
Islam 238,
Issue advocacy (ads) 35, 117, 417, 418,

Jacobs, Irwin 249,
Japan(ese) 241, 242, 251, 253, 259, 367,
Jet(s) 2, 125,
Job(s) 10, 39, 42, 92, 139, 146, 151, 187, 206, 212, 213, 244, 245, 250, 254, 262-264, 268, 269, 271, 272,
Jobs, Steve 207-209, 248,
Johnson, Lyndon 321,
Justice Department 416,

Know-how 139, 205, 207, 239, 240, 251,
Korea(n) 208, 253, 367,
Kosher prison meals 389, 390,

Lake Wobegon 284,
Las Vegas 3,
Law enforcement 69, 112, 133, 340, 374-376, 412, 415,
Legislation 8, 25,
Legislator(s) 7, 8, 9, 10, 23-26, 29, 33, 44-47, 82-86, 97, 101-105, 126-128, 134, 167, 200, 418,
Legislature(ive) 7, 9, 33, 35, 36, 83, 97, 102-105, 127, 376, 388, 408,
Less-developed country debt 194-196,
License(s) 164,
Lien filings 342, 343,
Life expectancies 273,
Life support 390, 391,
Limbaugh, Rush, 11,
Litigation playing field **337-341**, 366, 409, 410,
Living wage 262,

Lobbyist(s) 14, 35-38, 40-47, 101, 102, 134, 136, 137,
Locke, John 220,
Loophole(s) 39, 134, 141, 211, 218, 239,
Luxembourg 304,

Madagascar 349,
Made in U.S.A. label 210,
Mandatory arbitration 330, 332, 335, 336, 411,
Manufacture(ing) 139, 140, 183, 207-209, 213, 226, 251,
Marijuana 133,
Marine assistance 178,
Marine risks 318, 319,
Massachusetts formula 185, 186,
Matching funds 94, 113, 114,
Mathematics 246, 248, 249,
Media 118, 130, 192, 205, 213, 225, 256, 323, 326, 328, 335, 394,
Medical device(s) 41-43,
Medicare. *See* Health Care.

Melting pot 7, 75, 78, 384,
Mexico 216, 232,
Microsoft 280,
Military 4, 5, 10, 129, 130, 141, 210, 240, 242, 347, 378,
Milker(s) 16, 30,
Minimum wage 59, 264, 267-270, 274,
Minority(ies) 12, 48, 53-55, 70, 77, 89-91,
Missouri 68,
Mobility 264, 267, 273, 274,
Money 7, 9, 24, 25, 31, 34, 46, 115-118, 146, 154, 254,
Monopolies 164,
Mortgage interest 160, 177,
Municipal 160, 162,

National Institutes of Health 254,
National interest 214, 215, 253, 349, 356, 396,
National Rifle Association 377,
National Voter Registration Act 81,
Navy 179,
Nevada 413,
New Jersey 170, 180, 272,
New Jersey Turnpike 170,
New York 180, 272,
New York City 3, 232, 266, 289, 326,
Newspaper(s) 2, 19, 163,
Nobel Prize laureate 263,
Non-disclosure clauses 330,
Non-profit 24, 189, 191, 290,
Nuclear 2, 3, 55, 56,

Obama, Barack 54,
Occupy Movement 288, 289, 311,
Of, by, and for the people 5, 7, 35, 58, 115, 136, 309, 310, 341
Official Secrets Act 375, 395, 396,
Offshore 5, 39, 40, 140, 206, 211, 233, 248-251, 325,

INDEX

Ohio 380,
Oligopoly, oligarchy 224, 225, 279, 309, 310,
One nation out of the many 74, 75, 384,
One person, one vote 52, 71, 72,
Opportunity 264, 266, 275, 301,
Overtime pay 267, 274,

Parks 170, 231,
Partnership 211,
Patent abuse **366-367**,
Patents 165, 253, 257, 364, 365,
Patriot Act 373,
Payday loans 227,
Paying-to-play 30,
Pell grants 275, 353,
Penalties 416,
Pennsylvania 272, 273,
Pension(s) 169, 191, 192,
Periodic reviews 265, 266, 322,
Personal Freedoms **369-418**,
Pharmaceutical 3, 251, 255, 258,
Piketty, Thomas 281, 310-312,

Place-based programs 274,
Police state 27, 379,
Political Action Committees 15-20, 46,
Political contributions 14 21, 394,
Pollution 148, 228, 229,
Pope 288,
Pork 88, 147,
Poverty 267, 281, 300,
President 35, 47-55, 59, 63, 64, 88, 105,
Pressure groups 7, 14, 102, 103,
Primary(ies) 10, 22, 94, 98-100, 119-122,
Princeton University 348,
Privacy 29, 111,
Public policy 36, 37, 86, 160, 165, 167, 295, 315, 409, 412,
Public service 102,

Qualcomm 249,

Racehorses 167,
Radio 3,
Reagan, Ronald, 101

429

Recall 50, 51,
Reciprocity 179,
Re-election 9, 28, 46, 84, 103, 126, 134, 166,
Redistribution 9, 154, 155, 277, 278,
Redistricting 83, 96,
Religion(ous) 10, 123, 124, 155, 278,
Religious Freedom Restoration Act 388,
Regulation(s) 135, 182, **220-237**,
Rehabilitating prison inmates **360-363**,
Representatives 10, 94, 101,
Republican(s) 5, 6, 59, 99, 144, 270, 321,
Research (R&D) 5, 207, 208, 213, **237-259**,
Research tax credit 254,
Reserving, reserves 193, 194,
Retraining 325,
Right of Assembly 392, **397-398**,
Right to Bear Arms **377-381**,
Right to Equal Protection of the Law **398-402**,
Right to Privacy **370-376**,

Limitations 372,
Data mining 373-374,
Undercutting 374-376,
Right to be Civically Disobedient? 398,
Right to Choose? **405-406**,
Right to Protection? 376,
Rights of Corporations? **406-418**,
Corporate veils? 408-409,
Limiting lawsuits? 409-411,
Forcing arbitration? 411-412,
Cloak of secrecy? 412-417,
Free speech? 417-418,
Rights of Minorities Against Oppression? **403-405**,
Risk 193,
Risky areas 181,
Robin Hood 10,
Roe v. Wade 71, 372, 374,
Roman Empire 1,
Rome 1,
Roosevelt, Teddy, 310,
Russia 3, 238, 309,

Samsung 208, 252,
Satellites 3,
Savings bonds 170,
Science(s) 246-249,
Segregated communities 273, 274,
Self-improvement 274, 275,
Senate 8, 48-57, 61-64, 72-75, 83, 107-110,
Senator(s) 10, 42, 48, 49, 51-53, 56, 58-64, 94, 101,
Sequester 9, 141, 266, 300, 310,
Services 213,
Shareholder approval 284, 285, 288, 289, 294,
Shipping 180,
Social Progress Index 4,
Social Security 147, 327,
Socialism 281,
Slogan(s) 7, 10, 135, 151, 153, 154, 156, 157, 237, 278, 280, 310,
Snowden, Edward, 396,
Solutions 5, 134, 170, 230, 231, 264, 345, 365,
Speech 19, 115, 117,
Special interest(s) 9, 134,
Spending 132, 141, 145-148, 151, 231, 264, 267, 268, 272, 346,

Sports 246,
Stagnation 140, 206, 210,
Standard of living 4,
States' rights 68, 70,
Statute of limitations 345,
Stimulus 141, 146-149,
Stock bonuses 296, 297,
Stock options 197-199, 263, 292-297,
Subprime mortgage debt 195, 196,
Subsidies **159-188**, 213, 218,
Suffrage 74, 120,
Sunshine 286,
Superfunds 319,
Supremacy 65, 68,
Supreme Court 52, 56, 58, 60, 65-67, 72, 75, 80, 94, 106-108, 114, 116, 117, 163, 275, 351, 354, 364, 370-372, 375 381, 400, 401, 418,
Switzerland 255, 282, 283, 287, 288,

Tax(es), taxation 4, 5, 19, 20, 10, 39-42, 92, 119, 130, 133, 139-141, 150, 154, 166, 167, 171,

174, 182-188, 200, 205, 206, 209-211, 221, 231, 232, 239, 248, 249, 251, 253, 254, 268, 277, 278, 280, 294-305, 309, 341,
Tax burdens 298-302,
Tax cheats(ing) 199-202, 302-304, 413,
Tax deductible 119, 160,
Tax expenditures 175-178,
Tax-haven(s) 5, 303-305, **356-358**, 413,
Tax revenues 142, 200, 310,
Taxing estates 306-310,
Tea Party 144,
Teachers' and Professors' Tenure **358-360**,
Term limit(s) 26, 29, 44-46, 59, 98, 101-108,
Tesla 335, 336,
Texas 69, 178, 182, 186, 197, 233-235, 374, 375,
Thailand 11,
Tollbooth(s) 16, 30,
Top-two voting 94, 97-100, 122,
Toyota 182, 186, 197,
Trade 212, 215-217, 226, 256, 258, 259, 341,

Trade organizations 38, 39, 102,
Training 267, 271,
Treaty(ies) 52, 58, 212, 215-218, 259,
Tuesday voting 94, 123,

Unemployment benefits 271, 324,
United Nations 150, 355,
United States Postal Service 276,
University(ies) 3, 4, 248, 249, 349,
User fee(s) 170, 171, 231, 232,
Utilities 228,

Variance(s) 159, 161,
Voter registration 78, 112,
Voting Rights Act 80,

Wall Street 248, 289, 416,

Washington, George, 63, 89,
Washington (DC) 5, 8, 10, 37, 44, 46, 62, 80, 81, 95, 131,
Washington (State) 181, 336,
Whistleblower 29,
Wilson, Woodrow 53, 54,
Wisconsin 80, 81,
World Bank 221,
World Economic Forum 221
World War I 258,
World War II 75, 238, 298,
Wyoming 413,